Elizabeth Grant (1797–1885) was born in Edinburgh's fashionable New Town. Most of her childhood was spent in London and on the family estate, Rothiemurchus, on Speyside. She was educated by governesses and in the social graces by various tutors, finally entering Edinburgh society at the end of the Napoleonic wars.

The trauma of a broken engagement was followed by the disastrous failure of her father's career. This involved a huge burden of debt which, in 1820, forced the Grants to retreat to their highland home. As her contribution to improving the family fortunes Elizabeth and both her sisters wrote articles for popular magazines of the day.

In 1827 the family left Scotland for India when her father was appointed to a Judgeship in Bombay. It was here that she met and married Colonel Henry Smith, seventeen years her senior. They left for Ireland the following year to live at Baltiboys, her husband's newly inherited estate situated near Dublin.

She devoted herself to raising a family and took the leading role in managing and improving their impoverished estate. For over half a century Baltiboys was to be her home, her life and her occupation, her resolve never failing even after the death of her husband and her only son. Between 1845 and 1854 she wrote her Memoirs for her family's pleasure; they were later edited by her niece Lady Strachey and published in 1898, thirteen years after her death. The 1988 edition is the most complete ever to appear in print.

Elizabeth Grant of Rothiemurchus

MEMOIRS OF A
HIGHLAND
LADY

Edited by Andrew Tod

⟨ TWO ⟩

CANONGATE
CLASSICS
11

First published in 1898 by John Murray

This edition first published as a Canongate Classic in 1988
by Canongate Publishing Limited
17 Jeffrey Street
Edinburgh EH1 1DR

CANONGATE CLASSICS
Series Editor: Roderick Watson
Editorial Board: Tom Crawford, J. B. Pick

British Library Cataloguing in Publication Data
Grant, Elizabeth, *1797–1885*
Memoirs of a Highland lady.
1. Scotland. Grant, Elizabeth 1797–1885. Biography
I. Title   II. Tod, Andrew
941.107′3′0924
ISBN 0 86241 145 9 v.1
ISBN 0 86241 147 5 v.2

The publishers gratefully acknowledge
general subsidy from the Scottish Arts Council
towards the Canongate Classics series
and a specific grant towards the
publication of this volume

Set in 10pt Plantin
by Hewer Text Composition Services, Edinburgh
Cover printed by Wood Westworth, St. Helen's
Printed and bound in Great Britain
by Cox and Wyman, Reading

Contents

Volume I of Elizabeth Grant's *Memoirs of a Highland Lady* describes her recollections of early childhood in Rothiemurchus and London, painting a vivid picture of the life led by this landed highland family as her father's political and legal ambitions carried them to Edinburgh, London and back to Speyside.

The first volume ends in 1814 with the move to Edinburgh where John Peter Grant of Rothiemurchus, after spending more money than was wise in becoming Member of Parliament for the 'rotten borough' of Great Grimsby, was required to resume his career as an Advocate at the Scottish Bar. And this was to be the appropriate setting for his daughter, the seventeen-year-old Elizabeth Grant, to enter society and, as she wrote, 'commence life on her own account'.

CHAPTER SEVENTEEN

1814–1815

I HAVE always looked on our appearance at this Inverness Meeting as the second great era in my life. Although it so closely followed the first remarkable change, it more completely changed me myself although at the time I was hardly aware of it, reflexion being no part of my character. Our removal to the highlands, our regular break-in under the governess, the partial opening of young minds, had all gone on in company with Jane, who was in many respects much more of a woman than I was, by three years her elder. I was now to be alone. From henceforward, my occupations, pursuits, habits, ideas were all to be perfectly different from, indeed repudiated by, the Schoolroom. Miss Elphick thought, and she was not wrong, that I was a year too young for the trials awaiting me, and for which I had been in no way prepared. She was annoyed too at not having been consulted on the fitness of her pupil for commencing life on her own account, and so, she would neither help my inexperience nor allow me to take shelter under my usual employments. A head filled with nonsense, dress balls, beaux, was very unfit to be trusted near the still innocent brains of my sister.

I felt very lonely wandering about by myself, or seated in state in the library, with no one to speak to. There was no Company in the house. My Mother was little with me. Her hours were late, her habits indolent; besides, she never much cared for me, and she was busily engaged with my father revolving several serious projects for the good of the family, none of them proper for us to be made acquainted with till they were decided on. His Scotch friends were anxious that my father should return to their Bar. There was a want of just such an Advocate as it was expected he would prove and the state of his affairs, though none of us young people knew it, rendered some such step as this very desirable. Also my brother William had a home to look for while he continued in College. Mrs Gordon had had another baby, and in her small house, a flat in Buccleugh Place, there was no longer room for a lodger. Then there was the beautiful daughter! The pale thin girl had blossomed into a, let us tell the truth, why not, into a very lovely flower and fluttering hopes were raised of the consequences of her blushes being seen beyond the wilderness she had hitherto bloomed in. So Edinburgh was decided on, and Grace Baillie was written to, to engage us a house.

At this time Mrs Cameron died and was buried in our sacred corner of the kirk yard, her husband attending the funeral. He received the guests at his own house himself, walked as chief mourner, stood at the grave, returned home quietly with his son and grandsons and when the visits of condolence were paid, he appeared with the rest of the family. His manner had always been very calm, there was no difference perceptible in it. The faded eye alone and a certain drawn look about the mouth, evident only to a close observor, told the tale of the worn out heart. Yet, resigned, patient, Christian as he truly was, he might have survived the cherished wife of his youth, the companion of his age and many sorrows had not an accident shortened his life. He fell over a tub a few days before we left home, none of us thinking much of it but the blow, or cut indeed, was on the shin and it never healed. During the winter he died upwards of 78—young for a highlander, the last of his generation saving Miss Mary. When we went to take leave, he followed us down to the gate at the Lochan Mór; and there laying a hand on each young head, he bade God bless us with a fervour we recollected afterwards, and felt that he must have considered it as a final parting. Then wrapping his plaid round him and drawing his bonnet down over his eyes, he turned and moved away through the birch wood, our last sight of that dear, kind, worthy cousin from whom we had never heard but good. Rothiemurchus altered after all that old set were gone.

Our mourning did not interrupt our packing. We were all in great glee making our Edinburgh preparations, when late

one night we got a fright. One of the chimneys in the old part
of the house took fire, a common occurrence—it was the way
they were frequently cleaned!—but on this occasion the
flames communicated some sparks to a beam in the nearest
ceiling, and very soon part of the roof was burning. None of
us being in bed the house was soon roused, the masons sent
for, and a plentiful supply of water being at hand all danger
was soon over. My mother was however exceedingly frightened, could hardly be persuaded to retire to her room, and
kept us all near her to be ready for whatever might befall. At
last, when calmer, we missed Miss Elphick; she was no
where to be found, and we really feared some mischance had
happened to her. After a good search she was discovered as
far from the house as she could well get, dancing about on the
lawn in her night dress, without either a shoe or a stocking on
her; by which crazy proceeding she caught so severe a cold as
was nearly the death of her. The whole scene made a
beautiful picture, Jane said, and while the rest of us were
rather trembling for the fate of the poor old house, she was
actually studying the various groups as they moved about
under the flickering light of the blazing chimney.

We had no more adventures till we started on our journey,
nor any incidents deserving of notice during our three days'
travel, save indeed one, the most splendid bow with hat off
from my odiously persevering partner, who, from the top
of the Perth Coach as it passed us near Kinross, almost
prostrated himself before the barouche. It was cold wretched
weather, snow in the hills, frost in the plains, a fog over the
ferry. We were none of us sorry to find ourselves within the
warm cheerful house Miss Baillie had taken for us, at No. 4
Heriot Row. It was not a large house having no upper storey.
One floor only over the drawing room, but there were four
rooms on each floor and they were all of a good size. The
situation was pleasant, though not at all what it is now. There
were no prettily laid out gardens then between Heriot Row
and Queen Street, only a long slope of unsightly grass, a
green, fenced by an extremely untidy wall and abandoned to
the use of the washerwomen. It was an ugly prospect, and we
were daily indulged with it, the cleanliness of the inhabitants
being so excessive that, except on Sundays and the 'Saturdays

at e'en,' squares of bleaching linens and lines of drying ditto were ever before our eyes. Our arrival was notified to our acquaintance by what my father's brethren in the law called his advertisement, a large brass plate, really very little less than a page of this paper, on which in letters of suitable size were engraved the words—Mr Grant, Advocate.

We began our Edinburgh life in regular business fashion. My father established himself with a clerk and a quantity of law books in a study, where he really soon had a good deal of work to do. He went every morning to the parliament house, breakfasting rather before nine to suit William, who was to be at Dr Hope's chemistry class at that hour, and from thence proceed to Dr Brown's Moral Philosophy, and then to Mr Playfair's Natural Philosophy.[1] A Tutor for Greek and Latin awaited him at home, and in the evenings he had a good three hours' employment making notes and reading up, etc. Six masters were engaged for we three girls, three every day; Mr Penson for the pianoforte, M. Elouis for the Harp, M. L'Espinasse for French, Signor Something for Italian, and Mr I forget who for Drawing, Mr Scott for writing and cyphering. And oh, a seventh! I was near forgetting, the most important of all! Mr Smart for Dancing. I was occasionally to accompany my father and mother to a few select parties, provided I promised attention to this phalanx of instructors, and never omitted being up in the morning to make the breakfast in proper time. It was hoped that with Miss Elphick to look after us, such progress would be made and such order observed as would make this a profitable winter for every body. An eye over all was certainly wanted. My mother never left her room till mid day, she breakfasted in bed and took a good sleep afterwards, the marketing being made by Gouard, all the orders given the day before.

1. Thomas Charles Hope (1766–1844) was joint Professor of Chemistry with the celebrated Joseph Black; he is particularly remembered for his work on the newly discovered element, strontium. Thomas Brown (1778–1820), metaphysician, was awarded his chair in 1810. John Playfair (1748–1819), one of the leaders of the Scottish Enlightenment, was successively Professor of Maths from 1785 and Natural Philosophy, 1805.

On the same floor with the Drawing rooms which communicated with each other by means of folding doors, were my brother William's room and the Schoolroom. As I was never welcome in the Schoolroom, my studies were all carried on in the Drawing rooms, between the hours of ten, when breakfast was over, and one, when people began to call. It was just an hour apiece for each master, and very little spare time at any other period of the day for practising for them, invitations flowing in quick, and my occasional visiting resulting in an eternal round of gaieties that never left us one quiet evening except Sunday.

About two every day my mother went out to make calls or shop either on foot or most commonly in the carriage, taking me with her. On our return about four or maybe later the drawing room filled with men, who at about that time were at liberty from their different avocations to indulge themselves with a pleasant hour of gossip before dinner. After the first week or two, therefore, I gave up attempting to prepare for the masters, and when the Balls began I had frequently to miss their lessons, as the late hours coupled with the fatigue of frequently uninterrupted dancing exhausted me too much to make it possible for me to attend to their instructions regularly. The only lessons I never neglected were Mr Penson's. He brought his violin to accompany us, and sometimes a violincello, so that we got up trios occasionally, a very delightful treat to me without trouble, for I had no leisure for practising, just played at sight with him what ever he brought. Jane and Mary were kept more systematically to their business, yet Jane having to make breakfast after a while, and Mary having to wait on my Mother at that meal and afterwards assist at her toilette, rather interrupted the studies and extremely annoyed Miss Elphick. She found her evenings dull too without the Drawing room party and she could not bear dining early with the children when we either went out or had Company at home. She was ill too, a teasing cough and other bad symptoms from the effects of the cold she caught during her half naked dance upon the lawn. So cross and uncomfortable and disagreeable she became, the whole house was quite relieved when she announced her determination to take a holiday. She could be well spared, she said, when there were such excellent masters to replace her, and so she set off on a visit to her mother and sister.

On her departure my Mother's maid was deputed to walk out once a day with Jane, Mary, and Johnny, all the exercise they got. Jane taught Johnny, and she and Mary continued their own employments I really believe conscientiously. They said, at first, they found their days long and the evenings dull, but these complaints ceased when, as my Mother supposed, they became accustomed to live alone, and then they had to make tea for William, who was always a kind and cheerful companion for them. The real fact was, that whenever my father was out with my Mother and me, William had a very pleasant party at home—young College friends, and M. L'Espinasse the French Master. Every visitor brought a small supply of fruit and cakes, and Jane had plenty of tea, sugar, bread and butter for the substantial part of the feast. Conscientious as she was, she kept this secret faithfully and the servants who were all engaged in their own amusements were equally honourable. There were two very good rules observed by this pretty assemblage, no intoxicating liquors were allowed, and the company separated before eleven o'clock. No wonder Miss Elphick's absence was agreeable. William certainly must have neglected his studies—he was out riding for two or three hours daily on pretty little Fairy, a thorough bred by way of for which he had given rather a long price and had my father's permission to keep in the Stables.

Our visiting began with dinners from the heads of the Bar, the judges, some of the Professors, and a few others, all Whigs nearly, for the two political parties mixed very little in those days. The hour was six, the company generally numbered sixteen, plate, fine wines, middling cookery, bad attendance and beautiful rooms. One or two young people generally enlivened them. They were mostly got through before the Christmas vacation. In January began the routs and balls; they were over by Easter, and then a few more sociable meetings were thinly spread over the remainder of the Spring, when, having little else to do, I really began to profit by the lessons of our Masters. My career of dissipation was therefore but a four months thrown away. It left me a wreck, however, in more ways than one; I was never strong, and I was quite unequal to all we went through. Mrs Macpherson, who came up with Belleville in March for a week or two, started when she saw me. She thought me in a galloping consumption and very properly frightened my mother about me, who had observed no change, as of course it had come on imperceptibly. She had been extremely flattered and I believe a little surprised by my extraordinary success in our small world of fashion. I was high on the list of beauties, no ball could go on without me, ladies intending to open up their houses for dancing, solicited introductions to the mother for the sake of ensuring the daughter's presence. Crowds of beaux surrounded us when we walked out, filled our drawing rooms when we staid within. It was very intoxicating, but it did not intoxicate me, young and unformed as I was, and unused to admiration, personal beauty being little spoken of in the family. I owed my steadiness to neither good sense nor wise counsel, for neither of these were watching over me. A simple happy temper, a genuine love of dancing, a little highland pride that took every attention as the due of one of Grant blood, these were my safeguards, these and the one all absorbing feeling which early took possession of the young heart to the exclusion of other ideas.

The intimate friends of my father were among the cleverest of the Whigs. Lord Gillies and his charming wife, John Clerk and his sister, Sir David and Lady Brewster—more than suspected of Toryism, yet admitted on account of the Belleville connexion and his great reputation—Mr and Mrs Jeffrey, John Murray, Tommy Thomson, William Clerk. There were others attached to these brighter stars, who, judiciously mixed among them, improved the agreeableness of the dinner parties. My Mother's new and gay acquaintance were of all parties. Lady Molesworth, her handsome sister, Mrs Munro, Mrs Stein, Lady Arbuthnot, Mrs Grant of Kilgraston, etc. We had had the wisdom to begin the season with a Ball ourselves, before Balls were plenty. All the Beaux strove for tickets, because all the Belles of the season made their first appearance there. It was a decided hit, my Mother shining in the style of her preparations, and in her manner of receiving her company. The dancing was kept up till near the day dawn and every one departed pleased with the degree of attention paid to each individually. It struck me afterwards, in more reflecting days, that this Ball and my father's fir forest had no small share in my successful campaign, for my sister beauties were many of them so far beyond any loveliness I could pretend to. There were the two unmarried Dennistouns, afterwards Lady Campbell and Lady Baillie, Miss Farquhar Gray who became Mrs Ashburner, poor Betty Brown. Above all that really beautiful Miss Logan, the quite splendid Miss Dewar of Vogrie, Mrs Hastings Anderson, and several more pretty pleasing girls, who as usual married better than the more admired. Yet we none of us wanted for lovers, earnest, honest lovers, men that a few years later might have been listened to by the scornful fair who in the height of their pride considered them as just good enough to dance with. It is a great mistake sometimes to speak too soon.

The return to the Bar had answered pretty well; fees came in I know usefully, though certainly not in sufficient quantity to authorise our expensive way of living. We gave dinners of course, very pleasant ones, the dishes so well dressed, the wines so choice, and the company well selected that the parties always appeared to be more thoroughly at ease with us than elsewhere. My dress and my Mother's must have cost a fortune, it all came from London, from the *little* Miss Steuarts, who covered my mother with velvet, satin, rich silks, costly furs and loads of expensive lace while the variety of my nets, gauzes, Roman pearl trimmings and French wreaths, with a few more substantial morning and dinner dresses must have helped to swell up the bills to some very large amount. Some of the fashions were curious. I walked out like a hussar in a dark cloth pelisse trimmed with fur and braided like the coat of a Staff officer, boots to match, and a fur cap set on one side, and kept on the head by means of a cord with very long tassels. This equipment was copied by half the town, it was thought so exquisite. We wound up our gaieties too by a large evening party, so that all received civilities were fully repaid to the entire satisfaction of every body. This *Rout*, for so these mere card and conversation parties were called, made more stir than was at all intended.

It was given in the Easter holidays, or about that time, for my father was back with us after having been in London. He had gone up on some Appeal Cases, and took the opportunity of appearing in his place in the House of Commons, speaking a little, and voting on several occasions, particularly on the Corn Law Bill,[1] his opinion on which made him extremely unpopular with the Radical section of his own party, and with the lower orders throughout the country, who kept clamouring for cheap bread, while he supported the producer, the agriculturist. His name as a protectionist was very quickly remarked in Edinburgh where there was hardly another Member of Parliament to be had, and the mob being in its first fresh excitement the very evening of my Mother's rout, she and her acquaintance came in for a very unpleasant demonstration of its anger against their former favourite.

Our first intimation of danger was from a volley of stones rattling through the windows, which had been left without closed shutters on account of the heat of the crowded rooms. A great mob had collected unknown to us, as we had musick within, and much noise from the buzz of the crowd. A score of ladies fainted by way of improving matters. Lady Matilda Wynyard, who had always all her senses about her, came up to my mother and told her she need be under no alarm. The General, who had had some hint of what was preparing, had given the necessary orders, and one of the Company, a highland Captain Macpherson, had been despatched some time since for the military. A violent ringing of the door bell, and then the heavy tread of soldiers' feet announced to us our guard had come. Then followed voices of command outside, ironical cheers, groans, hisses, a sad confusion. At last came the tramp of dragoons, under whose polite attentions the company in some haste departed. Our Guard remained with us all night and ate up all the refreshments provided for our dismayed guests, with the addition of a cold round of beef which most fortunately was found in the larder. Next day quiet was perfectly restored, the mob molested us no more, and the incident served as conversation very usefully for a week or more. It also brought us better acquainted with

1. See *Hansard*, XXIX (1815), pp. 1026, 1123.

those excellent people, General and Lady Matilda Wynyard, whose English reserve had hitherto kept them merely on civil visiting terms with us. From her conduct, with a little help from a side remark or two of my father's, I got a good lesson in some of the trials of life.

There was a flirting, singing, not very wise Widow, rather in fashion in Edinburgh, a good natured Mrs General Anstruther whose principal merit was the having had her husband, a man of good Fifeshire family, killed in Egypt while serving under General Abercromby. She was far from handsome yet many men were much taken by her, amongst others General Wynyard, whose admiration was so very undisguised and all of whose spare time was so entirely occupied in attending on her, that his devotion was really the talk of the town and could not possibly have escaped the notice of Lady Matilda and yet she never seemed to observe it. She behaved with the same politeness to this illbehaved trifling woman as she did to her other acquaintance, invited her in her turn, spoke to her when necessary just as if she were neither more or less to her than any other of their society, always however in some unaccountable way throwing Mrs Anstruther back, as it were, putting herself and her requirements first, without effort either, when she and her husband were together so that in the end the General wearied of his unapproved flirtation and came to look upon this foolish woman with the same indifference he fancied his wife did. That Lady Matilda suffered, clear sighted bystanders could not but observe. And when her calmness had triumphed, every one most sincerely rejoiced.

A second lesson was on this wise. We had a party of rather noted people coming to dine with us. William Cameron, after his good father's death, and Mr Cooper arrived on some business in town. In Highland fashion they announced having merely ordered beds at an hotel, sure of a welcome at all meals with us. My mother wanted to tell them we had company and the table full; my father said no; he would hurt no one's feelings, they were fully entitled to a place at his board, let who would be invited to it. So a leaf was added; they were made extremely happy by eating on terms of equality with men whose names were before the world, and the celebrated guests were so charmed with new listeners to their witticisms that their conversation sparkled with unusual brilliancy. No dinner ever went off better, and though Mr Cooper added no lustre to the company, Mr Cameron in spectacles looked the quiet country gentleman to perfection. My Mother was perfectly satisfied.

The last large party of the season was given by Grace Baillie in her curious apartment on the ground floor of an old fashioned corner house in Queen Street. The rooms being small and ill furnished, she hit upon a curious way of arranging them. All the doors were taken away, all the movables carried off, the walls were covered with evergreens, through the leaves of which peeped the light of coloured lamps festooned about with garlands of coarse paper flowers. Her passages, parlours, bedrooms, closets, were all adorned *en suite*, and in odd corners were various surprises intended for the amusement of the visitors; a cage of birds here, a stuffed figure in a bower there, water trickling over mossy stones into an ivy covered basin, a shepherdess, in white muslin, a wreath of roses and a crook, offering ices, a highland laddie well-kilted presenting lemonade, a cupid with cake, a gypsey with fruit, intricacies purposefully contrived that no one might easily find a way through them, while a french horn, or a flute, or a harp at intervals from different directions served rather to delude than to guide the steps 'in wandering mazes lost.'[1] It was extremely ridiculous, and yet the effect was pretty, and the town so amused by the affair that the wits did it all into rhyme, and half a dozen poems were made upon this Arcadian entertainment, describing the scene and the Actors in it in every variety of style. Sir Alexander Boswell's production was the cleverest, because so very neatly sarcastick. My brother's most particular friend wrote the prettiest. In all, we beauties were enumerated with most flattering commendation, but in *the friend's* the encomium on me was so marked that it drew the attention of all our acquaintance, and most unluckily for me opened my Mother's eyes.

She knew enough of my father's embarrassments to feel

1. Milton, *Paradise Lost*, I, 555.

that my 'early establishment,' as the cant phrase went, was of importance to the future well being of the rest of us. She was not sure of the Bar and the House of Commons answering together. She feared another winter in Edinburgh might not come, or might not be a gay one, newer faces might supersede old favourites, a second season be less glorious than the first. She had been quite delighted with the crowd of admirers, but she had begun to be annoyed at no serious result following all these attentions. She counted the lovers, there was no scarcity of them, there were eligibles among them, some of whom she had believed prepared. How had it come that they had all slipt away. Poor dear mother, while you were straining your eyes abroad, it never struck you to use them at home. While you slept so quietly in the mornings you were unaware that others were broad awake. While you dreamed of Sheffield gold, and Perthshire acres, and Ross-shire principalities, my father and Miss Elphick both away, the daughter you intended disposing of for the benefit of the family had been left to enter upon a series of sorrows she never during the whole of her after life recovered from the effects of.

It is with pain, the most extreme pain, that I even now in my old age revert to this unhappy passage of my youth. I was wrong; my own version of my tale will prove my errours; but at the same time I was wronged—ay, and more sinned against than sinning. I would pass the matter over if I could, but unless I related it you would hardly understand my altered character; you would see no reason for my doing and not doing much that had been better either undone or done differently. You would wonder without comprehending, accuse without excusing; in short, you would know me not. Therefore, with as much fairness as can be expected from feelings deeply wounded and ill understood, I will recall the short romance which changed all things in life to me.

The first year my brother was at College he made acquaintance with a young man a few years older than himself, the son of one of the Professors. His friend was tall, dark, handsome, very engaging in his manners, very agreeable in his conversation, and considered by all who had been employed in his education to possess abilities quite worthy of the talented race he belonged to. The Bar was to be his profession, more by way of occupation for him in the meanwhile than for any need he would ever have to practise Law for a livelihood. He was an only son. His father was rich, his mother had been an heiress, and he was the heir of an old, nearly bedrid bachelour Uncle who possessed a very large landed property on the banks of the Tweed. Was it fair, when a marriage was impossible, to let two young people as him and me pass day after day for months familiarly together. My brother, introduced by his friend to the Professor's family during the first year he was at College, soon became extremely intimate in the house. The father was very attentive to him, the mother particularly liked him, the three sisters, none of them quite young, all treated him as a new found relation. William wrote constantly about them, and talked so much of them when at home at the Doune for the summer vacation that we rallied him perpetually on his excessive partiality, my mother frequently joining in our good humoured quizzing. It never struck us that on these occasions my father never by any chance entered into our pleasantry.

When we all removed to Edinburgh William lost no time in introducing his friend to us; all took to him amazingly; he was my constant partner, joined us in our walks, sat with us every morning, was invited frequently as company and was several times asked to stay and partake of the family dinner. It never entered my head that his serious attentions would be disagreeable, nor my Mother's, I really believe, that such would ever grow out of our brother and sister intimacy. I made acquaintance with the sisters at the houses of mutual friends. We visited and exchanged calls as young ladies did then in Edinburgh; and then I first thought it odd that the seniors of each family, so particularly obliging as they were to the junior members of each other's households, made no move towards an acquaintance on their own parts. The gentlemen, as much occupied with their affairs, were excusable, but the ladies, what could prevent the common forms of civility passing between them. I had by this time become shy of making any remarks on them, but Jane, who had marvelled too, one day asked my mother why she did not cultivate the society of such agreeable persons. My Mother's answer was quite satisfactory. She was the last comer, it was not her place to call first on old residents. I had no way of arriving at the reasons of the other side, but the fact of the non intercourse, the avoidance of intercourse, annoyed me, and frequently caused me a few minutes more of thought than I had ever before been conscious of indulging in.

Then came Miss Baillie's *fête*, and the poem in which I figured so gracefully. It was in every mouth, for in itself it was a gem, and I was so completely the genius of it, none but a lover could have mingled so much tenderness with his admiration. On the poet's next visit my Mother received him very coldly. At our next meeting she declined his now regular attendance. At the next party she forbade my dancing with him : after the indelicate manner in which he had brought my name before the publick in connexion with his own, it was necessary to meet so much forwardness by a reserve that would keep such presumption at a proper distance. I listened in silence, utterly amazed, and might in such perfectly submissive habits of obedience had we been brought up, have submitted sorrowfully and patiently, but she went too far. She added that she was not asking much of me, for this disagreeable young man had no attaching qualities ; he was neither good looking, nor well bred, nor clever, nor much considered by persons of judgment, and certainly by birth no way the equal of a Grant of Rothiemurchus.

I left the room, flew to my own little attick, what a comfort that corner all to myself was then and often afterwards to me. I laid my head upon my bed, and covering my face with my hands, vainly trying to keep back the tears. The words darted through my brain, 'all false, quite false—what can it be, what will become of us,' for I had reached that turning point, though till this bitter moment unconsciously. Long I staid there, half thinking, half dreaming, till a new turn took me, the turn of unmitigated anger. Were we puppets, to be moved about with strings. Were we supposed to have neither sense nor feeling. Was I so poor in heart as to be able to like today, and loathe tomorrow, so deficient in understanding as to be incapable of seeing with my eyes, hearing with my ears,

judging with my own perceptions. This long familiar intimacy permitted, then suddenly broken upon *false* pretences.
They don't know me, thought I; alas, I did not know myself.
To my mother throughout that memorable day I never
articulated one syllable. My father was in London.

My first determination was to see my poet and inquire of
him whether he were aware of any private enmity between
our houses. Fortunately he also had determined on seeking
an interview with me in order to find out what it was my
mother had so suddenly taken amiss in him. Both so
resolved, we made our Meeting out, and a pretty Romeo and
Juliet business it ended in. There *was* an ancient feud, a
College quarrel between our fathers which neither of them
had ever made a movement to forgive. It was more guessed at
from some words his mother had dropt than clearly ascertained, but so much he had too late discovered, that a more
intimate connexion would be as distasteful to the one side as
the other.

We were very young, we were very much in love, we were
very hopeful. Life looked so fair, it had been latterly so
happy. We could conceive of no old resentments between
parents that would not yield to the welfare of their children.
He remembered that his father's own marriage was an
elopement followed by forgiveness and a long lifetime of
perfect conjugal felicity. I recollected my mother telling me
of the Montague and Capulet feud between the Neshams and
the Ironsides, how my grandfather had sped so ill for years in
his wooing, and how my grandmother's constancy had
carried the day, and how all parties had 'as usual' been
reconciled. Also when my father had been reading some of
the old comedies to us, and hit upon the Clandestine
marriage,[1] though he affected to reprobate the conduct of
Miss Fanny, his whole sympathy was with her and her friend
Lord Ogleby, so that he leaned very lightly on her errour. He
would laugh so merrily too at the old ballads, Whistle and I'll

1. The best-known play (1766) of George Colman the
   Elder (1732–94); its most familiar lines ('Love and a
   cottage! Eh, Fanny! Ah, give me indifference and a
   coach and six.' II, ii) might also have come to mind.

come to ye, my lad, Low down in the broom,[1] and the girl who sent her love away deceived by a blink of the morn etc. These lessons had made quite as much impression as more moral ones. So, reassured by these arguments, we agreed to wait, to keep up our spirits, to give time to be true and faithful to each other, and to trust to the Chapter of accidents.

In all this there was nothing wrong, but a secret correspondence in which we indulged ourselves was a step into the wrong, certainly. We knew we should seldom meet, never without witnesses, and I had not the resolution to refuse the only method left us of softening our separation. One of these stray notes from him to me was intercepted by my mother, and some of the expressions employed were so startling to her that in a country like Scotland, where so little constitutes a marriage, she almost feared we had bound ourselves by ties sufficiently binding to cause considerable annoyance, to say the least of it. She therefore consulted Lord Gillies as her confidential adviser, and he had a conference with Lord Glenlee, the trusted lawyer on the other side, and then the young people were spoken to, to very little purpose.

What passed in the other house I could only guess at from after circumstances. In ours, Lord Gillies was left by my Mother in the room with me; he was always gruff, cold, short in manner, the reverse of agreeable and no favourite with me, he was ill selected therefore for the task of inducing a young lady to give up her lover. I heard him, of course, respectfully, the more so as he avoided all blame of either of us, neither did he attempt to approve of the conduct of our seniors; he restricted his arguments to the inexperience of youth, the unsurmountable aversion of the two fathers, the cruelty of

1. There is a poignancy about a couplet from Burns' song
   O, whistle an' I'll come to ye, my lad !
   Tho' father an' mother an' a' should gae mad,
   and the chorus of the other favourite ballad of E.G.'s
   father
   For he's low doun, he's in the brume,
   That's waitin' on me,
   Waiting on me, my love,
   He's waiting on me.
              (Alexander Whitelaw, *Songs of Scotland*).

separating family ties, dividing those hitherto living lovingly
together, the indecorum of a woman entering a family which
not only would not welcome her, but the head of which
repudiated her. He counselled me, by every consideration of
propriety, affection, and duty, to give 'this foolish matter
up.' Ah, Lord Gillies, thought I, did you give up Elizabeth
Carnegie? did she give up you. When you dared not meet
openly, what friend abetted you secretly. I wish I had had the
courage to say this, but I was so nervous at his knowing my
story, so abashed at our conversation that words would not
come, and I was silent. To my mother I found courage to say
that I had yet heard no reasons which would move me to
break the word solemnly given, the troth plighted, and could
only repeat what I had said at the beginning that we were
resigned to wait.

Lord Glenlee had made as little progress; he had had more
of a storm to encounter, indignation having produced a flow
of eloquence. Affairs therefore remained at a stand still. The
fathers kept aloof—mine indeed was still in London; but the
mothers agreed to meet and see what could be managed
through their agency. Nothing very satisfactory. I would
promise nothing, sign nothing, change nothing, without an
interview with my betrothed to hear from his own lips his
wishes. As if my mind had flown to meet his, he made exactly
the same reply to similar importunities. No interview would
be granted, so there we stopt again. A *growing* fancy early
perceived might have been easily diverted. It was a matter of
more difficulty to tear asunder two hearts too long united.

At length his mother proposed to come and see me, and to
bring with her a letter from him, which I was to burn in her
presence after reading, and might answer, and she would
carry the answer back on the same terms. I knew her well, for
she had been always kind to me and had encouraged my
intimacy with her daughters; she knew nothing of my more
intimate relations with her son. The letter was very lover like,
very tender to me, very indignant with every one else, very
undutiful and very devoted, less patient than we had agreed
on being, more audacious than I dared to be. I read it in much
agitation—read it, and then laid it on the fire. 'and now
before you answer it, my poor dear child,' said this most

excellent and most sensible woman, 'listen to the very words I must say to you,' and then in the gentlest manner, as a tender surgeon might cautiously touch a wound, rationally and truthfully, she laid all the circumstances of our unhappy case before me, and bade me judge for my self on what was fitting for me to do. She indeed altered all my high resolves, annihilated all my hopes, yet she soothed while she probed, she roused while seeming to crush and she called forth feelings of duty, of self respect, of proper self sacrifice, in the place of the mere passion that had hitherto governed me. She told me that although she considered my education to have been in many respects faulty, the life I led frivolous and that there was much in my own unformed character to condemn, she would have taken me to her heart as her daughter, for the pure, simple nature that shone through all imperfections, and for the true love I bore her son. She knew there was a noble disposition beneath the little follies, but her husband she said would never think so, never ever endure an alliance with my father's child. They had been friends, intimate friends, in their School and College days; they quarrelled, on what grounds neither of them ever had been known to give to any human being the most distant hint, but in proportion to their former affection was the inveteracy of their after dislike. All communication was over between them, they met as strangers, and were never known to allude to each other, nor to name either fine old name. My father had written to my mother that he would rather see me in the grave than the wife of that man's son. Her husband had said to her that if that marriage took place he would never speak to his son again, never notice him, nor allow of his being noticed by the family. She told me her husband had a vindictive as well as a violent and a positive temper, and that she suspected there must be a touch of the same evil dispositions in my father, or so determined an enmity could not have existed; they were, she thought, aware of what might be the consequences of such unchristian feelings, for they had swore never to have any intercourse and they felt that they were wrong, as was evidenced by the extra attention each had paid the other's children. At their age she feared there was no cure. She plainly shewed she had no hope of shaking any of the resolve in her house. She came then she added, to confide in me, to tell me the whole truth, as it would be safe with me, to shew me that, with such feelings active against us, nothing but serious unhappiness lay before us, in which distress all connexions must expect to share. She said we had been cruelly used, most undesignedly; she blamed neither so far, but she had satisfied her judgment that the peculiar situation of the families now demanded from me this sacrifice; I must set free her son, he could not give me up honourably. She added very, very kindly that great trials produced great characters, that fine natures rose up above difficulties, that few women, or men either, wedded their first love, that these disappointments were salutary. She said what she liked, for I seldom answered her; my doom was sealed; I was not going to bring misery in my train to any family, to divide it and humiliate myself, destroy perhaps the future of the man I loved, rather than give him or myself some present pain. The picture of the old gentleman too was far from pleasing, and perhaps affected, though unconsciously, the very timid nature that was now so crushed.

I told her I would write what she dictated, sign Lord Glenlee's 'renunciation,' promise to hold no secret communication with her son. I kept my word; she took back a short note in which, for the reasons his mother would explain to him, I gave him back his troth. He wrote, and I never opened his letter; he came and I would not speak, but as a cold acquaintance. What pain it was to me those who have gone through the same ordeal alone could comprehend. His angry disappointment was the worst to bear; I felt it was unjust, and yet it could not be explained away, and pacified. I caught a cold luckily, and kept my room awhile. I think I should have died if I had not been left to rest a bit.

My father on his return from London never once alluded to this heart breaking subject; I think he felt for me, for he was more considerate than usual, bought a nice little pony and took me rides, sent me twice a week to Seafield for warm baths, and used to beg me off the parties, saying I had been racketted to death, when she, my mother, would get angry and say such affectation was unendurable—girls in her day did as they were bid without fancying themselves heroines.

She was very hard upon me, and I am sure I provoked her not; I was utterly stricken down and to have lifted up my voice in any way was quite beyond me. What weary days dragged on till the month of July brought the change to the highlands.

CHAPTER EIGHTEEN

1815–1816

HAD I been left in quiet, to time—my own sense of duty, my conviction of having acted rightly, a natural spring of cheerfulness, with occupation, change, etc., all would have acted together to restore lost peace of mind, and the lesson, severe as it was, would have certainly worked for good, had it even done no more than to have sobered a too sanguine disposition. Had my father's judicious silence been observed by all, how much happier would it have been for every one. Miss Elphick returned to us in June, and I fancy received from my Mother her version of my delinquencies, for what I had to endure in the shape of rubs, snubs, and sneers and other impertinences, no impulsive temper such as mine could possibly have put up with. My poor Mother dealt too much in the hard hit line herself, and she worried me with another odious lover. Defenceless from being blameable, for I should have entered into no engagement unsanctioned, I had only to bear in silence this never ending series of irritations. Between them, I do think they crazed me. My own faults slid into the shade comfortably shrouded behind the cruelties of which I was the victim, and all my corruption rising, I actually in sober earnest formed a deliberate plan to punish my principal oppressor—not Miss Elphick, she could get a slap or two very well by the way. My resolve was to wound my Mother where she was most vulnerable, to tantalise her with the hope of what she most wished for, and then to disappoint her. I am ashamed now to think of the state of mind I was in; I was astray indeed, with none to guide me, and I suffered for it; but I caused suffering, and that satisfied me. It was many a year yet before my rebellious spirit learned to kiss the rod.

In journeying to the highlands we were to sleep at Perth.

We reached this pretty town early, and were surprised by a visit from Mr Anderson Blair, a young gentleman possessing property in the Carse of Gowrie, with whom our family had got very intimate during the winter. William was not with us, he had gone on a tour through the west highlands with a very nice person, a College friend, an Englishman. He came to Edinburgh as Mr Shore, rather later than was customary, for he was by no means so young as William and others attending the Classes, but being rich, having no profession, and not College bred, he thought a term or two under our Professors, our University was then deservedly celebrated,[1] would be a very profitable way of passing idle time. Just before he and my brother set out in their tandem with their servants, a second large fortune was left to this favoured son of a mercantile race, for which, however, he had to take the ridiculous name of Nightingale. Mr Blair owed this well sounding addition to the more humble Anderson, borne by all the other branches of his large and prosperous family, to the bequest of an old relation. Her legacy was very inferiour in amount to the one left to Mr Nightingale, but the pretty estate of Inchyra with a good modern house overlooking the Tay, was part of it, and old Mr John Anderson, the father, was supposed to have died rich. He was therefore a charming escort for my Mother about the town. We had none of us ever seen so much of Perth before. We were taken to sights of all kinds, to shops among the rest, and Perth being famous for whips and gloves, while we admired, Mr Blair bought, and Jane and I were desired to accept a very pretty riding whip each, and a packet of gloves was divided between us. Of course our gallant acquaintance was invited to dinner.

The walk had been so agreeable, the weather was so extremely beautiful, it was proposed, I can hardly tell by who, to drive no farther than to Dunkeld next morning, and spend the remainder of the day in wandering through all the beautiful grounds along the miles and miles of walks

1. Two near contemporaries who led the way were the future Prime Ministers, Lord Palmerston (1800–03) and Lord John Russell (1809–12), who lodged with Professor Playfair.

conducted by the riverside through the woods and up the mountains. 'Have you any objection to such an arrangement, Eli,' said my father to me. 'I, papa! none in the world.' It suited my tacticks exactly. Accordingly so it was settled, and a very enjoyable day we spent. The scenery is exquisite, every step leads to new beauties, and after the wanderings of the morning it was but a change of pleasure to return to the quiet inn at Inver to dine and rest, and have Neil Gow in the evening to play the violin. It was the last time we were ever there. The next time we travelled the road the new bridge over the Tay at Dunkeld was finished, the new inn, the Duke's Arms, opened, the ferry and the quiet inn at Inver done up, and Neil Gow dead.

Apropros of the Duke's Arms, ages after, when our dear amusing Uncle Ralph was visiting us in the highlands, he made a large party laugh, as indeed he did frequently, by his comical way of turning dry facts into fun. A coach was started by some enterprising individual to run between Dunkeld and Blair during the summer season, which announcement my Uncle read as if from the advertisement in the newspaper as follows: 'Pleasing intelligence. The Duchess of Athole starts every morning from the Duke's Arms at eight o'clock. . . .' There was no need to manufacture any more of the sentence.

The day had passed so agreeably at Dunkeld, it was decided on proceeding in the same way to Blair, a longer drive by a few miles, and through that most beautiful of all bits of mountain scenery, the pass of Killiecrankie. We did not spend our time near the Castle, we walked to the falls of the Bruar, first brought into notice by Burns, and then too much made of; as besides planting the banks and conducting a path up the stream,[1] so many summer houses and hermitages and peep bo places of one sort or another had

1. Burns' poem written about this tributary of the river
   Garry in 1787, took the form of a plea to the Duke of
   Athole for just this sort of development:
       Let lofty firs, and ashes cool,
           My lowly banks o'erspread . . .
       Let fragrant birks, in woodbines drest,
           My craggy cliffs adorn,
               ('The Humble Petition of Bruar Water').

been perched on favourite situations, that the proper character of the wild torrent was completely lost—nature was much
disturbed, but no ill taste could destroy so grand a scene. We
were fortunate in finding plenty of water leaping in wide
cascades over rocks of every size and shape, for there had
been rain a few days before.

Our obliging friend left us next morning with the consola-
tory information that we should meet again before the 12th of
August, as a letter from Mr Nightingale had brought his
agreement to a plan for them to spend the autumn in the
highlands. They had taken the Invereschie Shootings, and
were to lodge at the Dell of Killiehuntly with John and Betty
Campbell.

We had hardly got settled at the Doune before a note from
Mr Blair, a very nice pony, and a basket of most delicious
fruit, hothouse fruit, arrived from Inchyra; the fruit we ate
with the greatest pleasure, the pony had been sent to be
acclimatised as it would be used hereafter on the hill, and the
note said it would be conferring the greatest favour if the
young ladies would be so very kind as to ride and help to train
it. We were all perfectly willing to accept all civilities, and
Jane and I henceforth were able to ride out together, and
found our chief happiness in resuming our old wanderings,
which the encreasing stiffness of the poor old white pony had
made us fear must for the future have been undertaken
singly. Our excursions, however, were far from being as
enjoyable as formerly. Inverdruie was shut up. The attraction of the Croft was gone; Duncan McIntosh, broken by ill
health and distress of mind owing to the misconduct of his
eldest son, was no longer the animated companion of former
days. Aviemore was a painful visit. We had only Belleville
and Kinrara and the scenery. Belleville was almost always
our great resource. We young people were much liked there,
and we ourselves liked going there. Kinrara, it must be
confessed, was dull, too stiff, too constrained, although
kindness was never wanting; but the Marquis and Marchioness were not to arrive till the famous 12th of August. Our
first three weeks at home were very quiet, no company
arriving, and my father being absent at Inverness, Forres,
Garmouth, etc., on business. We had all our humble friends

to see, all our favourite spots to visit. To me the repose was delightful, and had I been spared all those unkind jibes, my irritated feelings might have calmed down and softened my temper; exasperated as they continually were by the most cutting allusions, the persuasion that I had been most unjustly treated and was now suffering unjustly for the faults of others, grew day by day stronger and stronger, and estranged me completely from those of the family who so perpetually annoyed me. Enough of this. So it was, so it ever was, blame me who will.

After this quiet beginning our highland autumn set in gaily. The 10th of August filled every house in the country in preparation for the 12th. Kinrara was full, though Lord Huntly had not come with the Marchioness; some family business detained him in the south, or he made pretence of it, in order that his very shy wife might have no assistance in doing the honours, and so rub off some of the awkward reserve which so very much annoyed him. Belleville was full, the inns were full, the farm houses attached to the shootings let were full, the whole country was alive, and Mr Nightingale, Mr Blair and my brother arrived at the Doune. Other guests succeeded them, and what with rides and walks in the mornings, dinners and dances in the evenings, expeditions to distant lakes or glens or other picturesque localities, the Pitmain tryst and the Inverness Meeting, a merrier shooting season was never passed. So every one said. I don't particularly remember any one person as very prominent among the crowd, nor any thing very interesting by way of conversation. The Battle of Waterloo and its heroes did duty for all else, our highlanders having had their full share of its glories.

We ladies went up for the first time this year to Glen Einich, our shooting friends with us. The way lay through the birch wood to Tullochgrue, past McAlpine's well and a corner of the fir forest and wide heath, till we reached the banks of the Luinach, up the rapid course of which we went till the heath narrowed to a Glen, rocks and hills closed in upon us, and we came upon a sheet of water terminating the *cul de sac*, fed by a cataract tumbling down for ever over the face of the precipice at the end of it. All the party rode on ponies caught about the country, each rider attended by a man at the bridle head. Jane and I were better mounted, for the Inchyra pony had never been reclaimed; it was not wanted, so she and I had it by turns on all occasions. The Edinburgh pony, poor Toper, so called from its love of porter, carried the one that was not honoured with *Paddle*. A very pleasant day we passed, many merry adventures of course taking place in so singular a cavalcade. We halted at a fine spring to pass round a refreshing drink of whiskey and water, but did not unload our sumpter horses[1] till we reached the granite pebbled shore of the lake. Fairy tales belong to this beautiful wilderness; the steep rock on the one hand is the dwelling of the Bodach[2] of the Scarigour, and the Castle like row of precipitous banks on the other is the domain of the Bodach of the Corriegowanthill—titles of honour these in fairy land, whose high condition did not however prevent their owners from quarrelling, for no mortal ever gained the good graces of the one without offending the other, loud laughing mockery ever filling the Glen from one potentate or the other, whenever their territories were invaded after certain hours. Good Mr Stalker the Dominie had been prevented continuing his fishing there by the extreme rudeness of the Corriegowanthill, although encouraged by his opposite neighbour and fortified by several glasses of stiff grog. We met with no opposition from either; probably the Laird and all belonging to him were unassailable. We had a stroll and our luncheon, and we filled our baskets with those delicious delicate char which abound in Loch Einich, and returned gaily home in safety.

Another much more adventurous expedition we made to the parallel roads, attended as usual. Our shooting friends did not thin their own moors too much. A tenant of the Duke of Gordon's who lived near Kingussie, a most excellent oddity of a little old man, had a large sheep farm up in Laggan with a better sort of bothie in a pretty glen, where he and Mrs Mitchell frequently remained a day or two at shearing time. The poor Captain's phaeton carried my Mother, Miss Elphick, and the carpet bags; the rest of us rode, and we

1. Pack or baggage horse.
2. An 'old man' or a 'hobgoblin'.

came up with Mr and Mrs Mitchell by the way, travelling in their gig, a cart following them containing one of their pretty daughters and plenty of provisions. The bothie had but two rooms, a parlour and a kitchen; the gentlemen occupied the kitchen, the ladies the parlour, all sleeping at night on beds of heather thickly strewed over the floor. The cooking kitchen was outside in the open air, near an old wall under a tree. We took all our meals out of doors, and so merry were we, so happy in this gypsy life, we could have enjoyed a good week of it instead of the two days my mother limited our visit to, out of consideration for the resources of Mrs Mitchell; particularly as two fiddlers were of the party, and after walking miles all day we danced for hours at night in the gentlemen's larger apartment. Our English friend, Mr Nightingale, was no great walker, nine miles there and back to fish for dinner in a beautiful little loch at the head of the Glen, where the trout actually leaped up by dozens to the hook, wore him and a fine pair of boots completely out, as he had the honesty to confess, and so declined a walk of sixteen miles on the morrow to the parallel roads in Glenroy. We suspected that our Scotch Mr Anderson Blair was little better able for such a highland amount of exercise, but this he would by no means allow, so he and William set out with a guide for the object of our enterprise, and lost their way, and returned very weary in the evening.

Some dinners at Kinrara were rather dull, pleasanter at Belleville, very agreeable at home, so they all said. The Pitmain Tryst was a very good one. My principal partner was old Mr Mitchell, with whom I finished off in the Haymakers, he, short and fat and no great dancer, doing his part so lovingly, the spectators were all in convulsions of laughter. Jane, though only fifteen, was taken to this country gathering and to all the dinners at Belleville. At one party there we met the two Charles Grants, father and son, and brought them back with us to Rothiemurchus.

At this time Mr Blair took leave, as he was one of the Stewards of the Perth Hunt, and their yearly Ball was approaching. He left us Paddle, and he sent us fruit and musick, and seemed much more to regret his going than some of us did to see him go. My Mother was consoled by retaining Mr Nightingale, whom really everybody liked–he staid, and went with us to the Inverness Meeting. It was a very bad one, I recollect, no new beauties, a failure of old friends, and a dearth of the family connexions. Having a party with us we went to Grant's hotel, much more in the midst of the fun than Mr Cooper's quiet house in Church Street. Chisholm and Mrs Chisholm were in rooms next ours, once such dear friends of my father and mother's. The connexion had long ceased, in spite of untiring efforts on the Chisholm part to renew it. She, in anticipation of the Meeting, had brought for me a french enamelled watch set with pearls, a venetian chain to hang it on, a large packet of french gloves, and a whole suit of embroidery. There was a great consultation about the propriety of my keeping them. No reason could be assigned for a refusal, so I, at any rate, gained by the civility. My last year's friend, the new Member for Ross-shire, Mr McKenzie of Applecross,[1] was at this Meeting, more agreeable than ever, but looking extremely ill. I introduced him by desire to my Cousin Charlotte Rose, who got on with him capitally. He was a plain man, and he had a buck tooth to which some one had called attention, and it was soon the only topick spoken of, for an old prophecy[2] ran that whenever a mad Lovat, a childless Chisholm, and an Applecross with a buck tooth met, there would be an end of Seaforth. The buck tooth all could see, the mad Lovat was equally conspicuous, and though Mrs Chisholm had two handsome sons born after several years of childless wedlock, nobody ever thought of fathering them on her husband. In the beginning of this year Seaforth, the Chief of the McKenzies, boasted of two promising sons; both were gone, died within a few months of each other. The Chieftainship went into another branch, but the lands and the old Castle of Brahan would descend after Lord Seaforth's death to his daughter, Lady Hood—an end of

1. Thomas McKenzie of Applecross was M.P. for Ross-shire, 1818–22.
2. One of the best-known of the prophesies of Coinneach Odhar, the seventeenth century 'Brahan Seer' from Lewis.

Caber-Feigh.¹ This made every one melancholy, and the deaths had of course kept many away from the Meeting.

Mr Nightingale left us soon after our return home to pay a visit to Mr Blair and his mother and sisters at Inchyra. We put all our home affairs in order for our long absence, and then we set out for Edinburgh. My father had taken there the most disagreeable house possible; a large gloomy No. 11 in Queen Street, on the front of which the sun never shone, and which was so built against behind there was no free circulation of air through it. It belonged to Lady Augusta Claverhouse, once Campbell, one of the handsome sisters of the handsome Duke of Argyll, who had run off from a masquerade with a lover who made her bitterly repent she ever took him for a husband.² It was comfortable within, plenty of rooms in it, four good ones on a floor, but they did not communicate. The drawing room was very large, four windows along the side of it. There were, however, no convenient rooms for refreshments for evening parties, so during our stay in it nothing could be given but dinners, and very few of them either, for none of us were in very good humour. It was well for me that my little bedroom was to the sunny and quiet back of the house, and on the Drawing room floor, for I had to spend many a week in it. A long illness beginning with a cold confined me there during the early part of the winter, and when I began to recover I was so weakened dear and kind Dr Gordon, who had attended me with the affection of a brother, positively forbade all hot rooms and late hours. It was a sentence I would have bribed him to pronounce, for I was sick of those everlasting gaieties, and with his encouragement and the assistance of a few other friends I was making for my self, I was able to find employment for my time infinitely more agreeable than that

1. The twenty-first Caber Feidh (the hereditary chief of the Clan McKenzie) had four sons, the last of whom died in 1814; the chief died of a broken heart the following year. The title went to Mackenzie of Allen-grange and the estates to his eldest daughter, who had married Admiral Sir Samuel Hood.
2. Lady Augusta (1760–1831) married Colonel Henry Clavering; she was the sister of the sixth Duke.

round of frivolous company. We were spared the train of masters. Harp and Italian alone were given to us this winter, a new Italian master, a fop and an oddity, very much superiour as a Teacher to the other poor old creature. M. L'Espinasse visited as a friend, and spent many pleasant evenings with us. My Mother did not at all approve of this secluded life. In heart she loved both dress and visiting; besides, she did not wish it to be thought that I was breaking my heart, or had had it broken by cruel parents. Spectre as I was, she really believed half my illness feigned. The Roses of Holm, too, had come to town, and Charlotte was dancing every where with Mr McKenzie. I am sure my ghostlike appearance would not have brought him back to his first fancy. Still, with her peculiar hopes and fears and wishes, it was rather hard upon her, but Dr Gordon was peremptory. My father supported him, and so he, that is my father, and my mother went out to the dinners together, and declined the evening parties till I was fit to accompany them. How I enjoyed our home tea circle. M. L'Espinasse generally with us, keeping Miss Elphick in good humour, but no College friends; those little domestick scenes were over.

Mr McKenzie and my father went up by the mail after Christmas together to attend their duties in Parliament. He had called frequently in the mornings after I was well enough to sit in the drawing room, and had once or twice dined with us. He and I were on the most friendly terms; my Mother could not understand us. We parted with the cordially expressed hope on both sides to meet soon again, I promising to cheer my cousin Charlotte's spirits during his absence—he really admired her, she was clever, pretty, and lively, though too flippant to secure the heart of a man like him. Mr Blair and Mr Nightingale then suddenly announced their intention of making a tour' on the Continent of some duration. They just remained for Mr Nightingale to get possession of a set of shirts my Mother had very obligingly offered that I should cut out for him, and then they set out, thus quite breaking up our home party.

We had two pieces of family news to raise our spirits after all these disappointments. Uncle Edward and Annie Grant were married—not to each other! He in Bombay, now a

Judge of the Sudder,[1] had married a Miss Rawlings, the daughter of an old Madras Civilian, a highly respectable connexion; and she in Bengal, had become the wife of Major General Need, commanding at Cawnpore, a King's Cavalry Officer.[2] I have quite forgot, I see, to mention that when we left London she had gone on a visit to Mrs Drury, the sister of Mr Hunter, the husband of one of the Malings. Mrs Drury took such a fancy to her that she would not part with her, at least not to a house of business. She proposed to my father to equip her for India. She went out with Miss Stairs, sister to Lady Bury and Mrs Vine, and she was received by Mrs Irwine Maling, from whose house she married. The Needs belonged to Arkwright, Need, and Strutt, names we British have cause to remember.[3]

By the end of February, this winter of 1816, I was able to indulge my Mother with my company even to a Ball or two. Though received by the world with as much indulgence as before, I had the prudence to dance little, generally sitting by Mrs Rose, or walking about with my steadiest of Admirers, the Colonel; my mother having the gratification of interrupting us frequently by bearing petitions from numerous partners for just one dance before the early hour at which we now retired. There was one I seldom refused—no lover, but a most true and agreeable friend, the best dancer in Edinburgh, Campbell Riddell, who, tho' a younger son and very little likely to make a living at the Bar, a profession quite unsuitable to him, was the favourite of all the belles, and more than tolerated by the mothers. We were very happy, he and I, together, I was hardly so intimate with any other young man, and long years after when we met in Ceylon we both recollected with equal pleasure the days of our innocent flirtation. The Roses were a great addition to us; we saw a great deal of them; she was kind, and clever, he was

1. Anglo-Indian for Chief or Supreme.
2. See II, pp. 175–7.
3. Jebediah Strutt and Need had a successful partnership joined by Richard Arkwright in 1768; their development of his water-frame played an important part in the Industrial Revolution.

charming, and I liked both the girls, tho' they were coheiresses and far from faultless. Old Miss Lawrence, who had just given herself brevet rank, and was to be Mrs Lawrence in future, came on a visit this year to the Man of Feeling.[1] I saw her for the first time, and thought her most extraordinary. She was greatly taken up with a poem old Mr McKenzie had made on me, and reminded me of it afterwards at Studley. Dr Ogle, of Oxford, an old Etonian, also made us out—he brought with him a very fine musical box he had bought at Geneva, a toy not common then.

A very singular set of persons, Nesham cousins, appeared to us about this time; Mr and Mrs Goodchild, and their son Jack. My mother's cousins in Durham were really innumerable. In one family, her Uncle John Nesham's, there had been nine handsome daughters, all married, and two sons. Mrs Goodchild was, I think, the third daughter. Her husband was a man of great wealth, deriving his income principally from the valuable lime quarries on his estates. He was rude, boisterous, and strangely ignorant of every gentlemanly acquisition, yet there was a natural frankness and kindness and clever fun, very redeeming, particularly when we knew him better. The wife was a very noisy, underbred, overdressed woman, evidently imbued with the idea that her money lifted her over the heads of almost every body. The son was worse than Tony Lumpkin[2], worse than Miss Jenny's booby of a brother, for to their ignorance and coarseness and loutishness he added a self sufficiency that kept him completely at his ease, while he was shocking all listeners. 'Well, *coosin*,' said he to me after sitting a while, 'got any prog? my stomach's been crying cupboard this hour.' We were delighted to shut such a mouth so easily. My Mother said these Goodchilds had always been remarkable for an affectation of vulgarity; from long practice it seemed to

1. Henry Mackenzie (1745–1831) whose *Man of Feeling* was published in 1771; for Scott he was the 'Northern Addison'.
2. An insensitive youth in Oliver Goldsmith's *She Stoops to Conquer* (1773).

me to have become natural. They were only passing through, so we saw no more of them at this time.

We were inundated this whole winter with a deluge of a dull ugly colour called Waterloo bleu, copied from the dye used in Flanders for the calico of which the peasantry make their smock frocks or blouses. Every thing new was Waterloo, not unreasonably, it had been such a victory, such an event, after so many years of exhausting suffering. And as a surname to hats, coats, trowsers, instruments, furniture, it was very well—a very fair way of trying to perpetuate the return of tranquillity; but to deluge us with that vile indigo, so unbecoming even to the fairest! It was really a punishment. Our *Albert* blue of this day is worth the wearing but that Waterloo was an infliction, none of us were sufficiently patriotick to deform ourselves by trying it. The fashions were remarkably ugly this season. I got nothing new, as I went out so little, till the spring, when white muslin frocks were the most suitable dress for the small parties then given. There was a dearth of news, too, a lull after the war excitement; or my feeling stupid might make all seem stupid. I know my memory recollects this as a disagreeable winter. The Lawyers were busy with a contemplated change in the Jury Court. Trial by jury in Civil cases had not, up to this date, been the custom in Scotland. In penal Cases the Scotch Jury law so far differed from the English that a majority of voices convicted the prisoner; unanimity was unnecessary; and this, which many very sagacious lawyers considered as the better rule, was not to be interfered with, it was only to be extended to Civil cases. The machinery of the Courts of Justice had of course to be slightly altered for this change of system. If I remember rightly, two new Barons were required, and a Chief Baron, whom we had never had before. Sir William Shepherd, from the London Bar, was sent in this capacity to set it all agoing. His very English wife came with him, and amused us more than I can tell with her Cockneyisms. He was very agreeable.

It may seem beyond the range of a girl of my then age to have entered into so grave a subject, but these sort of topicks were becoming my business. I wrote quick and clearly, and seldom made mistakes; my father, though he had a Clerk, frequently found it suit him to employ me as his more private Secretary. I even helped him to correct the press for some of his pamphlets,[1] sought out and marked his references, and could be trusted to make necessary notes. I delighted in this occupation, and was frequently indulged in it both in town and country at such odd times as help was wanted. Indeed from henceforward I was his assistant in almost all employments—work much more to my mind than that eternal 'outing.'

In July we returned again to the Doune. We had not many visitors, so far as I recollect: Miss Baillie on her way to Logie, Alexander so far with her on her return. Two brothers of the name of Davies, friends of Mrs Cumming's, one a merchant, the other a barrister, recreating themselves by a tour in the highlands, with the hope of a day or two's shooting here and there. Their first essay of the moors was with us, and a failure, for they waited for the late breakfast, came in dress coats to it, and were so long afterwards fitting on all the astonishing variety of their sportsman accoutrements, the day was too far advanced by the time they were completely equipped for the keepers to be able to take them to the best ground, although they rode ponies for the first half dozen miles. They were stupid specimens, and an elder brother whom we knew afterwards, a Colonel and an M.P., was positively disagreeable. The country was filled with half pay Officers, many of them returned wounded to very humble homes in search of a renewal of the health they had bartered for glory. A few of these had been raised to a rank they were certainly far from adorning; very unfit claimants got commissions occasionally in those war days. Lord Huntly had most improperly so advanced one or two of his servants and several of his servants' sons, and in the German legion there had been two lieutenants who began life as carpenters' apprentices to Donald Mclean. One of these, Sandy McBean, who lived the rest of his days at Guislich under the title of the *Offisher*, attended the church very smart, and dined once every season at our table, as was now his due, had helped to

1. He published in 1812 *Essays towards illustrating some Elementary Principles relating to Wealth and Currency*.

alter the staircase with the same hands that afterwards held his sword. Wagstaffe's son rose to be a Major. When he got his Company the father resigned his Stewardship, and received some situation from the Marquis more suited to the son's position.

Kinrara was very full this season, and very pleasant. The charming Duchess, whose heart was in the highlands, had left orders to be buried on the banks of the Spey in a field she had herself pointed out. Lord Huntly planted a few larch around the enclosure, but Lady Huntly laid out a beautiful shrubbery and extended the plantation, making paths through it. The grave was covered by a plain marble slab, but behind this rose a stunted obelisk of granite, bearing on its front by way of inscription the names of all her children with their marriages; this was by her own desire. Her youngest son, Alexander, died unmarried before herself; Lord Huntly she left a bachelour—her four younger daughters had all made distinguished connexions. The eldest, and the best bred amongst them, shewed to less effect among the list of great names, but then she had two husbands to make up for their being commoners. The first, Sir John Sinclair of Murkle, was a cousin of her own; they had one child only, the merry sailor son whom every one was fond of. The second husband, a Mr Palmer of Bedfordshire, it was supposed took her for the connexion as she was very oddly spoken of. The second daughter was Duchess of Richmond,[1] the third the Duchess of Manchester, the fourth the Marchioness of Cornwallis, the fifth the Duchess of Bedford. When the Duchess of Manchester was driven from the house of the husband she had disgraced, she left behind her two sons, and six daughters placed by their father under the care of a governess to be superintended by the Dowager Duchess; the boys were at Eton. The eldest of these girls, however, Lady Jane Montague, had almost always lived with her other

1. It was her second daughter, Madelina, who married
   twice and the eldest, Charlotte, who married Charles,
   the fourth Duke of Richmond and Lennox (it was she
   who gave the Ball before Waterloo—'There was a
   sound of revelry by night,' Byron, *Childe Harold's
   Pilgrimage*, III, xxi).

Grandmother, the Duchess of Gordon. She it was who danced the chantreuse, and trotted over to the Doune on her poney, as often nearly as she staid at home. My father and mother were dotingly fond of her, for she was a fine natural handsome creature, quite unspoiled. When our Duchess, as we always called her, died, Lady Jane was not happy at home with her younger sisters and their governess. She went to live with her aunt the Duchess of Bedford, and was shortly announced to be on the point of marriage with the second of the Duke's three sons by his first wife, Lord William Russell. Next we heard she was very ill, consumptive—dying—and that kind aunt of hers took her to Nice, and attended her like a mother till she laid her in her grave. It was a real grief to every one that knew her, particularly those who had watched the fair show of her childhood.

The second of these deserted girls was now of an age to be introduced into society, and Lord and Lady Huntly brought her with them to Kinrara. No, it was the third, Lady Susan, a beautiful creature; the second, Lady Elizabeth, was just married to a handsome Colonel Steele, whom she had become acquainted with through her Governess. It was on Lady Susan's account Kinrara was made so particularly agreeable. There were plenty of morning strolls and evening dances, a little tour of visits afterwards, all ending in her engagement to the Marquis of Tweeddale, a man liked I believe by men, and it was said by some women—of extraordinary taste, to my mind; for, thick set and square built and coarse mannered, with that flat Maitland face which when it once gets into a family never can be got out of it, he was altogether the ugliest boxer or bruiser looking sort of common order of prize fighter that ever was seen in or out of a ring. Yet he had a kind manner and a pleasant smile, and he made a tender husband to this sweet gentle creature, who accepted him of her own free will and never regretted the union.

Neither house went to the Tryst this year, nor to the Meeting. Lady Susan's approaching marriage prevented any publick displays from Kinrara, and my father having been called to a distance on business the Doune did not care to exhibit without him.

We had had some troubles in our usually quiet Duchus

this autumn. Urquhart Gale, the principal Saw miller, and George McIntosh, one of the returned officers, had each got into an unpleasant scrape. Urquhart Gale's backsliding was only suspected as yet, but George McIntosh's was a most miserable business; the young man was in the jail of Inverness for murder. Mrs McIntosh, as I am sure I must have mentioned[1] was one of the two very pretty daughters of Steuart of Pityoulish, an old tacksman on the Gordon property, very superiour in station to his forester son in law. He was devotedly attached to all of Gordon blood, but particularly so to the family of his Grace, and he insisted on his first grand child, a boy, being called after our Prince of Wales of the north, the Marquis of Huntly. At a proper age this piece of respect got George McIntosh a Commission. He had never joined his regiment in the field, but he had been away and come home, and finding other young officers in the country they one unlucky day entered the publick house at the Boat of Inverdruie, and ordering whiskey drank to one another till they fell to quarrelling. Very hard words passed between George McIntosh and one of the company; the rest took part against poor George, and Duncan Cameron the Landlord, fearing for unpleasant consequences, rushed amongst these half mad boys, as he said, to prevent mischief. A frightful scuffle ensued, at the end of which George McIntosh's first opponent was picked up senseless. Nor did he ever speak again. He died in a few hours without apparent injury except a small triangular wound near the temple, which, on the Doctor probing, was found to run deep into the brain. The whole party were taken up, lodged in prison, and indicted for murder; they could not, however, be tried till the Spring circuit, and the connexions had all to wear away the winter in this dreadful anxiety. Mr and Mrs McIntosh were completely overwhelmed by this calamity, the end of which I may as well tell now as keep it over to its proper season.

My father, feeling quite unable to conduct such a cause himself, engaged George Joseph Bell[2] to defend George

1. See I, pp. 233–4.
2. Bell (1770–1843) was six years later appointed to the Chair of Scots Law in Edinburgh.

McIntosh and Duncan Cameron, and he sent a very clever writer body, a regular rogue of the name of Lyon, to assist Mr Cooper in preparing the evidence. The friends of the other young men spared no means of assisting them, and they all got off easily, having been on the side of the poor murdered lad; his opponent and the Rothiemurchus man who had rushed in to help him were in a very different position. Nothing, however, transpired to criminate George McIntosh; he was acquitted; but the Landlord—he was by trade a tailor, and the wound had the appearance of having been made by closed scissors; this persuasion saved him; it was proved that it could not be scissors; neither was it—he had done it with the snuffers. The verdict was manslaughter, and he was transported for life. We all felt the whole affair as a disgrace to Rothiemurchus. My father was quite depressed by such an occurrence happening. Jane and I talking it over a year afterwards with Belleville, he said the fault lay with those who had put young men who were not gentlemen into a position only fit for gentlemen; had these lowly born uneducated youths been at the plough, they would neither have had time nor inclination for such a scandal.

My father actually got a Cadetship for George McIntosh after this, and sent him to India.

CHAPTER NINETEEN

1816–1817

In November 1816 we travelled back to Edinburgh to take possession of Sir John Hay's house in George Street, an infinitely more agreeable winter residence than Lady Augusta Clavering's very gloomy old barrack in Queen Street. It was an excellent family house, warm, cheerful, aery, with abundant accommodation for a larger party than ours; but there was the same fault of but one drawing room and a small study off of it. Perhaps my father wanted no space for a Ball. The town was much fuller than it had been before, of course gayer, many very pleasant people were added to our society. War was over. All its anxieties, all its sorrows had passed away, and though there must have been many sad homes made for ever, in a degree, desolate, these individual griefs did not affect the surface of our cheerful world. The bitterness of party still prevailed too much in the town, estranging many who would have been improved by mixing more with one another. Also it was a bad system that divided us all into small côteries; the bounds were not strictly defined, and far from strictly kept; still, the various little sections were all there, apart, each small set overvaluing itself and undervaluing its neighbours.

There was the fashionable set, headed by Lady Gray of Kinfauns, Lady Molesworth unwillingly admitted, her sister Mrs Munro, and several other regular party giving women, seeming to live for crowds at home and abroad. Lady Molesworth, the fast daughter of a managing man-oeuvring mother, very clever, no longer young, ran off with a boy at College of old Cornish family and large fortune, and made him an admirable wife—for he was little beyond a fool—and gave him a clever son, the present Sir William

Molesworth.[1] Within, or beyond this, was an exclusive set, the McLeods of McLeod, Cumming Gordons, Shaw Steuarts, Murrays of Ochtertyre, etc. Then there was a card playing set, of which old Mrs Oliphant of Rossie was the principal support, assisted by her daughters Mrs Grant of Kilgraston and Mrs Veitch, Mr and Mrs Massie, Mr and Mrs Richmond, she was sister to Sir Thomas Liddell, Lord Ravensworth, Miss Sinclair of Murkle the Duchess of Gordon's first cousin and the image of her, though a plain likeness, Sam Anderson and others. By the bye, Mrs Richmond was the heroine of the queer story in Mr Ward's Tremaine,[2] and she actually did wear the breeches. And there was a quiet country gentleman set, Lord and Lady Wemyss, all the Campbells, Lord and Lady Murray, Sir James and Lady Helen Hall, Sir John and Lady Steuart, Graemes, Hays, and so forth. A literary set, including College professors, Authours, and others pleased thus to represent themselves. A clever set with Mrs Fletcher. The law set. Strangers, and inferiours. All shook up together they would have done very well. Even when partially mingled they were very agreeable. When primmed up, each phalanx apart, on two sides of the turbulent stream of politicks, arrayed as if for battle, there was really some fear of a clash at times. We were so fortunate as to skim the cream, I think, off all varieties; though my father publickly was violent enough in his Whiggism he never let it interfere with the amenities of private life, and my Mother kept herself quite aloof from all party work.

The Lord Provost of Edinburgh was seldom in any of these sets; he was generally a tradesman of repute among his equals, and in their society he was content to abide. This winter the choice happened to fall on a little man of good family, highly connected in the mercantile world, married to

1. Sir William Molesworth, the politician (1810–55).
   His mother Mary Brown from Edinburgh married Sir
   Arscott-Ourry Molesworth, the seventh baronet,
   whose family had been of influence in Cornwall since
   the reign of Queen Elizabeth.
2. Robert Plumer Ward's *Tremaine, or the Man of Refinement* was to be published in 1825.

an Inverness Alves, and much liked. I don't remember what
his pursuit was, whether he was a Banker, or Agent for the
great Madras house his brother George was the head of,[1] but
he was a kind hospitable man, his wife Mrs Arbuthnot very
Highland, and though neither the one nor the other had
the least pretensions to good manners, they were general
favourites. He was chosen provost again when his three years
were out, so he received the king, George IV., on his
memorable visit, and was made a Baronet.[2] Just before him
we had had Sir John Marjoribanks of Lees, mercantile too.[3]
After him, the town Council went back to their own degree.
The name amongst us for Sir William Arbuthnot, I call him
by the name we knew him best by, was *Dicky Gossip*, and
richly he deserved it, for he knew all that was doing every
where to every body, all that was pleasant to know; a bit of
illnature or a bit of ill news he never uttered. After a visit
from him and his excellent wife, they were fond of going
about together, a deal of what was going on seemed to have
suddenly enlightened their listeners, and most agreeably. A
tale of scandal never spread from them, nor yet a sarcasm.
They, from their situation, saw a great deal of company, and
no parties could be pleasanter than those they gave. They
were much enlivened this year by the arrival of a sister from
Spain, the Widow of Sir John Hunter, the late Consul general
at Madrid. Lady Hunter, still in weeds, she did not shew
herself; her two very nice daughters appeared at home,
though they went out only to small gatherings of relations
till the spring. They were just sufficiently foreign to be
the more interesting, and they were so ladylike we took
greatly to them, became quite intimate, and never were

1. George Arbuthnot (1772–1843) founded this famous
   merchant company.
2. He was Provost from 1815–17 (when he was praised
   for setting up public works, such as the construction of
   a road round the King's Park, to help relieve distress)
   and then again from 1821 to 1823; George IV knighted
   him after the Town Council banquet in Parliament
   House.
3. His father had been a wine merchant in Bordeaux.

estranged although widely separated. Jane Hunter and Jane Grant more particularly remained faithful to their early friendship even after their names were changed, even to this day.

Locality has a good deal to do with intimacies. In Heriot Row and in Queen Street we had no acquaintance very near us. In Heriot Row the Cathcarts were next door, and Lord Alloway, who was a Widower, seemed anxious that his daughters should be a good deal with us; they were,—but that was all, for Agnes was merely gentle and pleasing, Mary very pretty, the brothers quite cloddish, so that we never got on very far, although we were much together. In George Street we were in the midst of agreeable neighbours. Near the Arbuthnots in Charlotte Square were the Cumming Gordons, the old Lady and her four unmarried daughters, Charles, and Sir William and his Bride on a visit to them. Young Lady Gordon Cumming, as she called herself for distinction, was not handsome, very tall—five feet ten and a half—thin, not well made, neither were her features good, yet all together, when well dressed, I have seen her look magnificent. The whole connexion was in a dream of joy at Sir Willie's wife being the daughter of Lady Charlotte Campbell, niece to the Duke of Argylle. It was Eliza here, and Eliza there, and Eliza only; they were awakened by and bye, and rather rudely, but this winter it was all an intoxication of happiness. Old Lady Cumming never went out, but every evening, when the rest of the family were in, the shutters were left open to shew the drawing rooms lighted up, and a general invitation was given to certain familiar friends on such occasions to enter if agreeable. There was a card table, always musick, for Sophy Cumming played delightfully, Charles very well on the violincello, Sir James Riddell, my friend Campbell's elder brother, equally well on the violin; there was a flute too sometimes, and in the flute's absence, a man whose name I can't remember *whistled* like a sweet double flageolet. When Sophy was out of the way I have taken the pianoforte for her—a very miserable substitute. Young Lady Cumming sang ballads neatly, all she had voice for. One of the married daughters, Mrs John Forbes, was observed by the old Lady to shirk these pleasant evenings rather, so the four sisters remonstrated. Mrs Forbes frankly acknowledged that she had not time, a houseful of children and an advocate's income left her little leisure for gadding; the sisters begged however she would come, as their mother liked to have as many of her family as she could gather round her, and they told her to bring her work, that would prevent her loss of time. So she did; I saw her there busy with a pair of coarse sheets, seaming down the long seam with a long thread, stitching and stretching, dragging this web bit by bit out of a great canvas bag as she wanted it; and yet she did not look unladylike. All the Cummings were queer, queerer than one ever sees people now, but the good blood kept order to a certain degree.

Lady Charlotte *Bury*, she had become, passed a few days in Edinburgh this season without the husband; her second daughter Eleanor, afterwards Lady Uxbridge, was with her, a pretty creature, the image of me! It was really curious the extraordinary likeness to us that ran through this whole Campbell connexion, and no relationship between us. Some two hundred years back or more an Argylle Campbell had married a Grant of Grant, and her daughter had married a Grant of Rothiemurchus, but that was too remote descent; besides, 'twas in the Gunning and the Ironside the likeness lay. My mother was so like Lady Wemyss they were frequently mistaken. Uncle Ralph and Walter Campbell the Uncle, the sailor, were like as two brothers. Lady Eleanor Charteris—afterwards Campbell, for she married her cousin Walter—was asked to dance for me, and I was congratulated on my approaching marriage for her. Lady Uxbridge and I were more alike. Even Charlotte Clavering, Lady Augusta's daughter, had a look of me after she dressed quietly as the wife of Miles Fletcher. Emma Campbell could hardly be known from my sister Mary, William and Walter Campbell ditto, Johnny and Johnny Campbell; and Mary and I were both so like the Miss Gunning, Duchess of Hamilton and Argylle, that they used at Altyre to dress us up and set us underneath her picture as a show and Mary certainly was as beautiful. After all, perhaps the surprise is that with so few features to work with nature is able to vary us all so much; that really is more wonderful than that some few of us should be alike. Where there is such near resemblance, character must have something to do with it.

Lady Ashburton's was another pleasant house; she was a Cuninghame of Lainshaw, niece to Lord Cranstoun[1] and to Dugald Stewart, one of the College professors.[2] He took pupils, and had among them this very eccentric son of the Speaker, Mr Dunning, Lord Ashburton,[2] he was ungainly in person, disagreeable in habits, some years younger than Miss Cuninghame, who would have him, despight both uncles; Lord Cranston felt it was a throwing away of a fine girl, Dugald Stewart took it a reflexion on himself that in his house, while under his care, a very wealthy nobleman should be while so young engaged to his niece. The niece did not care; she was cold and she was ambitious, so she married her Lord, and they had a fine country house and a beautiful town house—two houses thrown into one, which gave her a splendid suite of apartments for the grave style of receiving company that suited her taste; a dinner party every week, and in the evening her rooms thrown open to an assemblage that filled them. Her intimate acquaintance had cards for the season. Others she asked when she liked—there was no amusement provided, neither dancing nor musick nor cards, and yet it was always agreeable. In one of the many rooms was a counter spread with a variety of refreshments. In another were a number of small round tables where groups of any desired size were served with tea. Lord Ashburton delighted in company, and in people that were fat; like Julius Caesar he objected to all who had a lean and hungry look! He went about smiling, though saying little except to himself; he had a trick of soliloquising, so very oddly. We dined there one

1. George Cranstoun became a judge in 1826; one sister, Jane Anne, did marry the Count of Purgstall, and the other, Helen D'Arcy, married Professor Dugald Stewart. See Cockburn's *Memorials* for an interesting portrait.

2. Dugald Stewart (the distinguished figure of the Scottish Enlightenment, 1753–1828) was appointed to the Chair of Moral Philosophy in 1785.

3. John Dunning, first Lord Ashburton (1731–83); his son Richard married Ann Cunningham; the title died with him in 1823.

day, and it so happened that I sat next to him; he looked at me, after a while he looked again: 'That's a pretty girl—Miss Grant, I fancy; not fat enough. I must ask her to take wine.' All this was to himself, then aloud: 'Miss Grant, a glass of wine with me?' It was the fashion then to pay this civility to all ladies, who could not have got any otherwise, and who, some of them, liked a good deal. 'It's a pity she's so thin. What shall I say next to her?' He could not talk, converse, I mean, merely start out a few words thus, always however to the purpose. One of Lady Ashburton's sisters was married to McLeod of Cadboll, a Ross-shire laird, and an aunt was the Baroness Purgstall in Germany. This German aunt had given to two of her country men letters of introduction to her old friends in Edinburgh. Lady Ashburton presented them to my Mother. My Mother, who always liked foreigners, paid them a great deal of attention. The Styrian Baron Gudenus and the Saxon Chevalier Thinnfeldt were soon made free of our house, and very much indeed they enlivened it. They were well bred, well educated, sensible young men, great additions to our society. The Baron, the only son of an old Gratz family, was travelling for pleasure, or perhaps for health—he looked sickly. The Chevalier had a large property in mines, and came to our country to get some insight into a better method of working them.

There were very few large balls given this winter. Lady Gray, Mrs Grant of Kilgraston, Mrs McLeod, and a few others retained this old method of entertaining. A much pleasanter style of smaller parties had come into fashion with the new style of dancing. It was the first season of quadrilles, against the introduction of which there had been a great stand made by old fashioned respectables. Many resisted the new french figures altogether, and it was a pity so entirely to give up the merry country dance, in which the warfare between the two opinions resulted; but we were all the young people bit by the quadrille mania, and I was one of the set that brought them first into notice. We practised privately by the aid of a very much better master than Mr Smart. Finlay Dunn had been abroad, imported all the most graceful steps from Paris; and having kept our secret well, we burst upon the world at a select reunion at the White Melvilles', the

Spectators standing up the chairs and sofas to admire us. People danced in those days; we did not merely stand and talk, look about bewildered for our vis a vis, return to our partners either too soon or too late, without any regard to the completion of the figure, the conclusion of the measure, or the step belonging to it; we attended to our business, we moved in cadence, easily and quietly, embarrassing no one and appearing to considerable advantage ourselves. We were only eight; Mr White Melville and Nancy McLeod opposite to Charles Cochrane and me, Johnny Melville and Charles McLeod with Fanny Hall and Miss Melville. So well did we all perform, that our Exhibition was called for and repeated several times in the course of the evening. We had no trouble in enlisting cooperators, the rage for Cotillons[1] spread, the dancing master was in every house, and every other style discarded. Room being required for the display, much smaller numbers were invited to the quadrille parties. Two, or at the most three, instruments sufficed for band, refreshments suited us better than suppers, an economy that enabled the Inviters to give three or four of these little sociable dances at less cost than one ball; it was every way an improvement. My Mother gave several of these little parties so well suited to the accommodations of our house, and at no cost to my father, Uncle Edward having sent her for the purpose of being spent in any way she liked upon her daughter, a hundred pounds.

Of our first Edinburgh quadrille who are left. The White Melvilles were a family of two bachelour brothers and two unmarried sisters, protected by a married sister and her handsome Irish husband, Mr Jackson. Of the women I have never heard more; they were plain, well brought up, and had good fortunes. Robert the laird was a man of large property and very likeable, but he died, and Johnny, his brother, a very nice person, little thought of by the managing Committees, and small and plain, grew wonderfully in all ways on becoming great. But he remembered his younger brother days, and sought his Bride from afar; he married Lady

1. The name given to several French dances, including the quadrille.

Catherine Osborne, sister, half-sister rather, to the present Duke of Leeds; both are dead, and their children are married. Charles Cochrane, very handsome, a most perfect dancer, and always a great friend of mine, for I like all sailors, is still living, I think. He has been a great traveller, *walking* all over the world, is an authour,[1] a philanthropist, eccentrick but kindly. All the Cochranes are maddish. Charles had a brother Andrew, madly in love with one of the Ladies Charteris. He disguised himself first as a lamp lighter that he might look on her as she sat at dinner, and then as a gardener that he might watch her in her walks, Lord Wemyss having a large garden belonging to his house in Queen Street. Charles McLeod was brother to Harris, no way *nearly* related to Nancy. She was sister to *the* McLeod, as plain a man as she was a handsome girl; her brother's wife was a very underbred woman, City reared, daughter of a merchant, and sister to the Banker Stephenson, almost another Fauntleroy. Nancy McLeod married Spencer Percival, an old Italian love.[2] I met her afterwards at Cheltenham with nine not pretty daughters and two sons. I liked her much.

At our little parties Jane came out amazingly; she was never shy, always natural and gay and clever, and though not strictly handsome, she looked so bright, so well, with her fine eyes and her rosy mouth, she was in extreme request with all our Beaux. To the old set of the two former winters I had added considerably during the course of this more sociable one, and Jane went shares whenever she was seen. She carried one altogether away from me, the celebrated Basil Hall. He had just this very year returned from Loo Choo, had

1. *Journal of a Residence and Travels in Columbia during the years 1823 and 1824* by Captain Charles Stuart Cochrane of the Royal Navy (1825). Columbia, he wrote 'presents the gratifying spectacle of a nation successful in the vindication of its rights, and triumphant over the mean and mistaken policy that would have condemned it to a perpetuity of sloth, ignorance, bigoted superstition and slavery'. It was dedicated to Simon Bolivar.
2. This seems to be an uncharacteristic error as, according to the D.N.B., he married Jane Spencer-Wilson.

published his book,[1] brought home flat needles, and cloth made from wood, and a funny cap which he put on very good humouredly, and chop sticks which he ate with very obligingly; in short, he did the polite voyager to no end. Jane was quite taken with him, so was Jane Hunter; *Margaret Hunter*[2] and I used to be quite amused with them and him, and wonder how they could wait on the Lion so perseveringly. He was the second son of Sir James Hall, a man not actually crazy, but not far from it; so given up to scientifick pursuits as to be incapable of attending to his private affairs. They were in consequence much disordered, and they would have been entirely deranged but for the care of his wife, Lady Helen. Sir James had very lately published a truly ingenious work,[3] an attempt to deduce gothick architecture from the original wigwams made of reeds. The drawings were beautifully executed, not by himself, I fancy, and by them he clearly shewed the fluted pillars of stone copied from faggots of osier, groined arches from the slender shoots bent over and tyed together, buds originating ornaments; a fanciful theory may be, yet with some shew of reason in it. Lady Helen, a great friend of my Mother's, was sister to the Lord Selkirk[4] who went to colonise in America. How could the children of such a pair escape. Their eldest son was a fool merely; Basil, flighty, and his end miserable; a third, Jamie, used to cry unless Jane or I danced with him—nobody else would. Three or four beautiful girls died of consumption, Fanny among

1. Basil Hall (1788-1844) published his book *Account of a Voyage of Discovery to the West Coast of Corea and the Great Loo-Choo Islands* in 1818 not 1817.
2. In fact Margaret married Basil Hall in 1825; she was the daughter of Sir John Hunter, a diplomat.
3. Sir James Hall, Bart. (1761-1832), made many contributions to geological studies; this book, entitled *Essay on the Origin, History and Principles of Gothic Architecture*, was published in 1813.
4. Thomas Douglas, fifth Earl of Selkirk (he succeeded after the deaths of six elder brothers) organised a successful colonising expedition to Prince Edward's Island and one, fraught with controversy, to Red River in Manitoba.

them, two were idiots out at nurse some where in the country, and one had neither hands nor feet, only stumps. I used to wonder how Lady Helen[1] kept her senses; calm she always looked, very kind, she always was, wrapt up her affections were in Basil and the two daughters who lived and married—Magdalen, first Lady de Lancey and then Mrs Harvey, and Emily, the wife of an English clergyman. The eldest son married too, Julia Walker, Dr Hope's niece and heiress.

Dr Hope was the Professor of chemistry,[2] an old Admirer, nay I believe more, of my Aunt Mary's, and still the flutterer round every new beauty that appeared. I preferred him to Professor Leslie[3] because he was clean, but not to Professor Playfair; *he*, old, and ugly, and absent, was charming, fond of the young who none of them feared him, glad to be drawn away from his mathematical difficulties to laugh over a tea table with such as Jane and me. We were favourites too with Dr Brewster, who was particularly agreeable, and with John Clerk, who called Jane, Euphrosyne, and with Mr Jeffrey with whom we gradually came to spend a great deal of our time.[4] I had Lord Buchan all to myself though, he cared for no one else in the house. He lived very near us, and came in

1. Helen, daughter of the fourth Earl of Selkirk, had, in fact, three sons and three daughters; the eldest son may have been 'a fool merely' but he was also according to the D.N.B. an F.R.S.; Basil, the second son's end was indeed 'miserable' for he became insane in 1842 and died two years later in Haslar Hospital.
2. See I, p. 6.
3. Sir John Leslie (1766–1832): with the versatility of the Enlightenment, he succeeded Playfair to the Chair of Mathematics in 1805 when he moved to that of Natural Philosophy; and he in turn followed Playfair to that Chair on his death in 1819; Sir John was to be knighted in the year of his death.
4. Although Sir David Brewster was clearly suspected of Tory sympathies, he with Jeffrey and Clerk were 'the intimate friends of my father', and 'among the cleverest of the Whigs'. Euphrosyne was one of the Three Graces.

most mornings in his shepherd's plaid, with his long white hair flowing over his shoulders, to give me lessons in behaviour. He was particularly uneasy at my biting my nails, rated me well, examined the fingers and would give a smart rap where necessary. If he were pleased he would bring out some curiosity from his pockets—a tooth of Queen Mary's, a bone of James the 5th, imaginary relicks he set great store by. How many flighty people there were in Scotland—neither of his extraordinary brothers quite escaped the taint. Lord Erskine and Harry Erskine[1] were both of them at times excited. At a certain point judgment seems to desert genius. Another friend I made this year who remembered to ask about me very lately, Adam Hay, now Sir Adam. He was Sir John Hay's third son when I knew him. John died, Robert the very handsome sailor was drowned, so the Baronetcy fell to Adam. Are not the Memoirs of the old a catalogue of the deaths of all who were young with them. Adam Hay tried to shake my integrity; he advocated, as he thought, the cause of his dearest friend, whose mother, dear excellent woman, having died, their sophistry persuaded them so had my promise. We had many grave conversations on a sad subject, while people thought we were arranging our matrimonial excursion.[2] He told me I was blamed, and I told him I must bear it; I did add one day, it was no easy burden, he should not seek to make it heavier. His own sister, some time after this, succeeded to my place; lovely and most loveable she was, and truly loved I do believe. Adam Hay told me of it when he first knew it, long afterwards, and I said, so best; yet the end was not yet. I had never female friends, I don't know why; I never took to them unless they were quite elderly. I had only Jane, but she was a host.

Poor Jane—this very spring she sprained her ankle, that very ankle that never strengthened again. My Uncle William suddenly arrived from Houghton, and all of us running

1. See I, p. 143.
2. Sir Adam Hay (1795–1867) was M.P. for Linlithgow burghs (1826–30). This tantalising hint as to the identity of E.G.'s lover (see I, pp. 14–22), alas, does not appear to fit any of his four married sisters.

quickly down to welcome him, Jane slipt her left foot, turned it under her, and fell from the pain, tumbling on over the whole flight of the stairs. All that was proper was done for it, and we thought lightly of the accident, as she was only laid up three weeks or so. She felt it better not to use it much, and so for the present the matter rested. Our Uncle remained with us a few days only; he had come to consult my father on some business, and my Mother on an invitation he had received for his eldest daughter Kate to join Uncle Edward and his lately married wife in India. Soon after he went Aunt Leitch arrived—not to us. She liked being independant. She had taken lodgings at Leith for the purpose of sea bathing for Mary and Charlotte, two other daughters of Uncle William's, who had lived with her for some years. Charlotte had not been well and had been ordered to the sea, so on our account my Aunt thought she would try the East coast. Every second day they dined with us, at least, walking up that mile long Leith Walk[1] and our long street, and back again in the cool April evenings; fatigue enough to do away with all the good of the sea bathing. Charlotte was a mere rather pretty girl, nothing particular; Mary was most extremely beautiful. What a fate was hers! but I must not anticipate.

Aunt Leitch told us of Durham cousins living, poor people, very near us, within the rules of the Abbey,[2] on account of debt. Misfortunes had overtaken some of the husbands of the nine Miss Neshams. The Goodchilds were bankrupt, as were such of the connexions who had been engaged in business with them. Mr Carr, the husband of the eldest sister, had lost all; they had to fly with a very small portion of their personal property from their comfortable house at Stockton, and take refuge in a very sorry lodging inside the kennel at Holyrood. We found them out immediately, and from that time forward very much lightened their

1. Leith Walk was formed in 1774 and tolls were only abolished in 1835.
2. The Palace, its precincts and the Park were (until the ending of imprisonment for debt) a sanctuary for debtors so long so they only ventured out on Sunday; the peak numbers were 116 in 1816 (John Harrison, *History of Holyrood*).

banishment. At first there were only the poor silly old man and his wife, and two Stockton maidservants, not yet done with untiring efforts to clean up indifferent furniture. By and bye came George, their youngest son, not long from School, clever enough and the best of good creatures, but so unmitigably vulgar his company was frequently distressing. My Mother was quite disturbed by his conduct, and the roars of laughter it elicited from my father. They generally dined with us on Sunday, the only day the old man could go out, the carriage going for them and taking them home, George calling out 'my eye' and making faces at the coachman. He was a fit beau for a belle lately arrived amongst us.

Mrs Gillio, once Miss Peggy Grant of Craggan, niece to the old General and to Peter the Pensioner, had settled at Bath after her visit to the highlands. She intended leaving her youngest daughter and her son at good schools in England, and was preparing to return to Bombay with her two eldest girls when she heard of her husband's death. Her circumstances being much changed by this calamity, she thought of Edinburgh as uniting many advantages for all her children at a cheaper rate than she could procure them else where. We took lodgings for them which, by the bye, they changed; the boy was to attend the high School, the two younger girls the classes, and the elder ones to go a little out if they made desirable acquaintance. Amelia Gillio, with her brilliant eyes, was not a plain girl; she was worse, she was an impudent one, and many and many a time I should liked to have shipped her off to the antipodes for the annoyance she caused us. After a walk with Nancy McLeod, or a visit to Agnes Cathcart, or the Hunters, how this fourth rate young lady's tones grated rather on the ears all unaccustomed to them. It was the time of short waists and short petticoats, and the Bath, or Miss Amelia's, fashions were so extra short at both extremities, we were really ashamed of being seen with her; the black frock reached very little below the knee—she had certainly irreproachable feet and ankles. George Carr attracted equal attention by wearing his hat on the back of his head, never having a glove on, and besides talking very loudly, he snatched up all the notices of sales and such like carried about the streets by hawkers, and stuffed them with a meaning laugh into his pockets, saying they would do for 'summat,' he was very intolerable.

We had a visitor this spring of a different grade, Colonel d'Este, whom we had not seen since the old Prince Augustus days. He was just as natural as ever, asked himself to dinner, and talked of Ramsgate. He had not then given up his claim to Royalty,[1] therefore there was a little skilful arrangement on his part to avoid either assumption or renunciation. He entered unannounced, my father meeting him at the door and ushering him into the room, my mother, and all the ladies on her hint, rising till he begged them to be seated and on going to dinner he bowed all out, remaining beside my Mother as her escort. Other wise he conformed to common usage, let the servants wait on him, and perhaps did not observe that we had no finger glasses; which reminds me that a year or two after when Prince Leopold was at Kinrara, Lord Huntly, precise as he was, had forgotten to mention to his servants that nobody ever washed before royalty, and from the moment this omission struck him, he sat in such an agony as to be incapable of his usual happy knack of keeping the ball going. Very luckily some of the Prince's attendants had an eye to all, and stopt the offending chrystals on their way. I don't know what brought Colonel D'Este to Scotland at that season of year, he was probably going to some of his Mother's relations in the West.[2] I remember Lord Abercromby being asked to meet him, and after accepting, he sent an apology; 'an unavoidable accident which happily would never be repeated' set us all off on a train of conjectures wide of the truth, the newspapers next day announcing the marriage of this grave elderly friend of my father's.

We left Sir John Hay's house in May; he was coming to live in it himself with his pretty daughters; and we went for three months to the house of Mr Allan the Banker, in Charlotte Square, just while we should be considering where to fix for a permanency. Mrs Allan was ill, and was going to some

1. See 1, pp. 182–3; as late as 1831 he is reported as filing a Bill in chancery to prove the validity of his parents' marriage.
2. His mother's family were the Earls of Dunmore and Galloway.

watering place, and they were glad to have their house occupied. Before we moved we paid two country visits, my father, my mother and I.

Our first visit was to Dunbar, Lord Lauderdale's,[1] a mere family party, to last the two or three days my Lord and my father were arranging some political matters. They were always brimfull of party mysteries, having a constant correspondence on these subjects. My mother had so lectured me on the necessity of being any thing but myself on this startling occasion that in spite of all my experience a fit of *Kinrara feel* came over me for the first evening. I was so busy with the proper way to sit, and the proper mode to speak the few words I was to be allowed to say, and the attention I was to pay to all the nods and winks she was to give me, that a fit of shyness actually came on, and my spirits were quite crushed by these preliminaries and the curious state of household we fell upon. In the very large drawing room the family sat in there was plenty of comfortable furniture, including an abundance of easy chairs set in a wide circle around the fire. Before each easy chair was placed a stool rather higher than would have been agreeable for feet to rest on, but quite suited to the purpose it was prepared for—the kennel of a dog. I don't know how many of these pets the Ladies Maitland and their mother were provided with, but a black nose peeped out of an opening in the side of every stool immediately on the entrance of a visitor, and the barking was incessant. At this time four daughters were at home unmarried, and two or three sons. One daughter was dead, and one had disposed of herself some years before by running away with poor, very silly, and not wealthy Fraser of Torbreck, then quartered at Dunbar with the regiment of Militia in which he was a Captain. This proceeding of the Lady Anne quite changed the face of affairs in her father's family. Lord Lauderdale had rather late in his man of fashion life married the only child of one Mr Antony Tod, Citizen of London.[2] Pretty she had been never; she was a mere little painted doll when we knew

1. This visit to the eighth Earl (1759–1839) might be explained by Cockburn's description of him as 'the chief of the Whig party in Scotland.'
2. 'Secretary to the G.P.O.' (*Scots Peerage*).

her, a cypher as to intellect, but her fortune had been very large, and she was amiable and obedient, and her Lord, they said, really became fond of her and of all the many children she brought him. He was not vain, however, either of her or of them, he had no reason; so he kept them all greatly living in great retirement at Dunbar, never taking any of them with him to town, nor allowing them to visit either in Edinburgh or in their own neighbourhood, till the elopement of Lady Anne, the only beauty. From that sore time Lady Lauderdale and her remaining daughters lived much more in society. They had begun too to feel their own importance, and to venture on opposing my Lord, for Mr Tod was dead, and had left to each of his grandchildren, sons and daughters alike, £15,000. The rest to his daughter for her life, with remainder to her eldest son, Lord Maitland. To his son in law the Earl Mr Tod left nothing. Here was power to the weaker side, exerted, it was said, occasionally, but they were an united happy family, fondly attached to each other.[1]

The square Maitland face was not improved by the Tod connexion, though the family finances so greatly benefited by it. Sons and daughters of the house were alike plain in face and short in person, even Lady Anne, with her really lovely countenance, was a dwarf in size and ill proportioned; but there was a very redeeming expression generally thrown over the flat features, and they had all pleasant manners. The second day went off much more agreeably than the first, although I had to bear some quizzing on my horrour of gambling. In the morning the young people drove, or rode, and walked; before dinner the ladies worked a little, netting purses and knotting bags; the gentlemen played with the dogs. All the evenings were spent at cards, and such high play, Brag and Loo[2] unlimited. It was nothing for fifty or an hundred pounds to change hands among them. I was quite terrified. My few shillings, the first I had called my own for ages, given me for the occasion in a new purse bought to hold

1. After Lady Anne's marriage, three of the four remaining daughters were to marry.
2. Brag is an early form of poker; Loo was a version of whist where any player failing to take a trick pays an agreed sum or 'loo' to the pool.

them, were soon gone at Brag, under the management of
Captain Antony Maitland, R.N. He had undertaken to teach
me the game, of which I had acknowledged I knew nothing,
for we never saw cards at home except when a whist table was
made up for Belleville; and as the eternal cry 'Anty Anty'
did not repair my losses, and I sturdily refused to borrow,
declining therefore to play, and composing myself gravely
to look on, they could hardly keep their countenances; my
whole poor fortune was such a trifle to them. It was not
however my loss so much as what my Mother would say to it
that disturbed me. She was very economical in those little
ways, and her unwonted liberality upon this occasion would,
I knew, be referred to ever after as a bar to any further
supplies, the sum now given having been so squandered. I
sought her in her room before we went to bed to make the
confession, fully believing it had been a crime. The thoughts
of the whole scene make me laugh now, though I certainly
slept all the better then on being graciously forgiven 'under
the circumstances.'

There was no company, only Sir Philip Dirom, arranging
his marriage settlements with Lord Lauderdale, the guardian
of the Bride, the heiress Miss Henderson. He was a
handsome man, gentlemanly, and rather agreeable, not
clever in the least, and very vain. He had won honours in his
profession, the navy, and his latest acquisition, a diamond
star of some order, was the single object of his thoughts, after
Miss Henderson's acres. Lord Lauderdale laid a bet that
Sir Philip would not be two hours in the house without
producing it; nor was he. In the middle of dinner, having
dexterously turned the conversation on the orders of knighthood, he sent his servant for it, sure, he said, that some of the
ladies would like to see the pretty bauble—one of the
principal insignia of the *Bath* I suppose it was. Lord Maitland
received and handed the little red case round with a mock
gravity that nearly overset the decorum of the company. How
little, when laughing at these foibles, did we foresee that
the vain knight's great niece was to be my cousin Edmund's
wife, or fancy that he would be so kind, so generous, to that
thoughtless pair.

The other visit was only for the day. We did not even sleep

from home, but returned very late at night, for Almondell was twelve miles good from Edinburgh. Henry Erskine had added to a small cottage prettily situated on the river from which he named his retirement, and there, tired of politicks, he wore away time that I believed sometimes lagged with him, in such country pursuits as he could follow on an income that gave him little beyond the necessaries of life. He and Mrs Erskine had no greater pleasure than to receive a few friends to an early dinner; they had a large connexion, a choice acquaintance, and were in themselves so particularly agreeable that, company or no, a few hours passed with them were always a treat. Each had been twice married; his first wife I never heard more of than that she had left him children, two sons no way worthy of him, Mrs Callander, and another married daughter. The last wife had no children, either Erskines or Turnbulls, and her father, Mr Munro, a merchant in Glasgow, having failed, her youth was a struggling one. She had even had to draw patterns for tambour work for her bread. Her sister Meg Munro, afterwards Mrs Harley Drummond, was a much more conspicuous person than Mrs Erskine. Their brothers were Sir Thomas Munro and Mr Alexander Munro, the husband of Lady Molesworth's handsome sister. Mrs Cumming and Grace Baillie had an old intimacy with these Munros; they were all from Ayrshire, and that is a bond in Scotland.

In May we removed to Charlotte Square, a house I found the most agreeable of any we had ever lived in in Edinburgh. The shrubbery in front, and the peep from the upper windows behind, of the Firth of Forth with its wooded shores and distant hills, made the look out each way so very cheerful. We were in the midst, too, of our friends. We made two new acquaintances, the Wolfe Murrays next door, and Sir James and Lady Henrietta Ferguson in my father's old house, in which Jane and I were born. Nothing could be pleasanter than our sociable life. The gaiety was over, but every day some meeting took place among us young people. My Mother's tea table was, I think, the general gathering point. The two Hunters were almost always with us in the evenings; they danced their Spanish dances, fandangoes and boleros, striking the castagnettes so prettily in time to the musick, Agnes Cathcart often; and for Beaux our German friends, George and Henry Lindsay, at College then, Basil Hall, and sometimes a class fellow of my brother's. In the mornings we made walking parties, and one day we went to Roslin and Lasswade, a merry company. Another day we spent at sea.

The Captain of the frigate lying in the roads gallantly determined to make a return to Edinburgh for all the attention Edinburgh had paid him. He invited all left of his winter acquaintance to a breakfast and a dance on board. We all drove down to the pier at Newhaven in large merry parties, where now the splendid Granton pier shames its predecessors,[1] and there found boats awaiting us, manned by the merry sailors in their best suits, and we were quickly rowed across the sparkling water, for it was a beautiful day, such a gay little fleet, and hoisted up on the deck. There an awning was spread, flags, etc., waving, a quadrille and a military Band all ready, and Jane, who was in high good looks, soon took her place among the dancers, having been engaged by the little monkey of a Middy who had piloted us over. The collation was below, all along the lower deck. We sat down to it at four o'clock, and then danced on again till near midnight, plentifully served with refreshments, most hospitably pressed upon us by our entertainers. Sailors are so hearty, and every Officer of the ship seemed to feel he had the part of host to play. There never was a merrier *fête*.

Jane always considered this her *début*. She was nicely dressed, was very happy, much admired, and danced so well. She and I were never dressed alike; indeed there was so little resemblance then between us that probably the same style of dress would not have become us. Her figure was not good, yet when any one with better taste than herself presided at her toilette, it could be made to look light and pleasing; her complexion was not good either, at least the skin was far from fair, but there was such a bright healthy colour in her rounded cheek, and such a pair of deep blue brilliant eyes,

1. Newhaven pier was destroyed by a storm in 1797 and replaced in 1812 by a slip; the new Granton pier was where Queen Victoria landed in 1842.

and such a rosy mouth which laughter suited, two such rows
of even pearls for teeth, she well deserved her names,
Euphrosyne and Hebe;[1] and she was such a clever creature,
had such a power of conversation, without pedantry or
blueism, it all flowed so naturally from a well stored head and
warm honest heart. The little Middy's fancy was not the only
one she touched that day. We were, like the best bred of the
company, in half dress, white frocks made half high and with
long sleeves. Jane's frock was abundantly flounced, but it
had no other trimming; she wore a white belt, and had a
hanging bunch of lilacks with a number of green leaves in her
hair. My frock was white too, but all its flounces were headed
with pink ribbon run through muslin, a pink sash, and all my
load of hair quite plain. A few unhappy girls were in full
dress, short sleeves, low necks, white shoes. Miss Cochrane,
the Admiral's daughter,[2] was the most properly dressed
amongst us; she was more accustomed to the sort of thing.
She wore a white well frilled petticoat, an open silk spenser,
and a little Swiss hat, from one side of which hung a bunch of
roses. She and the dress together conquered Captain Darling; they were married a few months after.

Just before we left Charlotte Square we had a visit from the
whole family of Goodchild. They were on their way from
their handsome old home of High Pallion to a cottage in
Perthshire, very cheap, with a good garden, and quite out of
the way of expense of any kind. Mr Goodchild shipped a good
deal of his lime to Dundee and thereabouts, it was therefore a
good situation for him. Mrs Goodchild was glad to leave her
old neighbourhood. Since their misfortunes she had come
out quite in a new character. All her harshness, all her
sarcasms, all her follies indeed, were gone. She had put her
shoulder to the wheel in earnest, and tho' she could never
make herself agreeable, she had become respectable. Still we
were not prepared for the storming party by which we were
assaulted; six daughters, I think, the father, mother, and two
sons. The girls, all in coloured cotton frocks, close coarse

1. Hebe was a daughter of Zeus, seen as the personification of Youth.
2. See I, p. 187.

cottage bonnets, thick shoes, talking loud in sharp Durham voices, chose to walk about to see the town, with the brothers and George Carr attending. They were quite at their ease in the streets, gloves off or on, bonnets untied for the heat, shop windows inspected, remarks of all sorts made, George Carr perpetrating his usual series of misdemeanours with a gay effrontery unparalleled. Jane and I deputed to escort this assemblage, rejoiced we had so few acquaintances left in town, the lawyers only remaining for the summer. I was more remarkable myself if I had but known it! My walking dress was a white gown, a pink spenser, yellow tan boots with tassels dangling, and a fine straw, high crowned, deep poked bonnet, trimmed with white satin, in the front of which were stuck up there three white tall Ostrich feathers in a Prince's plume, nodding their tops forward with every step, unless the wind held them straight up like poplar trees. 'Fair and feathery Artizan' must have brought up this fashion; it was very ungraceful.

Mrs Goodchild and her younger children proceeded almost immediately on their journey. Mr Goodchild had to remain a short time on account of business. After this time he was frequently with us on his way backwards and forwards, and became quite a favourite in spite of his very strange manners, he was so cleverly original and so good natured. He took amazingly to our Germans, particularly to the Cheva*leer*, as he called him, and the Chevalier to him, and more especially to Bessy, the eldest daughter, whom my Mother had consented to receive for a week or so as she had occasion to see a dentist, and wished besides to remain to travel home with her father. She was a pleasant person, very amusing, but not to my mind likeable. I was forced to admire her very pretty feet, but M. Thinnfeldt could not get me any farther. To be rid of *Jack* was such a blessing, we cheerfully put up with his rather too lively sister. She was an addition too to the tea table and dancing, making her way with every body. Early in July we moved to a large house in Picardy Place, No. 8, with four windows in front, a great many rooms all of handsome size, and every accommodation, as the advertisements say, for a family of distinction. My father took a lease of it for three years, hiring the furniture from Mr

Trotter.[1] It was a sad change to us young people, down in the
fogs of Leith, far from any country walk, quite away from all
our friends, and an additional mile from Craigcrook too,
reckoning both ways. We had got very intimate with Mr and
Mrs Jeffrey, Jane and I, and we had frequently from
Charlotte Square walked out to their beautiful old place on
Corstorphine hill, spent the day there, and returned late
when any one was with us, earlier when alone. Mr Jeffrey was
enchanted with Jane, he had never seen any girl at all like
her; he liked me too, but he did not find me out till long after.
He left me now more to Mrs Jeffrey and their little Charlotte,
a pretty child in those days.[2]

We had been at Craigcrook on a visit of some days, and
William had come out to walk home to Picardy Place with us,
looking strangely sad; and on the road he told us there was
very little hope of the life of Dr Gordon. What a shock it was.
Our intimacy had continued unbroken from the hour of our
first acquaintance, William and I more particularly having
been very much with him. He had got on in his profession
as he deserved to do, and had lately got a Chair in the
University[3] and a very full class, and they had left the old flat
in Buccleuch Place in the old town off by the meadows, and
lived in a nice house in Castle Street. All was prospering with
them, but he died. It was some kind of fever he had neglected
the first symptoms of, and I believe he had injured himself by
too exclusive a meat diet. He was the first physician who had
ever tried checking a certain sort of consumptive tendency
by high feeding; he had succeeded so well with patients
requiring this extra stimulus that he tried the plan on

1. The Trotter family were well-known for the quality of
   the furniture they supplied to the houses of this early
   stage of the development of the New Town of Edinburgh; Picardy Place, on the edge of one of its most
   fashionable areas, is scarcely in 'the fogs of Leith'.
2. For Lord Jeffrey see I, p. 76; the D.N.B. commented he
   was 'chivalrous to women, with whom he liked to
   cultivate little flirtations'.
3. Dr Gordon (see I, p. 298), whose Chair was Anatomy,
   died in June 1818; for Henry Cockburn his death
   'clouded our city'.

himself, he who overstudying and under exercising should have given his system rest. Deeply we lamented him; William felt the lost most sincerely, nor did any other friend, I think, ever replace him. Mrs Gordon was left with three children, and only tolerably well off. She was unable to remain in Castle Street. She therefore removed soon to some place in Ayrshire, where there was good and cheap education to be had for her boys. Gogar, or some such name—her little boy, died; so, I think, did her pretty Jane. John only lived and was hardly a comfort to her. He has got steadier since his marriage but he is not what his father's son should have been.

We went late to the highlands and staid very quietly there. Kinrara was deserted this season, Belleville less gay than usual, and we did not go to the Meeting. My mother was not in spirits, my father was away; he went to Ireland to defend some rebels, trials that made a great stir at the time, being made quite a political battle field. The junior Counsel was little Erskine Sandford, the Bishop's son,[1] who went with us by the name of Portia, as it was his gown Mrs Henry Siddons[2] borrowed when she acted that character; it fitted her well, for he was only about her size, and she did not look unlike him, for he was handsome, though so small. They were some weeks absent. While in the north of Ireland my father took up his quarters in the house of an old acquaintance, the Marquis of Donegal, whose brother, Lord Spenser Chichester, my mother was once expected to marry. The Marquis was in some perplexity about his own marriage; he was ultimately obliged to go to the serious expense of having an act of parliament passed to legalise it, the Marchioness having been under age at the time it was celebrated. She was a natural child, so without a parent, consequently the Chancellor was her guardian. She had been brought up, indeed adopted, by a worthy couple somewhere in Wales; they supposed their consent sufficient, but it was not.[3]

1. Erskine Sandford (1793–1861), son of the bishop of Edinburgh, was to become Sheriff of Galloway.
2. Daughter-in-law to Sarah Siddons.
3. George Augustus, second Marquess and sixth Earl of Donegal (1769–1844), married Anna May, illegitimate daughter of Sir Edmund May, Bart., in 1795. Until this act of Parliament, this brother was the rightful heir.

I spent most of the Autumn rubbing dear Jane's ankle, on the Oxford Mr Grosvenor's plan.[1] We sat under the large ash tree, while I rubbed and she read aloud to me. We got through many interesting books this way. She had hurt herself dancing so very much on board the frigate. We rode too; Paddle was gone back to Inchyra, but a big Bogtrotter was there instead, on which Jane, who knew not fear, was mounted. Mr Blair had returned from abroad, and had not come near us, and my Mother bore it well, for after hearing that he had asked the Duc de Bcrri to drink wine with him, she had given him quite up. At a publick dinner in Paris this Prince had paid an unusual compliment to some of the English by proposing to 'troquer' with them in their fashion; he was certainly unprepared for the civility being returned.[2] Mr Nightingale could not get over this and a few other such instances, so they parted company. Mr Nightingale had come home too; we heard from him once or twice, and then we heard of him. He was married to his old love, Fanny Smith.

1. John Grosvenor (1742–1823): 'for long the most noted practical surgeon in Oxford . . . he was specially successful in his treatment of stiff and diseased joints by friction.' (D.N.B.)
2. If E.G.'s mother shared her husband's Whig principles then she would not have cared for the Duc de Berry, nephew to Louis XVIII and great hope of the 'ultra', legitimist faction in restoration France; he was assassinated in 1820. The verb 'troquer' (to barter) should be 'triquer' (to toast) . . . a rare error for E.G.

CHAPTER TWENTY

1817–1818

AFTER a very short stay in the highlands we all came up to Picardy Place the end of October 1817, to meet my father on his return from Ireland. We soon settled ourselves in our spacious house, making ourselves more really at home than we had hitherto felt ourselves to be in town, having the certainty of no removal for three years. Still we younger ones were not soon reconciled to the situation, all our habits being disturbed by the separation from the West End! Three winters we spent here, none of them worthy of particular note, neither indeed can I at this distance of time separate the occurrences of each from the others. The usual routine seemed to be followed in all. My father and his new, very queer clerk, Mr Caw, worked away in their law chambers till my father went up to London late in Spring. The second winter he lost his seat for Grimsby, a richer competitor carried all votes, and for a few months he was out of Parliament. How much better it would have been for him had he remained out, stuck to the Bar, at which he really would have done well had he not left ever so many cases in the lurch when attending the 'House,' where he made no figure—he seldom spoke, said little when he did speak, and never in any way made himself of consequence. Only once, when all his party censured the Speaker, he made a little reputation by the polite severity of his few words, called by Sir Alexander Boswell his bit of brimstone and butter, a witticism that ran through all *côteries*, almost turning the laugh against the really clever speech.[1] He dined out every where with my

1. E.G. does her father less than justice; during these years
   he spoke regularly on Ireland, the Corn trade, Army
   expenditure, banking and, of course, Scots Law.
   Boswell himself was an M.P. 1816–21.

Mother while he was in Edinburgh, but hardly ever went out in an evening. He seemed, from his daily letters to my Mother, to go a good deal into society while he was in London, dining at Holland House, Lord Lansdowne's, Lord Grey's, all the Whigs in fact, for he got into Parliament again. The Duke of Bedford gave him Tavistock till one of his own sons should be ready for it.

Five or six dinners, two small evening parties, and one large one, a regular rout, paid my mother's debts in the visiting line each winter. She understood the management of company so well, every assembly of whatever kind always went off admirably at her house. In particular she lighted her rooms brilliantly, had plenty of refreshments, abundance of attendants, always a piece of matting spread from the carriage steps to the house door, and two dressing rooms with toilettes, good fires, hot water, and in the one prepared for the ladies stood a maid with thread and needle in case of accident. Every body praised, though few imitated; such preparations involved a little trouble, besides requiring more rooms than many people had to dispose of. We dined out a great deal, Jane and I taking the dinners in turns. We both went out in the evenings except when I could manage an escape, which was easier than formerly, my Mother having given me up as a matrimonial speculation, and Jane really delighting in Society. We got into rather a graver set than we had belonged to while in the sunshine of George Street and Charlotte Square, not quite giving up our gayer companions, but the distance from them was so great our easy sociable intercourse was very much broken. In our own short street we knew only John Clerk, not then a judge, and his truly agreeable sister Miss Bessy. We half lived in their house, William, Jane and I. They never gave a dinner without one of us being wanted to fill the place of an apology, and none of us ever shirked the summons feeling so at home, and meeting always such pleasant people. All the Law set of course, judges, barristers, and Writers; some of the literary, some of the scientifick, and a great many country families. The drawing rooms, four of them, were just a picture gallery, hung with paintings by the 'ancient masters,' some of them genuine! There were besides portfolios of prints, clever caricatures, and original sketches, these last undoubted and very valuable. John Clerk was a Collector; a thousand curiosities were spread about. He made more of his profession than any man at the Bar, and with his ready money commanded the market to a certain extent. The last purchase was the favourite always, indeed the only one worth possessing, so that it almost seemed as if the enjoyment was in the acquisition, not in the intrinsick merit of the object. A hideous daub called a Rubens, a crowd of fat lumps of children miscalled angels, with as much to spare of 'de quoi' as would have supplied the deficiencies of the whole cherubim, was the wonder of the world for ever so long; my wonder too, for if it was a Rubens it must have been a mere sketch, and never finished. I think I have heard that at the sale of this museum on Lord Eldin's death, a great many of his best loved pictures were acknowledged to be trash.[1]

I did not like him; the immorality of his private life was very discreditable; he was cynical too, severe, very, when offended, though of a kindly nature in the main. His talents there was no dispute about, though his reputation certainly was enhanced by his eccentricities and by his personal appearance, which was truly hideous. He was very lame, one leg being many inches shorter than the other, and his countenance, harsh and heavy when composed, became demoniack when illumined by the mocking smile that sometimes relaxed it. I always thought him the personification of the devil on two sticks, a living, actual Mephistopheles. He spoke but little to his guests, uttering some caustick remark, cruelly applicable, at rare intervals, treasured up by every body around as another saying of the Wise man's deserving of being written in gold, eastern fashion. When he did rouse up beyond this, his exposition of any subject he warmed on was really luminous, masterly, carried one away. The young men were all frightened to death of him; he did look as if he could bite, and as if the bite would be

1. John Clerk, who took the title Lord Eldin, died in 1832. The sale of his principal pictures, held in Picardy House, was remembered because a floor of the house fell in.

deadly. The young ladies played with the monster, for he was very gentle to us.

In the parliament house, as the Courts of Justice are called in Scotland, he was a very tiger, seizing on his adversary with tooth and nail, and demolishing him without mercy, often without justice, for he was a true Advocate, heart and soul, right or wrong, in his client's cause. Standing very upright on the long leg, half a dozen pair of spectacles shoved up over his forehead, his wickedest countenance on, beaming with energy, he poured forth in his broad scotch a torrent of flaming rhetorick too bewildering to be often very success-fully opposed. There was a story went of his once having mistaken a case, and so in his most vehement manner pleading on the wrong side, the Attorneys, called writers with us, in vain whispering and touching and pulling, trying in their agony every possible means of recalling his attention. At last he was made to comprehend the mischief he was doing. So he paused—for breath, readjusted his notes, probably never before looked at, held out his hand for the spectacles his old fat clerk Mr George had always a packet of ready, put them on, shoved them up over all the series sent up before, and then turning to the Judge resumed his address thus, 'Having now, my lord, to the best of my ability stated my opponent's case as strongly as it is possible for even my learned brother'—bowing to the opposite Counsel with a peculiar swing of the short leg—'to argue it, I shall proceed point by point to refute every plea advanced, etc. etc.'; and he did, amid a convulsion of laughter. As a consulting lawyer he was calm and clear, a favourite Arbitrator, making indeed most of his heavy fees by chamber practice.[1]

The sort of tart things he said at dinner were like this. Some one having died, a man of birth and fortune in the West country, rather celebrated during his life for drawing pretty freely with the long bow in conversation, it was remarked that the heir had buried him with much pomp, and had ordered for his remains a handsome monument: 'wi' an epitaph,' said John Clerk in his broadest border dialect; 'he must hae an epitaph, an appropriate epitaph, an' we'll

1. For a contemporary assessment of his legal reputation,
   see Cockburn.

change the exordium out o' respect. Instead o' the usual *Here lies*, we'll begin his epitaph wi' *Here* continues *to lie*' . . . I wish I could remember more of them; they were scattered broadcast, and too many fell by the wayside. The sister who lived with him and kept his house must in her youth have been a beauty. Indeed she acknowledged this, and told how to enhance it, she had when about fifteen possessed herself of her mother's patch box, and not content with one or two black spots to brighten her complexion, had stuck on a whole shower, and thus speckled had set out on a very satisfactory walk, every one she met staring at her admiringly. A deal of such quiet fun enlivened her conversation, adding considerably to the attraction of a thoroughly well bred manner. She painted a little, modelled in clay beautifully, sometimes finishing her small groups in ivory, and her busts in stone or marble. She was well read in French and English Classicks, had seen much, suffered some, reflected a good deal. She was a most charming companion, saying often in few words what one could think over at good length. She was very proud—the Clerks of Eldin had every right so to be—and the patronising pity with which she folded up her ancient skirts from contact with the *snobs*, as we call them now,[1] whom she met and visited and was studiously polite to, was often my amusement to watch. She never disparaged them by a syllable individually, but she would describe a rather *fast* family as 'the sort of people you never see in mourning,' 'persons likely to make the mistake of being in advance of the fashion—so busy trying to push themselves into a place and not succeeding,' added with a smile a trifle akin to her brother's.

There was a younger brother William who, likewise a bachelour, had some office with a small salary and lived in lodgings, dining out every day, for no party was complete without him. He was less kindly than John, but his manner concealed this. He was as clever, if not cleverer, but too indolent to make any use of his great natural abilities. He had never practised at the Bar, and was quite content with his small income and his large reputation, though I have heard

1. Thackery's *The Snobs of England by One of Themselves*
   appeared in *Punch* the year after E.G. began her
   Memoirs.

say, when wondering at the extent of his information, that his memory was regularly refreshed for society, it being his habit to read up in the morning for his display in the evening, and then dexterously turn the Conversation into the prepared channel. He told a story better than any one in the world, except his friend Sir Adam Ferguson. He one dark winter's evening over the fire gave us a whole murder case so graphically that when he seized me to illustrate the manner of the strangling, I and the whole of the rest of us shrieked. I never trembled so much in my life.

Sir Adam Ferguson was the son of the 'Roman Anti-quities';[1] another idler. He was fond in the summer of walking excursions in two or three localities where he had friends, in the Perthshire highlands, along the coasts of Fife and Forfar, and in the border country, the heights along the Tweed, etc. Mark the points well. His acquaintance were of all ranks. He had eyes, ears, observation of all kinds, a wonderful memory, extraordinary powers of imitation, a pleasure in detailing—acting, in fact, all that occurred to him. He was the bosom friend of Walter Scott; he and William Clerk lived half their time with the 'great novelist,' and it was very ungenerous in him and Mr Lockhart to have made so little mention of them in the biography, for most undoubtedly Sir Adam Ferguson was the 'nature' from which many of these lifelike pictures were drawn.[2] We, who

1. He was Scott's staunchest friend from school and college; his father during his long life (1723–1816) was successively Professor of Natural and Moral Philosophy at the University of Edinburgh—the book referred to is his *History of the Progress and Termination of the Roman Republic* (1782).
2. John Gibson Lockhart's biography of his father-in-law was published in 1837–8; he *was* generous enough to write that Scott's 'intimacy with Adam was thus his first means of introduction to the higher literary society of Edinburgh'. (I, p. 153). Ferguson's long and eventful life (1771–1855) saw him Secretary to the Governor of the Channel Islands, Captain in Portugal during the Peninsular War, a prisoner of war for two years in France and, thanks to Sir Walter, Custodian of the Crown Jewels of Scotland.

knew all, recognised our old familiar stories, nay, characters, and afterwards accounted for the silence on the subject of the friends from the desire to avoid acknowledging the rich source that had been so constantly drawn on. Walter Scott had never crossed the Firth of Forth as far as I know.[1]

Waverley came out, I think it must have been in the autumn of 1814, just before we went first to Edinburgh. It was brought to us to the Doune, I know, by 'little Jemmy Simpson,' as that good man, since so famous, was then most irreverently called. Some liked the book, he said; he thought himself it was in parts quite beyond the common run, and the determined mystery as to the Authour added much to its vogue. I did not like it. The opening English scenes were to me intolerably dull, so lengthy, and so prosy, and the persons introduced so uninteresting, the hero contemptible, the two heroines unnatural and disagreeable, and the whole idea given of the highlands so utterly at variance with truth. I read it again long afterwards, and remained of the same mind. Then burst out *Guy Mannering*, carrying all the world before it, in spite of the very pitiful setting, the gipsies, the smugglers, and Dandie Dinmont are surrounded by. Here again is the copyist, the scenery Dumfries and Galloway, the dialect Forfar. People now began to feel these works could come but from one Authour, particularly as a few acres began to be added to the recent purchase of the old tower of Abbotsford, and Mrs Scott set up a carriage, a Barouche landau built in London, and which from the time she got it she was seldom out of, appearing indeed to spend her life in driving about the streets all day. I forget which came next, the Baronetcy or *the Antiquary*—the one was very quickly succeeded by the other[2]—and were followed by the *Castle* at

1. This increasingly uncharitable portrait is here quite
    wrong. Scott and Ferguson had travelled through the
    territory of *The Lady of the Lake* (1810), for example,
    and four years later he joined the Commissioners for
    the Northern Lights in a circumnavigation of Scot-
    land, that provided material for his Orcadian novel *The
    Pirate* (1822).
2. *The Antiquary* was published in 1816 and George IV
    conferred the baronetcy four years later.

Abbotsford, that monument of vanity, human absurdity, or madness, William Clerk used to speak of this most melancholy act of folly almost with tears.

I was never in company with Walter Scott; he went very little out, and when he did go he was not agreeable, generally sitting very silent, looking dull and listless, unless an occasional flash lighted up his heavy countenance. In his own house he was another character, especially if he liked his guests. His family were all inferiour. I have often thought that this was the reason of the insipidity of his ideal gentlemen and ladies—he knew none better. Lady Scott,[1] a natural daughter of a Marquis of Downshire, her mother French of low degree, herself half educated in Paris, very silly and very foolish, was a most unfortunate mate for such a man. When I saw her she had no remains of beauty, dressed fantastically, spoke the greatest nonsense in her broken English—and very frequently had taken too much wine. I recollect one evening at the Miss Pringles', she was actually unconscious of her actions, poor Anne Scott vainly trying to conceal her condition, till catching sight of William Clerk they got her to go away. The excuse was Asthma, a particular Asthmatick affection, which a glass or more of Madeira relieved. Such a Mother could scarcely do much for or with her children. The eldest son, Walter, was a mere good-natured goose forced into a marriage he hated and never able to get over the annoyance his unsuitable partner gave him. The younger, Charles, was thought more of, he died on his travels before being in any way brought to notice. Sophy,

1. The mysterious circumstances of the early years of Charlotte Charpentier (Carpenter) are described in Edgar Johnson *Sir Walter Scott: The Great Unknown*. The second Marquis of Downshire was certainly her guardian from as early as 1786, but at the time she was conceived he was a sixteen year old at Eton. Her mother was far from being 'of low degree'; M. Charpentier had worked in the French Embassy in Constantinople and became Master of the Military Academy at Lyons. The explanation for this hostile portrait probably lies in E.G.'s distaste for Scott's Tory politics and social pretensions.

Mrs Lockhart, was an awkward, very ignorant girl, not exactly plain yet scarcely otherwise, her husband did a great deal with her. She was liked in London, her manner remaining simple after it was softened. Anne was odious—very ugly and very pretending and very unpopular, which she should not have been, would not, had she been less exacting, less irritable, for she was a good daughter in different ways to both parents.[1] It was odd, but Sir Walter never had the reputation in Edinburgh he had elsewhere—was not the Lion, I mean. His wonderful works were looked for, read with avidity, praised on all hands, still the Authour made far less noise at home than he did abroad. The fat, very vulgar Mrs Jobson, whose low husband had made his large fortune at Dundee by pickling herrings, on being congratulated at the approaching marriage of her daughter to Sir Walter's son, said the young people were attached, which was not true, otherwise her Jane might have looked higher. It was only a baronetcy, and quite a late creation.[2]

Another family in the Clerk set and ours were the Dalzels; they lived in a small house just behind Picardy Place, in Albany or Forth Street. They were a Professor's Widow,[3] her sister, and her sons and daughters, reduced in the short space of a few years to the one son and one daughter who still survive. Mary Dalzel played well on the piano forte; there was no other talent among them. The Professor had been a learned but a singularly simple man. He had been tutor to

1. The eldest son Walter (1801–47) married Jane Jobson, a match which was set up by the joint efforts of his father and Sir Adam Ferguson; Charlotte Sophia (1799–1837) married John Gibson Lockhart whose biography of his father-in-law was the cause of his literary success in London; Anne (1803–33) and Charles (1805–41) both died unmarried.
2. Mrs Jobson was an Athole Stewart, descending from Robert II through Alexander, the 'Wolf of Badenoch'; another attraction for the Scotts was that the prospective bride, Jane, was heiress to the estate of Lochore in Fife.
3. Andrew Dalzel was Professor of Greek at the University of Edinburgh between 1772 and 1806.

either Lord Lauderdale or to his eldest son, and they had a story of him which Lady Mary told us, that at dinner at Dunbar—a large party—a guest alluding to the profligacy of some prominent political character, Mr Dalzel burst in with, 'There has not been such a rogue unhanged since the days of the wicked Duke of Lauderdale.' John Dalzel was a great companion of my brother William's; they had gone through College, and were now studying for their Civil Law trials together. He was dull but persevering, and might have risen to respectability at least in his profession had he lived.

In York Place we had only the old Miss Pringles, chiefly remarkable for never in the morning going out together— always different ways, that when they met at dinner there might be the more to say; and Miss Kate Sinclair; and two families which, all unguessed by us, were destined to have such close connexion with us hereafter, Mrs Henry Siddons and the Gibson Craigs.[1] Mrs Siddons was now a Widow living with her two very nice daughters and her two charming little boys, quietly as became her circumstances. She acted regularly, as the main prop of the Theatre on which the principal part of her income depended. She went a little into society. She had pleasure in seeing her friends in a morning in her own house, and the friends were always delighted to go to see her, she was so very agreeable. The girls were great friends of my sister Mary's. The little boys were my Mother's passion, they were with us for ever, quite little pets. The Gibsons, who were not Craigs then, we got more intimate with after they moved to a fine large house Mr Gibson was building in Picardy Place when we went there. There were two sons, and seven daughters of every age, all of them younger than the brothers. Mr Shannon, the Irish chaplain of the Episcopal chapel we attended, the fashionable one, lived in York Place, and the Gillies's, with whom we were as intimate as with the Clerks, and on the same easy terms; we young people being called on when wanted, and never loth to

1. E.G.'s brother William married her daughter Sally; sister Jane took as her second husband Sir James Gibson Craig of Riccarton.

answer the call, Lord Gillies being kind in his rough way, and Mrs Gillies then, as now, delightful. Their nieces Mary and Margaret at this time lived with them.

Jane and I added to our private list of so called friends Mr Kennedy of Dunure, whose sister wrote *Father Clement*, whose Mother, beautiful at eighty, was sister to the Mother of Lord Brougham, who himself married Sir Samuel Romilly's daughter and held for many years a high situation here in Ireland.[1] Archy Allison, now Sir Archibald, heavy, awkward, plain, and yet foredoomed to greatness by the united testimony of every one sufficiently acquainted with him. His father, one of the Episcopal Chaplains and author of a work on Taste, had married Mrs Montague's Miss Gregory, so there was celebrity on all sides.[2] Willy and Walter Campbell, Uncle and nephew the same age. Willy Campbell of Winton was really a favourite with all the world, and most certainly would have shone in it had he been spared; he died in Greece, bequeathing his immense fortune equally between his two sisters, Lady Ruthven and Lady Belhaven; they were all three the children of a second marriage of old Campbell of Shawfield's with the heiress of Winton. Robert Hay, Captain Dalzel who lent us the whole of M. Jouy's then published works beginning with L'hermite de la Chaussée d'Antin, and the *Scots Greys*, completed our first winter's List. There was always a Cavalry regiment at the barracks at Piers Hill, and in this fine corps was a nephew of General Need's, Tom

1. Thomas Francis Kennedy of Dunure and Dalquarran Castle (1788–1871), and M.P. for Ayr, was appointed by Melbourne's Whig government to be Paymaster of the Civil Service in Ireland in 1837, a post he held until 1856. His sister Grace (1782–1825) was well known for her religious tales. For once E.G.'s memory has let her down, for Kennedy's mother was in fact Jane Adam, a daughter of the eldest of the famous architect brothers.

2. This was Sir Archibald Allison (1797–1867) the historian, whose father had published an *Essay on the Nature and Principles of Taste* in 1790. His mother was Dorothea, daughter of Dr John Gregory, author of *A Father's Legacy to his Daughters*.

Walker, who was the means of introducing us to the rest of the Officers.

The gay set in Edinburgh was increased by the advent of Mr and Mrs Inglis, Mr and Mrs Horrocks, the McLeods of Harris, and others. Mr Inglis was but a Writer to the Signet, but a hospitable man reputed to be thriving in business; his Wife, sister to Mr Stein, the rich distiller, with a sister married to General Duff, Lord Fife's brother, kept a sort of open dancing house, thus, as she fancied, ushering her two very pretty little daughters, really nice natural girls, into the world with every advantage. Her aim was to marry them well, that is, highly or wealthily. She fixed on McLeod of Harris for the younger, and got him; the elder fixed on Davidson of Tulloch for herself, and lost him. Did I forget to name Duncan Davidson among our peculiar friends. A finer, simpler, handsomer, more attractive young man was never ruined. Spoiled by flattery, and not very judiciously managed at home, year by year with sorrow we saw him falling from the better road, till at last no one named him. He was much in love with Catherine Inglis, and there was no doubt meant to marry her. He might perhaps have turned out better had his early inclinations not been thwarted. The old stock broker was as ambitious as Mrs Inglis, and expected a very much superiour connexion for his eldest son. Harris, having no father, could choose his own wife, too blind to see how very distasteful he was to her. This miserable beginning had a wretched ending hereafter. Charles McLeod, the brother, would have been more likely to take a young girl's fancy. The McLeod sisters were nothing particular. Mr Horrocks was the very rich and extremely under bred son of a Liverpool merchant, a handsome little man married to a Glasgow beauty, a cold, reserved woman, who did not care for him a bit. They could do nothing better than give balls.

Of course Miss Baillie gave her annual *fête*, no longer an amusing one. An Ayrshire aunt had died and left her and Mrs Cumming handsome legacies, upon the strength of which the Lady Logie came up to live in Edinburgh, and Grace Baillie bought a good house, furnished it neatly, and became quite humdrum. She had taken charge of a 'decent man,' for whom she wanted a proper wife—Sir Ewan Cameron of

Fassiefern, made a Baronet as a mark of honour to the reputation of two, if not three, elder brothers all killed in the battlefield, leaving this poor body the only representative of the old family. She offered him both to Jane and me, and that we might not buy a pig in a poke, she paraded him several times before our windows on the opposite side of the street. These old kind of men were beginning to fancy us. I suppose we were considered, like them, on the decline. Mr Crawford, of Japan reputation, was seriously attracted first by one and then the other, but Jane carried the day, got all the languishing looks from such bilious eyes, an ivory fan, and the two heavy volumes of his Eastern history.[1] A year or two after, he married Miss Perry, the Morning Chronicle,[2] she being referred to me for his character, like a servant, and getting Mary Gillies to write to me to beg for a candid opinion of her elderly lover. When ladies arrive at asking for such opinions, one only answer can be given. Mine was highly satisfactory. We really knew no ill of the man; his appearance was the worst of him, and there was a drowned wife too, lost on her voyage home. She might have been saved on a desert island, and so start up some day like the old woman in the farce, to destroy the happiness of the younger bride and the bridegroom.

But I had an old lover all to myself, unshared with any rival, won, not by my bright eyes, but by my spirited fingers, from playing the highland marches as Lady Huntly had taught me them. Old Colonel Steuart of Garth, seventy, I should think, always in a green coat, and silver broad rimmed spectacles, was writing the history of the 42nd Regiment, and the slow Black Watch, and the quickstep of the Highland Laddie, given better, he said, than by the band of his old love, so over excited or over enchanted him that he hardly

1. A later mention of this learned orientalist suggests he was John Crawford (1783–1868), author of *History of the Indian Archipelago*, written in three volumes by 1820.
2. James Perry (1756–1821) purchased the *Morning Chronicle* in 1789; it became a leading Whig party journal.

ever quitted my side, and he gave me his precious work on its publication. I had my two thick volumes too, but they were not heavy ones. He was a fine old soldier, though a little of a bore sometimes, so very enthusiastick about the deeds of his warrior country men.[1] He never went further in his love making than to wish he were a young man for my sake, so that Jane had the advantage over me of a real offer. As for poor little Sir Ewan, we left him to Grace Baillie.

It was a great addition to the quiet home society we were beginning to prefer to the regular gaiety, the having Mrs Cumming settled near us. Her two elder sons had already gone out to India, Alexander in the Civil Service, Robert in the Artillery, both to Bengal. The three younger it was necessary to educate better, as it was gradually becoming more difficult to get passed through the examinations, and all were destined for the East. Besides, there was May Anne, who had hitherto, happy child, been let to run wild on the beautiful banks of the Findhorn, and who was now declared to be of an age requiring taming and training. John Peter, the third son, whom you know best as the Colonel, soon got his Cadetship and sailed away to Bombay. George and Willie, intended for army surgeons, were to study medicine, and were also to have their manners formed by appearing occasionally in society. Willie made his entrance into fashionable life at a large evening party of my mother's. He was a handsome lad, very desirous of being thought a Beau, so he dressed himself in his best carefully, and noticing that all the fine young men were scented, he provided himself with a large white cotton pockethandkerchief of his mother's which he steeped in peppermint water, a large bottle of this useful corrective always standing on the chimney piece in her room. Thus perfumed, and hair and whiskers oiled and curled, Willie, in a flutter of shyness and happiness, entered our

1. David Stewart published his *Sketches of the Character, Manners and Present State of the Highlanders of Scotland, with details of the Military Service of the Highland Regiments* in two volumes in 1822, written as propaganda against emigration; he became governor of St Lucia in 1825.

brilliant drawing rooms, when he was pounced on by Miss Shearer, the very plain sister of Mrs James Grant, an oldish woman of no sort of fashion and cruelly marked with the small pox. 'We'll keep together, Willie,' said Miss Shearer, at every attempt of poor Willie's to shake himself clear of such an encumbrance in the crowd. How Dr Cumming laughed at these recollections when he and I met again after a lifetime's separation. Up and down this ill assorted pair paraded, Miss Shearer seeming determined to shew off her beau. 'There's an extraordinary smell of peppermint here,' said Lord Erskine to Mrs Henry Siddons, as the couple turned and twirled round to pass them, Willie flourishing the large pockethandkerchief in most approved style. It was really overpowering, nor could we contrive to get rid of it, nor to detect the offending distributor of such pharmaceutical perfume, till next day, talking over the party with the Lady Logie, she enlightened us, more amused herself by the incident than almost any of the rest of us.

She was right to keep the bottle of peppermint where it could easily be found, as the sort of housekeeping she practised must have made a frequent appeal to it necessary. She bought every Saturday a leg of mutton and a round of beef; when the one was finished, the other was begun; the leg was roasted, the round was boiled, and after the first day they were eaten cold, and served herself, her daughter, her two sons, and her two maid servants the week. There were potatoes, and in summer cabbage, and peas that rattled, in winter oranges, and by the help of the peppermint the family throve. We never heard of illness among them; the minds expanded too, after their own queer fashion, even George, the most eccentrick of human beings, doing credit to the rearing. He was so very singular in his ways, his Mother was really uncertain about his getting through the College of surgeons. She made cautious enquiries now and then as to his studies, attention to lectures, notes of them, visits to the hospital, preparation for his thesis and so on, and getting very unsatisfactory replies, grew very fidgetty. One day one of the Medical Examiners stopt her in the street to congratulate her on the admirable appearance made by her son George when he was passed at Surgeon's hall; his answers had been remarkable, and his thesis, dedicated to my father, had been No. 2 or No. 3 out of fifty. She was really amazed. 'George,' said she, when they met, 'when did you get your degree?' When did you pass your trials?' 'Eh!' said George, looking up with his most vacant expression. 'Oh! just when I was ready for them.' 'You never told me a word about it?' 'No? Humph! you'd have heard fast enough if I'd failed.' That was all she could get out of him; but he told us, that seeing the door of the Surgeon's hall open and finding it was an examining day, it just struck him that he would go in and get the job over; it was very easy to pass, he added. He has since at Madras risen high in his profession, been twice publickly thanked for the care of the troops, made money, married a wife; yet when he was at home on furlough he acted more like Dominie Sampson[1] than any other character ever heard of.

George Carr was also a medical student, a very attentive one, making up by diligence for no great natural capacity; he was kept in order by his sister, a young lady lately from Bath, as we were without ceasing reminded. She was a ladylike, rather nice looking person, without being at all handsome; beautifully neat and neat handed, and amiable, I believe, in her home, though dreadfully tiresome in ours; for when asked for a day, she staid a week, sharing my small room and civilly begging the loan of pins, oils, gloves, ribbons, handkerchiefs, and other small articles with none of which I was particularly well provided, and yet none were ever returned. We were not comfortably managed with regard to our private expenses, Jane and I. My Mother bought for us what she judged necessary, and she was apt to lay out more on handsome gowns than left her sufficient for clean gloves, neat shoes, fresh flowers; a way of proceeding that greatly distressed us—distressed me at least, for I was by nature tidy, had all the Raper methodically pricknickity ways, and a five guinea blonde trimmed dress, with calico or dirty gloves and ill made shoes, made me wretched; besides, there was no pleasure in managing a wardrobe not under my own controul. Out of economy I made most of my own clothes, many of my mother's and Jane's, yet reaped no benefit from this diligence, as what I disliked was often chosen for me, and

1. The learned but gauche tutor in Scott's *Guy Mannering*.

what I hated I had to wear. The extreme neatness of Miss
Carr exactly suited me; all her under clothes, made by herself, were perfection; her dresses of simple materials, except
such as had been presents, were well fitting and fresh, so that
she looked always nicer in a room than many much more
expensively attired. She had the fault of hinting for presents,
but then she loved dress, she loved company, she was not
very wise, and her purse was very scanty. She amused us
another way. She had such a string of lovers—had had; it
was poor Miss Elphick and her early adorers over again; and
if any one danced twice with her, she wriggled about like an
eel when his name was mentioned. Every now and then we
were informed in confidence that she was going to be
married, or to try make up her mind to marry—that was the
form. However, these affairs never progressed. A Mr Lloyd
did 'make his offer'; mother and daughter walked up in
pleased agitation to tell us. He was an ugly, little, shabby old
man, a friend of Mr Massie's, who wanted a wife and was
taken with her, but when they came to particulars, there was
not money enough on either side to make the connexion
prudent. It was a great feather though in Miss Carr's thirty
year cap, and she shook it out on all occasions with much
complacency.

Bessie Goodchild likewise favoured us with another visit;
her teeth again required attention. She did not trust to a
request and a favourable answer, but very sagaciously made
sure she would be welcome for three days, and then contrived
one way or another to stay above a month. She was very
entertaining, and made herself very agreeable to my Mother
with funny gossip about all the old Durham relations. She
was no plague in the house, but we had been brought up too
honestly to approve of her carrying tales from family to
family, and mimicking the oddities of persons from whom
she had received kindness. We had an odd family party
sometimes—a Carr, a Goodchild, a Gillio, and Grace Baillie
who thrice a week at least walked in at dinner time. My
brother's young men friends continued popping in morning
and evening, when it suited them. He brought us most
frequently William Gibson, Germaine Lavie, Robert Ferguson, now the superfine colonel, Mr Beauclerk, grandson of

Topham's[1] John Dalzel, and the two Lindsays while they remained at College. Mary, now grown into a very handsome girl, did her part well in all home company. Johnny also was made a little man of; he had a Tutor for Latin, attended the French and dancing classes, and read English history with Jane. We had given up all masters except the Italian and the harp, which last taught us in classes, and thereby hangs a tale.

Monsieur Elouis, the Harp master, charged so high for his private lessons, that my Mother suggested to him to follow the Edinburgh fashion of Classes at so much a quarter, three lessons a week. He made quite a fortune. There were eight pupils in a Class, the lessons lasting two hours. We three, the two Hunters, Grace Stein, afterwards Lady Don, Amelia Gillio and Catherine Inglis were his best scholars. We played concerted pieces doubling the parts. Chorus's arranged by him, and sometimes duetts or solos, practising in other rooms. The fame of our execution spread over the town, and many persons entreated permission to mount up the long Common Stair to the poor frenchman's garret to listen to such a number of harps played by such handsome girls. One or two of the Mamas would have had no objection, but my mother and Lady Hunter would not hear of their daughters being part of an exhibition. We went there to learn, not to shew off. Miss Elphick, too, had her own ideas upon the subject. She always went with us, and was extremely annoyed by the group of young men so frequently happening to pass down the street just at the time our Class dispersed, some of them our dancing partners, so that there were bows and speeches and attendance home, much to her disgust. She waited once or twice till the Second Class assembled, but the Beaux waited too. So then she carried *us* all of a quarter of an hour too soon, leaving our five companions to their fate; and this not answering long, she set to scold Monsieur Elouis, and called the Edinburgh gentlemen all sorts of vile names. In the midst of her season of wrath the door of our musick room opened one day, and a

1. Topham Beauclerk (1739–80) was a member of Dr
   Johnson's circle.

very large fine looking military man, braided and belted and moustached, entered and was invited to be seated. Every harp was silent. 'Mesdemoiselles,' said Monsieur Elouis with his most polished air of command, 'recommence if you please; this gentleman is my most particular friend, a musical amateur, etc.' Miss Elphick was all in a flame; up she rose, up she made us rise, gather our musick together, and driving us and Amelia Gillio before her, we were shawled and bonnetted in less time than I am writing of it, and on our way down stairs before poor Monsieur had finished his apologies to the officer and the other young ladies. Never was little woman in such a fury. We never returned to the Harp Classes, neither did the Hunters, and very soon they were given up. It was certainly an unwarrantable liberty, an impertinence, and the man must either have been totally unaware of the sort of pupils he was to find, or else an illbred ignorant person. Poor Elouis never recovered the mistake; he had to leave for want of business.

Margaret Gillio and I went shares in another master, mistress rather. She had a sweet, flexible, bird like voice and sang her little English ballads very prettily. I tried higher flights, but my singing was very so so till we had some lessons from Mrs Bianchi Lacey. She came with her husband and her apprentice, a Miss Simmons, to give a Concert or two and take a few pupils by the way. The concerts were delightful, the three sang so well together, the musick they gave us was so good, and it was all so simply done; her pianoforte the only accompaniment, and in the small Assembly room so that they were perfectly heard. It was a style of singing, hers, that we may call peculiarly ladylike; no very powerful voice, and it was now going, for she was no longer young; still it was round and true and sweet in the upper notes, and the finish of her whole song, the neatness of every passage, the perfect expression she gave both to musick and words, was all new to me. I could now understand it, and it gave to me a different notion of the *art* from any that had ever entered into my head before. The first Concert she gave we were so much amused with old Sir John Hay, one of the Directors, squiring her about, bringing her negus,[1] a shawl, a chair, and what not,

1. Spiced wine or sherry with hot water.

and my brother William doing ditto by Miss Simmons, that
the first song by that young lady, '*H*angels ever bright and
fair,'[1] she was Birmingham, made less impression than it
should have done, for her voice was splendid. We never
heard what became of her; she was pretty, so perhaps she
married a pinmaker and led a private, instead of a hazardous
publick, life. But the moment Mr Lacey and his Wife began
their delightful duetts we had ears for none else. My father
offered me a dozen lessons. We had time for only ten—all, I
may say, I ever got—but we went to her three concerts. They
dined with us twice, and sang as much as we liked, and my
mother gave an evening party for them at which their singing
enchanted every body. It was essentially suited to the
Drawing room. She was taught by old Bianchi, who made her
a perfect musician. She played admirably and had a thorough
knowledge of the Science. She was his apprentice and he
married her. After a short widowhood she rather threw
herself away on too young a husband,[2] a very vulgar man
with so much presumption of manner as to keep one in a
fright lest he should commit some atrocity. It was like sitting
on needles and pins, that young monkey our brother Johnny
said, to sit in company with him. However, he never
offended, and if he had, his fine voice would have secured his
pardon.

Mrs Lacey took a fancy to me, gave me extra long lessons,
and the kindest directions for the management of my voice in
her absence. She was very particular about the erect position
of the head and chest, the smile with which the mouth was to
be opened, the clear pronunciation of every word. She gave
me a set of exercises to develop the powers of the voice, every
tone, every half tone being brought out in every one of them;
the inequalities were to be carefully marked and carefully
improved. When we came to songs, she made me study one.
First the poet's meaning; his intentions were to be accurately
ascertained, as accurately expressed *aided* by the musick,

1. An aria from Handel's oratorio, *Theodora* (1755).
2. Francesco Bianchi committed suicide in 1810; his
   widow married another singer, John Lacey, two years
   later.

which was to accompany the words and follow out the idea. In fact the song was to be acted. Next it was to be embellished with a *few* occasional graces, very neatly executed, applied in fit pauses, the whole got up so perfectly as to be poured forth with ease, any effort, such as straining or forcing the voice or unduly emphasising a passage, being altogether so much out of taste as to produce pain instead of pleasure. Lastly she bid me practise what I liked, but never inflict on other ears what was not completely *within* my compass—no effort to myself. I owed her much, very much, and yet she did not teach me singing, at least not altogether. Her valuable advice, and her care of the form of the mouth, were the foundation of my after fame. My finishing instructress was Mrs Robert Campbell. She and her sister Mrs James Hamilton were two little Jewesses four feet high, whose father had been Consul at some of the Italian ports. One evening, at a small party at Mrs Munro's, Mrs Robert Campbell sang a simple Italian ballad so beautifully, so exactly according to Mrs Lacey's rules, it was all so easy, so satisfying, my lesson in singing was then, I felt, given me. She was encored by acclamation; this enabled me to follow every note. On going home I sat down to the piano forte, sang the ballad myself with every little grace that she had given it, next day repeated it, took another from a store sent us by Eliza Cottam, Ironside, then decorated it after my own taste, got every little turn to flow as from a flute, and in the evening treated my father to both. His surprise was only equalled by his extreme pleasure. It seemed to be the height of his musical expectations. However, we did more for him than that. He really loved musick, he loved us and was proud of us, and though he could sternly express his dissatisfaction, he was no niggard of praise when praise was due. We worked with a heart for a person so discriminating.

Mr Loder[1] brought an Opera company with him, and gave, not whole Operas, he had not strength enough for that, but very well got up scenes from several most in favour. It was a most agreeable variety in a place where publick

1. John David Loder (1788–1846), violinist and musical publisher.

amusements were but scantily supplied to the inhabitants. We had de Begnis and his wife,[1] and scenes from Figaro, Don Giovanni, etc.; the rest of the artistes were very fair, but I forget their names. Going into a musick shop we saw on the Counter two numbers of a new work—the opera of Don Juan arranged for two performers on the pianoforte; the first attempt in a kind that had such success, and that brought real good musick within the power of the family circle. We secured our prize, Jane and I, hurried home, tried the first Scena, were delighted, gave a week to private, very diligent study, and when we had it all by heart, the first afternoon my father came up to spend the *gloaming* napping in an easy chair, we arrested his sleepy fit by 'notte e giorno,' to his amazement.[2] He liked our Opera better, I think, than 'Sul margine dun rio' or 'Ninetta cara,'[3] for we had so lately heard all the airs we played that we were quite up to the proper style, and had ourselves all the desire in the world to give the musick we loved the expression intended by our then favourite composer, Mozart. William also began to try a few tenor duetts with me. Mrs Lacey had taken the trouble to teach him half a dozen for love. It is surprising how well he could do both tender and buffo. His ear either was slightly defective naturally, or from want of early exercise; this made it difficult to keep his voice in order, otherwise he was a most agreeable singer, and once set out kept the key well, but after a pause *might* begin flat again, never sharp luckily. Really our home concerts, with Mary Dalzel's help, were very much applauded by our partial audience.

Edinburgh did not afford much publick amusement. Except these Operas which were a chance, a stray Concert now and then, catches and glees being the most popular, and the six Assemblies, there were none other. The Assemblies

1. The bass Guiseppi de Begnis married the soprano Giusepina Roazi in 1816.
2. Leperello's opening aria in *Don Giovanni*.
3. The first, an Italian Arietta, was written by Vincenzo Pucitta (1778–1861) around this year 1818; the second is probably based on one of Ninette's arias from *La gazza ludra* (*Thieving Magpie*) which Rossini had completed the year before.

were very ill attended, the small room never half full, the large, which held with ease twelve hundred people, was never entered except upon occasion of the Caledonian Hunt Ball, when the Members presented the tickets, and their friends graciously accepted the free entertainment. The very crowded dances at home, inconvenient, and troublesome and expensive as they were, seemed to be more popular than those easy balls, where for five shillings we had space, spring, a full orchestra, and plenty of slight refreshments. I heard afterwards that as private houses became more fully and handsomely furnished, the fashion of attending the Assemblies revived. McLeod of Harris did a very sensible thing the winter he married poor, pretty little Richmond Inglis. They were living with her father and mother, and so very much invited out that he did not think Mrs Inglis' perpetual entertainments sufficient return for the many civilities he and his young wife had received. He therefore hired Smart's rooms where the dancing master had his Academy, asked every one he knew far and near, contracted for a supper, and gave the best ball I was ever at in my young days; a ball that finally established waltzing among us. This much persecuted dance had been struggling on for a season, gaining far less ground than the quadrilles; but a strong band mustering on this occasion, the very 'propers' gave in as by magick touch, and the whole large room was one whirligig. Harris himself danced for the first time at his own ball, and beautifully; his brother Charles was the Vestris[1] of our Society—acknowledged. The Laird was even more graceful in his movements. 'Ah!' said poor Richmond, 'if I had ever seen my husband dance, Mama would not have found it so difficult to get me to marry him.' She saw his perfections too late, I fancy, for she left him and seven children afterwards.

1. Born Lucia Elizabeth Mathews, Madame Vestris (1797-1856), a well-known actress.

CHAPTER TWENTY-ONE

1818–1819

THE first summer we were in Picardy Place, 1818, we younger ones, or rather we girls remained there protected by Miss Elphick during the whole of it. When the fine weather came on in Spring we had resumed our excursions to Craig Crook, and it was then we got so intimate with Basil Hall. We could not have been acquainted with him while we lived in George Street, because he only returned from his Loo Choo cruise late in the Autumn of 1817. During the following winter we saw a good deal of him both before he went to London, and after they had tried to spoil him there, for he was made such a wonder of there, it was a miracle his head kept steady; but it was at Craig Crook that we became such friends. Cruel Lord Jeffrey limited his two young favourites to friendship; the Halls and the Selkirks were all so crazy that he forbid any warmer feelings, closetting Jane in his pretty Cabinet, and under the shades of the wood on Corstorphine Hill, to explain all the melancholy particulars. And then Basil went off to sea. The Jeffreys generally went out on Friday evenings, or, at any rate, on Saturdays, to a late dinner at Craig Crook, and came back to town on Monday morning, till the 12th of July released him from law labours. Jane and I frequently went with them, sometimes only to them for one day, returning in the evening. We never met any lady there but Mrs George Russell occasionally; a clever woman, not to my mind agreeable. The men were John Murray, now and then his elder brother, Tommy Thomson, Robert Graeme, Mr Fullerton till he married, James Keay till he married, William Clerk very seldom, Mr Cockburn always, John Jeffrey, the Moreheads now and then, chance celebrities, and a London friend at intervals. It was not a big wig set at all.[1] My father, Lord Gillies, and such like dignitaries would have been quite out of place in this rather riotous crew; indeed, the prevailing free and easy tone did not altogether suit *me*. Individually, almost all of our party were agreeable, cleverly amusing. Collectively, there was far too much boisterous mirth for my taste. I preferred being with Mrs Jeffrey, that *naturally* charming woman, not then by any means sufficiently appreciated by those so much her inferiours. She and I spent our time gardening, she was a perfect florist, playing with little Charlotte, to whom all my old nursery tales and songs were new, preparing for the company, and chattering to one another. My gentleman friends were William Murray of Henderland, and Robert Graeme of Lynedoch; they used to find Mrs Jeffrey, chatty and stout, where we were weeding our borders, and often carry us off up the hill, Jane remaining queen of the bowling green. How much she was admired by all those clever heads.

The dinners were delightful, so little form, so much fun, real wit sometimes, and always cheerfulness. The windows open to the garden, the sight and the scent of the flowers heightening the flavour of repasts unequalled for excellence. Wines, all our set were famous for having of the best and in startling variety–it was a mania; their cellars and their books divided the attention of the husband; the wife, alas, was more easily satisfied with the cookery. Except in a real old fashioned Scotch house, where no dish was attempted that was not national, the various abominations served up in corner dishes under French names were merely libels upon housekeeping. Mrs Jeffrey presented nothing upon her table but what her Cook could dress; her home fed fowl and home made bread, and fine cream and sweet butter, and juicy vegetables, all so good, served so well, the hot things *hot*, the fruits, creams, and butter so cold, gave such a feeling of comfort every one got good humoured, even cranky William Clerk. They were bright days, those happy summer days at Craig Crook.

Another country house we were very much in was one the

1. This is the only mention of Henry Cockburn, author of the indispensable *Memorials of his Time*.

Gibsons had a lease of, Woodside. It was six miles from town, a good ride. We went out early, staid all day, and came back in the cool of the summer evening. They were kind people, the father and mother very little in our way, the sons not much, the seven daughters of all ages our great friends. Mrs Kaye and Jane drew most together, Cecilia and I; the little ones were pets, and very pretty ones. We rode a good deal, one at a time, with the Coachman attending. We had struck up a friendship with a Captain and Mrs Bingham through the medium of their three fine little boys. He commanded the frigate in the Roads, had succeeded Captain Dalling. In winter, they lived in lodgings in the town; in summer, took a small house close to the sea at Newhaven. They gave a very pretty party in town, towards the end of a winter, inviting people simply to spend the evening. We found tea, and a good many friends, and a very hearty Sailor's welcome. After tea, said the Captain, 'Couldn't we get up a dance, don't you think, for the young people,' and pulling out a whistle gave a shrill call, on which in skipt half a dozen smart young sailors in their best, who wheeled out the tables, lifted up the carpet, settled the seats round the room, and then ushered in a Band. It had all been prepared before, but it was nicely done and a surprise, and put us all in high spirits. The sailors brought in supper at the proper time, and whilst we were enjoying our refreshments in the one room, they danced us a hornpipe in the other. When we *rode* to see them at Newhaven our luncheon was strawberries and cream. More than once we afterwards *rowed* to the frigate, and they gave us one little *fête* there on board; a dozen friends and a collation; the boats took us up the Forth for an hour instead of any dancing.

Captain Bingham's 'impromptu fait à loisir' party puts me in mind of Johnny Bell's. He was the celebrated Surgeon,[1] a morsel of a man married to a Wife as small, and they lived in rooms proportioned to their size, in a flat in George Street. He was extremely musical, of course collected a musical society about him; his instrument, the bass viol or double bass, bigger a great deal than himself; his hands could just

1. He was 'the best surgeon that Scotland had then produced' (Cockburn); he died in 1820 aged 57.

meet on it, the bow producing sounds from those thick strings a giant could only have emulated. It was a Grace Baillie affair, their single Concert, the return for all they went to; their whole apartment thrown open, kitchen and bed-room and all, made to communicate not only by doors but by windows, oval windows cut in the walls, filled by book shelves at ordinary times and opened on this state occasion, having all the effect of mirrours, spectators fancying at first that the moving mob seen through these openings was a reflexion. The many tiny rooms were by this means really made into one large enough for the company, nearly all of whom met the eye at any spot, by turning round the head. Some one wondering where the little couple slept on this gala night, Lord Jeffrey gravely answered, 'In the case of the bass viol.' A brother, George Bell, a barrister, was a great friend of my father's, a very first rate man; it was he who helped poor Duncan Cameron so well out of his scrape.

In August my father and Mother and William went to the highlands. Johnny accompanied M. L'Espinasse to France. The little monkey had a turn for languages, was making good progress in French, so as a reward this pleasant trip was arranged for him. We three young ladies were left to amuse ourselves—and Miss Elphick. John Dalzel was good enough to take us long walks frequently, sometimes as far as Portobello, where Mrs Gillio had taken lodgings for sea bathing. She had been in considerable difficulties, poor woman, on account of her children. Amelia was very unmanageable, a forward flirting girl, by no means pleased when found fault with. George, her only son, had run away; after a search of some days he was discovered on board a collier, bent on going to sea. He made stipulations before consenting to return home, one of which was that he should no more attend the High School. One of her Indian friends placed him some where in England under a Tutor, who prepared young men for Cadetships; he got his appointment in proper time, and went out to Bombay, where he died. Just as he left Edinburgh the mother broke her leg, and it was to recover her strength that she was sent to the seaside. Nobody could be kinder than she ever was to us, and in every way by attention on our part we tried to repay her warmth of feeling, but we could not go the length of having Amelia much with us, or of at all forming part of Amelia's own society. She had picked up a very under set of girl acquaintance, with Beaux of manners agreeable to them, principally young medical students, as a Class, the lowest of all at college. She had a 'Morris' and a 'Turnbull' she called them all thus by their plain surnames, and 'two Goldwires,' and I really forget how many more, with whom she seemed to be equally intimate; for, by her account, extraordinary personal liberties seemed to be taken by these young men with those young ladies without much offence, though she confessed she did not approve of all proceedings. She 'hated,' she said, 'pawing men.' 'Morris was not a pawing man, nor one of the Goldwires's, but the other was, and so was Hogg, and it was quite unpleasant,' she thought, 'to have a great hot hand feeling all over one.' We used to wonder at what School in Bath this girl could possibly have been educated.

We were obliged to offend poor Mrs Gillio about a trip to Roslin. She had hired a carriage, and made sure of our delighted acceptance of seats in it. We were to have cold meat and strawberries and cream at Lasswade, a day of thorough enjoyment; but as Amelia's Beaux were to have joined the party, Miss Elphick took it upon herself to say that she could not sanction the excursion. Amelia gave us a very lively description of the pleasures we had lost, concluding by a fine trick she had played her Mother. Going, Mrs Gillio had packed up all her young ladies inside the carriage with herself; two gentlemen going on the box, the rest in a gig. Returning Miss Amelia had no intention of a continuance of 'such old fudge'; so forming a respectable league with a 'Goldwire,' not the 'pawing one' it was to be hoped, 'off him and me set, and jumped upon the dickey box.' Dislodgement was stoutly resisted, and so there was rather a riotous journey home. Margaret, a pretty, gentle girl, was quite innocent of all these illbreedings. She occupied herself with her masters, her needleworks and her birds, and as a child, a companion for Mary, was very much with us, improving herself in every way with Mary in the schoolroom. A little spoiled Isabella, once so pretty, growing plain, was the plague of every body.

We did not neglect our unfortunate Cousins in the Abbey.

We never failed to visit them as when my Mother ordered the visit. Miss Carr, however, did not so much care to come to us, our ways were rather dull for her; Jane spent most of her time drawing, I worked a robe in imitation point, appliquée, intended for Mary's first Northern Meeting. We were so quiet, so orderly, so very correct in our whole conduct during the absence of the Heads of the family, that on their return my father was addressed in the Parliament House by our opposite neighbour, a Writer who lived on a flat, a second storey, high enough for good observation, and assured by him of the perfect propriety of our behaviour.

Jane's turn for drawing had been considerably increased by some lessons from Mr Wilson, the head of the Academy of painting, to whom Lord Eldin had most especially recommended her. She went twice a week to his painting rooms, where she worked away in earnest with several clever companions, among them poor Marianne Grant of Kilgraston, who very soon married James Lindsay, and Grace Fletcher, both of them good painters in oils. Mr Wilson sometimes read a picture or a drawing or a print with his pupils, and as I sometimes took my work and went with Jane, I came in for the lecture. He began with the general effect, went on to the grouping, the shading, the light, the distance, the peculiar propriety of certain objects in certain situations, directing our attention to an apparent trifle on which perhaps the whole beauty depended. Always afterwards, whether viewing fine scenery or examining paintings, we applied these explanations to our pictures, and found our pleasure in them heightened beyond any previous idea. It was like opening another eye, an eye with brains behind it; and we had ample opportunity for exercising our newly perceived faculty, for not only was the surrounding sea and land and our own town beautiful as art and nature could make them, but we had access to an admirable collection of paintings by the best Ancient and modern Artists, gathered from all quarters early the following winter, and exhibited at small cost to all who chose to buy a ticket. An empty house in York Place was hired for the purpose, and open every morning to the publick. Once a week in the evening the holders of season tickets were admitted; the rooms were well warmed, well lighted, and there were plenty of seats and it really was the most agreeable of assemblies, there being a paramount object to engage the attention and furnish an unfailing subject of discourse. All the possessors of good paintings had contributed to this Collection. We used to know the owners of particular gems by the air of triumph with which they stood contemplating what they were thoroughly acquainted with, instead of searching out stranger beauties. Mr Wilson frequently called us to him there, when surrounded by eager listeners to his criticisms. He and I did not always agree! I never would at any time surrender my private judgment, tho' I had sense enough to keep my free rights to myself.

Before my father and Mother went north, Jane and I had spent a week with them at Hermandstone, an ugly but comfortable place which Lord Gillies rented of Lord St Clair. I had been there before, and we were often there again, and when they were quietly leading a country life with only a few intimate friends visiting them, it was very pleasant. But when they had all their rich, grand, formal East Lothian neighbours, we young people hated going there. Lord Gillies was extremely fond of aristocratick company; the more grandees he could seat together at his very splendidly furnished table the better pleased he seemed to be. How often we see this in those of humble birth, as if the having risen to a place in that 'charmed circle' did not add a lustre to it, when talents and probity such as his had been the passport. Mrs Gillies, well born and highly bred, took her position naturally, content with what contented him. Neither of them, for all this, ever neglected the poor relations. His one prosperous brother, the doctor and authour,[1] was never as kindly welcomed as poor William, and poorer, more primitive Colin. At this very time William Gillies' three children found their home with their uncle Adam; for years they had had no other, the two girls going to the different classes while in Edinburgh, the boy placed first at the High School and then sent to the Charter House; and every Saturday when in town there was a dinner

---

1. John Gillies (1747-1836) was, in fact, not a M.D.; he
   was an historian who succeeded Principal Robertson as
   Historiographer Royal for Scotland.

for the young family connexions, school boys and girls, and College boys, all made as welcome as the grandees, and appearing a good deal happier. Miss Bessy Clerk and others used to fear that young people like William Gillies' children, brought up in such society, in a house so luxurious, would be spoiled for a ruder life, should such a change, as was most likely, come to them. But it did not so turn out; the change did come, and they bore it perfectly. Robert the corn factor, Mary the Authouress, and Margaret the professional painter, have followed their different employments better than if they had never had their intellects improved by their superiour education. The Authouress and the painter in particular benefited by the early cultivation of their taste, neither did I ever hear that Robert did less in Mark Lane because he was capable of enjoying in his Villa at Kensington the refinements of a gentleman's leisure. Margaret was never agreeable, but she was very clever. She did not wait to be turned out of Lord Gillies' house by his death or any accident. 'Uncle Adam,' said she one day, 'do you mean to leave Mary and me any thing in your Will?' 'Perhaps a trifle,' answered the Uncle. 'Not an independance?' pursued the niece. 'Certainly not, by no means; these are strange questions, Margaret.' 'Necessary ones, Uncle. My father has nothing to give us; he has married a second wife. We shall have then to work for our bread some time; we had better begin now while we are young, have health, activity, and friends to help us. I go to London next week.' She did, to her father's, where she was not welcome; so she hired two rooms, sent for Mary, began painting dauby portraits while learning her art more thoroughly; and when I saw them in their pretty home at Highgate they told me they had never been in want, nor ever regretted the decisive step they had taken.[1] The friends were at first seriously displeased; but the success of the nieces in time appeased the Uncles, and both the doctor and Lord Gillies left them legacies.

1. Margaret Gillies (1803–87) earned a reputation as a
   miniaturist and water-colour painter. Her sister Mary,
   the author of many books for children (often using the
   pseudonym Harriet Myrtle), died in 1860.

In the early part of the Edinburgh summers a good many very pleasant, quiet parties went on among such of us as had to remain in town till the Courts rose in July. I remember several very agreeable dinners at this season at the Arbuthnots, foreigners generally bringing their introductions about this time of year. At the Brewsters they had foreigners sent to them too, and they entertained them now, not in the flat where we first found them, but in their own house in Athole Crescent newly built out of the profits of the Kaleidoscope,[1] a toy that was ridiculously the rage from its humble beginning in the tin tube with a perforated card in the end, to the fine brass instrument set on a stand, that was quite an ornament to a drawing room. Had Sir David managed matters well, this would have turned out quite a fortune to him; he missed the moment and only made a few thousand pounds; still they gave him ease, and that was a blessing. The little dinners at his house were always pleasant. *She* was charming, and they selected their guests so well and were so particularly agreeable themselves, I don't remember any where passing more thoroughly enjoyable evenings than at their house. He was then, and is still, not only among the first of scientifick men, but in manners and in conversation utterly delightful; no such favourite every where as Sir David Brewster, except at home or with anyone engaged with him in business. Irritable as a husband, careless of his wife, thankless for her unceasing attentions, tyrannical and penurious, her life was rendered miserable; harsh, even cruel, as a father, his children were terrified by him. Nobody ever had dealings with him and escaped a quarrel. Whether he were ill, the brain overworked and the body thus overweighted, or whether his wife did not understand him, or did not know and exert himself, there is no saying. His temper has much improved since his sensible very patient daughter grew up, and since Lady Brewster died before her sister Miss Macpherson, and so put the succession to Belleville out of his head.[2] I have

1. Brewster's *Treatise on the Kaleidoscope* was published in 1819—he had invented it in 1816, but the patents were faulty so it was pirated.
2. This is explained on 1, p. 258.

sometimes spent the greater part of a day with them, when he would leave all his calculations and devote himself to our amusement, keeping close by the side of our worktable for hours, without giving expression to one cross word, and at dinner he would be in high spirits. Holy days poor Lady Brewster called those bright gleams in her much vexed existence.

At one of their small dinners my father and I could not take our eyes off a Tweedside neighbour, Miss Cochrane Johnstone. The Kaleidoscope had bought a few acres near Galla Water and built a small house upon them, where the Brewsters for some years passed every summer. She was one of the loveliest creatures that ever inherited broad lands, and she became the prize of a tall, red haired, rough sailor, who did not make her happy. She had a round beautiful figure, beautiful complexion, regular features, finely formed head, and a pair of almond shaped, warm, hazel, sleepy eyes, that must have killed every man they glanced on—gently. When I was reintroduced, in 1842 was it, to the widowed Lady Napier, a little thin, prim looking body surrounded by unmistakeably their father's daughters, I could not recall a trace of her youthful beauty. It quite grieved me. Perhaps, if she remembered me, I may have struck her as as much changed.

Miss Cochrane Wishart was another heiress that was thought handsome in a masculine way. She married a pretty little ladylike Sir Thomas Trowbridge, a sailor. A real beauty who was no heiress was a Miss Maclean. She made a perfect hubbub, and it was so odd a story altogether, the rights of it, as they say, not known till long afterwards.

At a mess dinner the conversation turning on beauties, their varieties, their reputations, their fashion, their merits, etc., a young officer laid a bet that he would bring any pretty girl into notice and have her cried up as a wonder, by properly preparing for her reception by the publick. The bet was taken and the plot laid. The Barrack Master at Berwick had several pretty daughters; the handsomest was selected, and very soon a whisper grew to an inquiry, and the inquiry to a strong desire to see either herself, or some one who had seen the beautiful Miss Maclean. She was very judiciously kept just long enough in retirement to excite curiosity, and then she appeared on a visit to Mrs Major somebody. The accomplices praised her to the skies, her fame increased, the few that saw her reported in exstasies. Presently crowds followed her out goings and her in comings. She lived in a mob, and so interested everybody. Mrs Major became suddenly the rage, she had more invitations for herself and her friend than there was a possibility of accepting, and in a room the rudeness of Admirers quite blocked up the poor girl's position, every eye too fixed on her. She really was a pretty creature, with a fine clear skin, dark hair and eyes, and a modest manner. She was not to be named by the side of many who had been less noticed, however. What stamped her celebrity was the notice taken of her by the Count and Countess Flahault; they invited her to stay with them, and as they saw company in an easy way every evening, Miss Maclean was at once raised into our great world. The Countess, Miss Mercer Elphinstone by birth, Baroness Keith in expectancy, had fallen in love with this most attractive foreigner and would marry him.[1] An heir to her vast fortune was of consequence, and an heir did not come; all sorts of accidents preventing it. Little Dr Hamilton was consulted, and when the next occasion presented itself Madame de Flahault was condemned to her sofa; but as her mind was to be amused she was to pass her time cheerfully. There she lay, covered with a lace overlay lined with pink silk, her hair nicely arranged, chattering at a great rate to thirty or forty guests. She was a very ugly woman and not a clever one and very far from being generally agreeable. I do not think she would have continued to attract much company, men at least, whom she greatly preferred, without some such magnet as her new protégée. Miss Maclean's reign

1. Margaret Elphinstone, Viscountess Keith
   (1788–1867) married Auguste Charles Joseph,
   Comte de Flahault de la Billardrie, in Edinburgh in
   1817. A natural son of Tallyrand, he became aide-de-
   camp to Napoleon. He was exiled but returned to
   favour after the Restoration, becoming ambassador in
   Rome, Vienna and London.

was short, but like Miss Manie Dreghorn's long before, Oh!, it was glorious. She had to return to Berwick, where she married poorly enough, a lieutenant in a marching regiment, a Mr Clarke; went with him to Bombay and died; and the young Officer won his bet.

M. de Flahault was in manner perfection, a finished frenchman, than which one can go no further in describing a gentleman; very handsome too, of a lively conversation truly agreeable. One small trait much struck me and set me thinking too. Mrs Munro had a small party, a good many young people at it, so she wished to set them dancing. Who would play? Mrs This had not any musick, and Mrs That made some other excuse. My Mother desired me to go to the instrument, which of course I did. 'Oh, no,' said M. de Flahault, 'that would be too severe a punishment to the gentlemen; let me relieve you, I can keep good time.' He played particularly well, so that it was a treat to dance to him, but what I thought over was his putting himself and his playing out of the question; his intention was to assist the amusement of the evening, make every body happy, and pay a neat compliment the while. It was all so high bred, so very un British. He behaved very well to his somewhat haughty wife, and she got on very well with him always. They had in time three daughters, one married to Lord Shelburne, I think, and one dead, but no son ever.

Lady Wiseman came to Edinburgh this summer; she was staying with her mother's relations the old Miss Steuarts, Annie Need's old friends, or foes, who on retiring from business had settled in their native town. She and two sisters, Mrs Rich and Mrs Erskine, were Sir James Mackintosh's children by his first wife. She was a clever, flighty creature, very foolish in her conduct, plain in face, but very pleasant, and a great friend of Jane's in a short time. After parting they corresponded. Sir William Wiseman being at sea, she had been left at Hertford College with her father, where she had picked up an admirer with whom her proceedings went rather beyond discretion, and so she was sent out of his way. No heart break for she very soon replaced him, first by Basil Hall, and then by Sir James Ramsay. It is to be hoped she *then* found safety in numbers. Afterwards, when she joined her husband on the Jamaica Station, she did not escape so well. She had two fine little boys : Willie, the present Baronet, who went to sea, and has come through life well, and dear little clever Jamie, who went all entirely wrong and shot himself in India. What has not a mother to answer for who deserts her children. How could she ever smile as Mrs Turnball. Above all, be saucy as she was at Grandville.

I think it was about the May or June of this year that old Mrs Siddons returned to the stage for twelve nights to act for the benefit of her grandchildren.[1] Henry Siddons was dead, leaving his affairs in much perplexity. He had purchased the theatre and never made it a paying concern, altho' his Wife acted perseveringly, and all the Kemble family came regularly and drew good houses. His ordinary company was not good ; he was a dreadful stick himself, and he would keep the best parts for himself, and in every way managed badly. She did better after his death ; her clever brother William Murray conducting affairs much more wisely for her, and certainly for himself in the end, slow as she was in perceiving this. Some pressing debts, however, required to be met, and Mrs Siddons came forward. We were all great play goers, often attending our own poor third rates, Mrs Harry redeeming all else in our eyes, and never missing the stars, John and Charles Kemble, Young, Liston, Matthews, Miss Stephens, etc. But to see the great queen again we had never dreamed of. She had taken leave of the stage before we left London. She was little changed, not at all in appearance, neither had her voice suffered ; the limbs were just hardly stiffer, more slowly moved rather, therefore in the older characters she was the finest, most natural ; they suited her age. Queen Catherine she took leave in. To my dying hour I never shall forget the trial scene ; the silver tone of her severely cold 'My Lord Cardinal,' and then on the wrong one starting up, the

1. See I, pp. 198–9 for the great Sarah Siddons' triumphant 'final' appearance as Lady Macbeth in 1812.
After her son Henry's death in 1815, she returned ten times to the stage of the Theatre Royal in Edinburgh (on which he had taken a twenty-one year lease in 1809) in benefit performances for her grand-children.

scorn of her attitude, and the outraged dignity of the voice in which she uttered 'To *You* I speak.'[1] We were breathless. Her sick room was very fine too. Then her Lady Macbeth, Volumnia, Constance[2]—ah, no such acting since, for she was nature, on stilts in her private life. 'Bring me some beer, boy, and another plate,' is a true anecdote, blank verse and a tragick tone being her daily wear.

Once when Liston was down I longed to see him in Lubin Log; for some reason I could not manage it, and Mrs Harry let me go to her private box. He had been Tony Lumpkin in the Play, and we were talking him over, waiting for his appearance in the farce. 'I have heard,' said I, 'of his giving a look with that queer face of his, not uttering a word, yet sending people into convulsions of laughter not to be checked while he remained in sight.' 'Hush,' said Mrs Harry, 'here he comes.' Enter Lubin from the Coach with all his parcels. Between his first two inquiries for his 'numbrella' and his ''at,' he threw up at our hidden box, at *me, the* look—perfectly oversetting; there never could be such another grotesque expression of fun since the days of fauns and satyrs, and when composure in a degree returned, a sly twinkle of one squinting eye, or the buck tooth interrupting a smile, or some indescribable secret sign of intelligence, would reach us and set us off again. We were ill with laughing. He played that whole farce to us, to Mrs Harry and me, and not to the House, and every one agreed he had surpassed himself.[3]

The early part of the next summer, 1819, passed much in the same way as the one before; sociable small parties among our friends in town, and visits to those in the country. Messages to the Abbey of course, and we were always the messengers. My Mother was very careful of the servants;

1. *Henry VIII*, iv, 69.
2. Mother of *Coriolanus*; Arthur's mother in *King John*.
3. John Liston (1776?–1846) is described by the D.N.B. as the highest paid comic actor of his day; it adds he was 'unjustly charged with a mere power of grimace'. Lubin Log was a rôle he created in *Love, Law & Physic* (1812); Goldsmith's Tony Lumpkin appears in *She Stoops to Conquer*.

Johnny declared that one extremely rainy day when it was proper the Newcastle Chronicle should be returned to Mrs General Maxwell, my Mother called out to him, 'Johnny, my dear, I wish you would run to George Street with this; it's such a dreadful day I don't like sending out poor Richard'—a colossus of a footman, weighing heavier every day from having too little to do. Poor Johnny! I can't somehow separate him in boyhood, dear Jack, from you. My recollection of him is so like you while he was little, before he grew to six foot one. This very spring he, may be, thought with regret of even Mrs Maxwell's newspaper, for my father took him up to town with himself and sent him to Eton. They first paid a visit to the Electors of Tavistock, and on their way spent a day or two with Dugald Stewart, who lived then near the Duke of Bedford's cottage at Endsleigh. The old philosopher predicted the boy's future eminence, although we at home had not seen through his reserve. He was idle, slow, quiet, passing as almost stupid beside his brilliant brother. 'Take care of that boy, Grant,' said Dugald Stewart at their parting; 'he will make a great name for himself, or I am much mistaken.' And has he not? Quiet he has remained, indolent too, and eccentrick, but in his own field of action where is his parallel? My Mother and I thought of no honourable future when our pet left us. We watched him from the window, stepping into the travelling chariot after my father in the new great coat that had been made for him, the little tearful face not daring to venture a last glance back to us. He was small of his age, and from being the youngest he was childish. We did not see him for fifteen months. He came back to us an Eton boy; how much those three small words imply. My poor Mother, I can understand now the sob with which she threw herself back upon the sofa, exclaiming, as the carriage rolled away 'I have lost my Johnny!' His cousin John Frere went to Eton at the same time, and our John spent all short holidays at Hampstead, only coming home to the highlands once a year in the summer. The two cousins remained attached friends ever, and though widely separated, never lost sight of one another till poor John Frere died.

The next event was the arrival of Uncle Ralph, his wife, daughter Eliza, and sister Fanny, to have just a peep of us before settling again at Tennochside. They had tired of England and were glad to return home, leaving Edmund behind at School. Jane, who was a great favourite with Mrs Ralph, went to see them soon afterwards, and spent a very happy three weeks at that comfortable place. During her absence we had a visit from Aunt Leitch and our cousin Kate. Kate had been with us before, which I have neglected to mention. Uncle Edward, soon after his marriage, invited her out to India, funds were sent home for her equipment and passage, and it was decided by the family that Aunt Leitch should have the charge of all matters concerning her departure. She was to spend the winter in Glasgow, and the following spring proceed to London to be outfitted before embarking. She came direct from Houghton to us, and remained with us two months, going to any parties that offered, and very much admired. She was not pretty, in spite of fine eyes, but the expression of her countenance was very bright; she was clever and natural and lively, with modest, simple manners, and she was tall and her figure was good. She dressed very becomingly, scanty and plain as her wardrobe was when she arrived; it increased in size and value considerably during her stay at Picardy Place. We were all quite sorry when she left us, the more so that she sadly deteriorated during her visit to Glasgow. Aunt Leitch's temper ruffled Kate's, want of exercise destroyed her looks. She returned to us fat, and dark, and pert, and quite unlike herself. This all went off after she reached India, although Mrs Edward Ironside's humours tried her *im*patience sorely. She married very happily, and as Mrs Barnwall was one of the most agreeable women in all Bombay. Glasgow was not a place to improve in. We were there once, I forget in what year. My father went to collect evidence in some political business, my Mother and I with him, as a cloke I suppose. We were at Aunt Leitch's pretty new house in St Vincent Street, and she took a great deal of trouble for us in making up parties at home, engagements abroad, and even directed an Assembly. We were not very refined in manners in Edinburgh, some of us, but there were brains with us, abilities of a high order, turned to a more intellectual account than could be the general employment of them in a mere manufacturing seaport town, for into that had Glasgow sunk. Its College, as to renown, was gone; its merchants no longer the Cadets of the neighbouring old County families, but their clerks of low degree shot up into the high places. 'Some *did* remain who in vain mourned the *better* days when they were young,' but as a whole the Society was indescribably underbred. I should have been very much out of my element in that Assembly had it not been for an accidental meeting with the little merry sailor Houston Steuart, and Dick Honeyman, a son of Lord Armidale's.

About July the Scots Grays got the route for Ireland. Tom Walker was in despair. He was a fine looking young man, truly amiable, played the flute to Jane's pianoforte, a performance suitable in every respect and unimprovable, for in spite of daily very lengthened practisings neither artist made much progress. He had a handsome private fortune. Altogether, Annie Need had hoped this favourite nephew of her general's would have brought them a Scotch niece back; but his knowledge of history was so defective! It was not possible for a moment to think seriously of a companion for life with whom there could be no rational conversation! So the handsome Cavalry officer *walked* away—no, *rode*. I daresay the Band master was glad, for most of his spare time had been occupied copying out Waltzes. An Irish love soon replaced the 'bonnie Jean' so honestly wooed. A Miss Constantia Beresford made no educational difficulties. She caused a few, however, of many another kind, and poor Tom Walker bore them.

General Need had returned home very soon after his marriage to our dear Annie. They had settled amidst his rich manufacturing relations near Nottingham, who had all received her most kindly. We heard from her constantly and were always planning to meet, yet never managed it. My father had seen her with her two nice little boys, and found her perfectly happy; her General no genius, but an excellent man.

I cannot recollect much else that is worthy of note before our little tour upon the Continent. We set out in August, and were two months and a half away. My father was not inclined for such a movement at all, it was probably very inconvenient

to the treasury, but my mother had so set her heart upon it,
he, as usual, good naturedly gave way. Johnny was to spend
his holidays with the Freres. Miss Elphick went to the
Kirkman Finlays,[1] her parting was quite a dreadful scene,
screams, convulsions, sobs, hystericks. The poor woman was
attached to some of us, and had of late been much more
agreeable to the rest; but she was a plague in the house, did a
deal of mischief, and was no guide, no help. She had been
seven years with us, so there was a chain of habit to loosen at
any rate.

1. Kirkman Finlay (1773–1842) was a famous Glasgow
    merchant, who prospered in the difficult conditions
    after the American War to become Lord Provost in
    1812 and one of the M.P.s for the city 1812–18.

CHAPTER TWENTY-TWO

1819

IN the month of August, then, of this year 1819 we set out on our foreign travels, my father, my Mother, William, Jane, Mary and I; rather too large a party as we found when we had more experience, particularly as we were attended by a man, a maid, and a dog. The maid, a thoroughly stupid creature, and the dog, poor Dowran, went with us; the man, a black, and a deal too clever, joined us in Holland, for to the Netherlands we were bound. My father had always had a passion for Dutch and Flemish paintings, farming, buildings, and politicks; besides, he was so very kind as to wish to take me to the waters at Aix la Chapelle. I had been attacked in the Spring with the same sort of strange suffering that has fallen upon me several times since, at intervals often of years, after any disturbance of mind, a failure as it seemed of all powers of body, the whole system paralysed, as it were, without any apparent cause other than that reserve of disposition inherited from my Mother, which threw all grief back inwardly while the outward manner was unchanged. She never told me that anxiety for me made her anxious for the complete change of scene we were entering on. I only guessed it many years afterwards.

We embarked at Leith in a common trading vessel, a tub, with but moderate accommodation, the Van Egmont, bound for Rotterdam. Its very slow rate of sailing kept us nine days at sea; luckily the weather the whole time was beautiful, and our few fellow passengers accommodating, with the exception of one unhappy looking man, a merchant in some embarrassment with regard to his affairs. He used to watch the wind so nervously, it being of consequence to him to appear before a certain day in the Counting House of his Dutch Correspondent. We had some difficulty in sweetening the disturbed moments of this anxious minded poor man, but we succeeded in a degree, the wind, the last few days, aiding us. His father was a light hearted very old man, taking the voyage for pleasure, probably unaware of the full extent of his son's perplexities. A very grave Merchant's Clerk and two young Officers completed our party. One of the Officers, now Colonel Clunie, has been to India and back, found Jane out in Edinburgh, and has several times dined with her in York Place, recurring with delight to the happy nine days on board the Van Egmont. We all did our best to make them pass cheerfully. We watched the land, the sea, the sky, the day's work. Our skipper was extremely civil; his mate, a merry scapegrace, inventing all sorts of fun to amuse every body; the fare was good, the Cabin clean, and living out on deck in the open air even I regained an appetite.

On nearing the Dutch Coast the scene became very interesting. All at once we found ourselves amid a crowd of little fishing vessels, rigged with three cornered sails of a deep orange colour. We passed then a few larger boats, a merchantman or two, and then there suddenly rose upon us from the waves, steeples, treetops, towers and windmills, without any more stable foundation seemingly than the water. There was some delay in crossing the Bar, an accumulation of sand at the mouth of the Maas that can only be crossed at the full tide; once over that we sailed quietly on, the windmills and steeples closing in upon us, till the sedgy banks of the river appeared on either hand, with houses, gardens, small fields full of cattle, all as it seemed below the level of the water. It was a curious sight, and a pretty one; for as the river narrowed and so enabled us to distinguish the objects we were passing, the total difference they exhibited from any of the kind we had been accustomed to look on created the most lively feelings of surprise. The villages looked all like toys, little, formal, green, round topped trees in rows, small baby houses painted in such bright colours—red, and blue, and green, and yellow, and dazzling white—with window panes that shone like diamonds, door steps clean enough to dine on, neat gravel paths, and palings without a blemish. One could not fancy the large, heavy looking, heavily clothed men we saw in all the Craft on the river being allowed to enter such fairy premises. It now became a matter of nice piloting to get our heavy barge through the thickening throng of vessels of all sizes, but the big Dutchman in his big balloon breeches, and his big overcoat covered with great big dollars for buttons, and his red night Cap, whom we had taken on board below the Bar, carried us safe in and out and all round all obstacles, and brought us up easily to the quay in the heart of the busy and very beautiful City of Rotterdam.

The extent of the Bompjes I really don't remember. A row of fine elms runs all along the parapet by the river's edge.[1] A broad road, so clean, is beyond, then a narrow pavement in front of the street of irregularly built houses, some high, some low, some palaces, some cottages, some with a handsome façade, and others with picturesque gable ends, *portes cochères* every here and there admitting to the Court- yard and the ware rooms as well as the dwelling house of the Merchants, even cranes at intervals impending over head. A large, long, low building, a capital hotel, the Badthouse, was where we were bound, gladly availing ourselves of all its name promising hot water luxuries, to refresh bodies wearied by near a fortnight of a sea toilette.

We arrived in the very midst of the Kermess, the annual fair, the most favourable of all times for the visit of strangers. The wares of all the world were exposed for sale in streets of booths tastefully decorated, lighted up brilliantly at night, and crowded at all hours by purchasers from every province in the two united kingdoms,[2] all in their best and very handsome and perfectly distinct attire. Like Venice, Rotter- dam is built in the water, long canals intersect it in every direction, on which the traffick is constant; there are mere footpaths on either side, with quantities of narrow bridges for

1. It was this avenue of elms that gave its name to the Boompjes, the quarter mile long quay in the heart of the city.
2. The former Austrian Netherlands had been joined to the Kingdom of Holland by the victorious allies four years earlier at Vienna; E.G. seemed well aware of this union's deficiencies.

the convenience of crossing. The tall houses forming the
street must have been gloomy abodes, just looking over the
narrow stream to one another. Outside they were gay enough
from the excessive cleanliness observed, and the bright paint,
and the shining brass knockers, and the old fashioned
solidity of the building. It was quite amusement enough to
wander all about this fine old City, every now and then
getting back into the throng of the fair, where indeed I could
have spent the day most agreeably, every object presented to
the eye was so totally different from any ever seen at home.
The people were of course the most dissimilar, national
features varying as much as national dress. The men were
merely sturdy, healthy, sailor like persons, enveloped in a
great quantity of substantial clothing, each coat and pair of
breeches containing stuff enough for two; the women were
quite superiour, the younger ones beautiful, with the
loveliest of fair clear skins; even the old were agreeable from
the perfect cleanliness and good order of their appearance; a
rag, a tatter, is never seen, nor a speck of dirt either, and the
peculiarity of the costume of every province, all so befitting
the station of the wearers, made every little group we fell in
with a picture. Full stuff petticoats rather short, such clean
white stockings, neat, very black, polished shoes, pretty
ankles too, snow white handkerchiefs, smart aprons, clear
muslin caps edged with the finest lace in good quantity,
varying in shape according to the district that sent it forth,
and often very valuable gold ornaments about the head,
round the throat, and in the ears. The north Hollanders
especially were remarkable for thus adorning themselves;
their style of head was particularly becoming, or else they
were so pretty that whatever they wore would have suited
them.

After the people came the vehicles, the queerest assort-
ment of strangely shaped post waagens not unlike our
omnibus's with open sides, or some of the third class
carriages on our railways. Quantities of these, of all sizes,
were running through the paved streets all day, and for the
narrow pathways by the canals there were very small carts
drawn by dogs to convey such market produce as it was not
worth while to send by water to every door; larger carts with

or without tilts plied in the more accessible thoroughfares. It was a very busy scene, very cheerful, and very curious to us who had never been out of our own country before.

The excessive cleanliness was almost more to be admired than all else; it pervaded the habits of the nation throughout. The streets were daily swept, the pavements daily washed, the railings daily wiped, the windows daily rubbed, the brasses daily brightened. Within it was the same; no corner left unvisited by the busy maid, the very door keys were polished, like the small bunches we keep in our pockets, cupboards, closets, shelves, not only spotless but neatly ornamental; white paper with a cut fringe, or white linen frilled, laid along under the shining wares they were appropriated to hold. Yet nobody seemed overworked. In the afternoons all the women were spinning or knitting, as beautifully tidy in their own persons as was all the property around them. There were no dirty children, even no beggars. They are all early risers, and very active in their movements—regardless of consequences too! In our before breakfast walks we often got more from the whirl of the mop than we liked, while the regular splashing and dashing was going on during the hour all the houses were having their faces washed. A girl with long gold ear rings dangling, would be out in the street with her pail, too intent on the freshening up of her master's dwelling to think of the passers by. In Ireland here we can't get our maids to wash our doorsteps—must not propose such an indignity—some of the very particular ones object to kneel to wash the kitchen flags; and as for dusting, or bright rubbing! alas! damp as is our climate we must put up not only with rusty keys, but rusty fire irons, for a generation or two yet. Our lady wives not thinking the care of their families a duty, as does the comfortable Dutch *vrow*. The damp in Holland was the original cause of all this care, destruction would have followed carelessness, and does follow it here. The hotel was just as admirably kept as any private house. We had no sitting room, but the bedrooms were very large, and we took our meals in the saloon, breakfast at a small table at our own hour, dinner at the *table d'hôte*. The eating was very good, abundance of it, nice fruit, wine, beer, and most delicious tea; never before nor since nor any where else did

I ever drink any equal to it. The coffee was very strong of *chicorée*, but well made, and I believe the bitter made it more wholesome. The bread was either too heavy or too spongy for our taste.

The *table d'hôte* was very pleasant; many of the townspeople seemed to dine there, bachelours mostly, without homes, and travellers, all of whom spoke to those they happened to sit next, charitably acting to one another as if there were no convicts in the company. The Dutch are called a silent people, yet some of them at least had plenty to say, French being our medium of conversation—a foreign language both to them and us. We found the low Dutch commonly spoken by no means hard to learn a little of. Jane and I were very soon able to carry on all the business of our travelling party so as to be perfectly understood by servants and tradespeople. We were bargaining at the door steps with a flower girl, when a very smart English group, new arrivals, elbowed their way past us. Some of the faces were familiar to us, and a lady's loud, shrill, very English voice gave me quite a start I remembered it so well, but where, I could not puzzle out. When we were assembled at three o'clock to dinner a door opened and the party entered, the ladies in great dress, all in rich silks, one with a bare neck, all with the smartest heads, a turban, a blonde cap with flowers, ribbons, trinkets—making themselves in every way so conspicuous that we really felt ashamed of our compatriots. Imagine the feelings then with which *I* received the most gracious of bows from the turban, and heard the sharp provincial voice pronounce my name, adding that the owner of these two properties could give me a better than ordinary report of my 'poor dear Uncle at Oxford.' It was the President of Trinity and Mrs Lee! her sister and a soldier husband, Captain English by name, and two or three other Ipswich friends who had made a run across the Channel to see some of the wonders of Holland. Introductions all round followed of course as soon as we rose from the table, and we agreed to take tea together in one of our bedrooms. Very obliging they all were, and Mrs Lee did give my mother a more comfortable account of Dr Griffith's health than my Aunt Mary had latterly been able to send us. Still the case looked melancholy enough, and this kind hearted woman seemed to feel it so sincerely that even William forgave the midday turban. They were going on to Antwerp next day, so that we were saved another full dress daylight dinner. My father, who extremely enjoyed my Mother's discomfiture on this rather startling occasion, had behaved very ill by drawing Mrs English out, as he called it, and so he was banished after their departure to take a walk till his extraordinary paroxisms of laughter were over. I went with him along the Bompjes under the trees by the side of the water, and reaching the part at which the Harwich packet landed the passengers, who should step ashore but Mr Canning—the only time I ever saw him. He and my father seemed glad to meet,[1] and while they were conversing I had an opportunity of correcting all my imaginary impressions of the great man. He was not so tall and much more slender than I expected. His countenance was pale, anxious almost, and certainly no longer handsome; the high, well developed forehead alone reminded me of the prints of him. He was travelling with his sick son, a boy of seventeen or so, a cripple confined to a Merlin chair, and supported in that by many cushions. An elderly, very attentive servant never left the invalid's side, while another looked after the luggage and a carriage fitted up with a sort of sofa bed. They did not come to the Badthouse, so we saw no more of them; but I could not forget them, and often after, when the world was ringing with Mr Canning's fame, this scene of his private life returned to me, for he lost the son. It was Mr Burke and his son over again[2] as to many of the circumstances, only Mr Canning had another son, and one daughter whose marriage to Lord Clanricarde helped to kill him. Mrs Canning, the wife, was sister to the Duchess of Portland and the Countess of Moray. They were co-heiresses with very large fortunes,

1. Although of different parties, they knew each other well. Canning was Prime Minister for a few months before his death in 1827.
2. His eldest son died next year aged 19; Edmund Burke's son, Christopher, had died in childhood; a Merlin chair was an invalid wheel chair named after its inventor.

something like a hundred thousand pounds apiece; indeed I believe the eldest sister had more. It was all made by whist, their father, General Scott, being the most accomplished player of his day. He pursued it as a business, ate an early dinner of mutton or chicken with a glass of wine, no more, and then encountered any body, every body, *full* or fasting, taking good care however of who was his partner. He was never accused of the slightest approach to any incorrect practices, he merely took the advantage of a sober man over those who had dined well; it was not called dishonourable, this!, his opponents were free Agents. He left a curious will. He ordered his daughters to marry into the peerage under the penalty of forfeiting all share of their inheritance should any of them give herself to a Commoner. How absurd are these meddlers with the future. Mrs Canning, of course, lost her fortune, but her ennobled sisters each presented her with fifty thousand pounds as a wedding present.

We remained above a week in Rotterdam. Besides that this first specimen of foreign lands extremely interested us, we had made acquaintance with a very agreeable family long residents in the town, Mr Ferrier's our consul, a native of Brechin, not then knighted, to whom Lord Gillies had given us an introduction. They had been schoolfellows and friends; for the civilities we received could hardly, at first at least, have been paid us on our own account. The handsomest house on the Bompjes was Sir Alexander Ferrier's; it was quite a palace, far too splendid for a private family, having belonged to some great functionary during the reign of Louis Buonaparte.[1] The principal Staircase and the pavement of the hall and the door steps were of polished marble. One room was of such large dimensions it had never been furnished by Lady Ferrier; it occupied the height of two storeys, and was opened only on occasion of the Consul's annual ball. Even the dining room was much larger than any room at Russborough,[2] the daily parties of fourteen, sixteen, or so, were lost in it. They dined late for Holland, six

1. He ruled Holland for his brother, 1805–10.
2. The beautiful house of E.G.'s Co. Wicklow neighbour, the Earl of Milltown.

o'clock, and had musick and dancing among a large society of young people every evening. The daughters of the house were of all ages, and all of them were handsome, Amelia the eldest perhaps the least so; neither was she clever; she was amiable, gentle, and most obliging in manner to every one, and soon became quite a favourite with us. We suspected her of a little tender interest in the handsome son of her father's Dutch partner, young Mr Blankenhelm, for she certainly looked grave when he chose any other lady to drive out with him in his pea green gig on either of the only two roads available for carriage exercise, the one to Dort and the one to the Hague. The second sister was in School in England, quite a beauty, young enough, yet old enough to be in love too, and engaged to Sir James Turing, a very old Aberdeenshire Baronet, whose father while a Cadet had settled in Holland. The third and fourth, very pretty girls, afterwards married well among their father's mercantile friends. One of them, Eliza, was the mother of Mrs George Lauder! There were only two sons, John, married to a tiresome little heiress who had been a ward of his father's, a Walter Scott story, I am afraid,[1] and little Alex, who with a little Georgy still younger, two beautiful children, was in the nursery. Sir James, or Sir *Robert* Turing, I believe he was, had a brother, a very small little man; he arrived with a ship full of valuables from Batavia while we were in Rotterdam. Much of the Merchandise had been a venture of Mr Ferrier's. We saw it arrive, enter the great gates, be unloaded from the trucks. Some of it was arranged in the extensive surrounding warerooms on the ground floor; some of it raised by the crane into the upper storeys, and one small bale left at the Counting house door. We saw all this from Amelia's apartments high up at the back of the house overlooking the yard. She had a bedroom and sitting room to herself beautifully furnished. 'Come,' said she, 'now's *our* time for the Indian curiosities,' and she led the way running lightly downstairs. The unpacking of the cases in the Office had begun. There were China crapes, and China silks, and India muslins, ivory, Japan, Bombay pretty

1. For Scott's securing an heiress for his eldest son,
    see II, pp. 73–4.

things, preserved fruits, an infinite variety. Some of these were commissions and would be sold well; some were for the general market, and some for presents. My share was a box of dates, and the black lacquer fan I gave to you, Annie, dear. Mrs Ferrier had pieces of damask for new drawing room curtains. We highly approved of the generosity of the Mercantile profession, though Mr Blankenhelm took care to repeat more than once that his partner was not usually so liberal; his heart had evidently warmed to his country folk.

Sir James Gambier was another visitor. He was the Consul General for the Netherlands, a very fine looking, most agreeable man, though the father of a grown up family. He lived at the Hague, but had business at Rotterdam during our stay which kept him with us almost the whole time. Mr Blankenhelm said these affairs were of that mysterious nature no one could form the least idea of them. He was a busy body evidently, that tall, slender, handsome, gentlemanly Dutchman. The father and mother were formed after the old squat type, as were one or two other native heads of firms; the ladies belonging to them we did not see; they were either at Schevening bathing, or at their pleasure houses in the country. We had Mr Anderson Blair however for a couple of days. He was on his road to the German Spas and wanted to engage us to extend our travels so far. He liked every thing and every body at Rotterdam, except the pea green gig and Mr Blankenhelm; however sunny were our morning drives, clouds obscured our return from that quarter.

At last we were to move, the quicker because the low fever common to the place had seized on me and change of air was the cure, assisted by a glass every morning of gin bitters the first thing, ordered peremptorily by Mr Ferrier, and sent in in a dumpy bottle bulging out on either side from a long neck, sometimes ages ago seen of alike shape and larger size in our own country, and called a tappit hen. How they were to get on without us, without Jane's highland fling and my rebel songs, they were afraid to think of in that palace house. We were quite grieved ourselves to leave them, they had made us so very happy. We settled to return and embark for home from thence, and that during the time we were at Brussels Mr Ferrier should bring Amelia to us and leave her there for the

few weeks we intended remaining, and so bidding farewell
overnight, we set out early next morning for the Hague,
twelve miles only along a paved road by the side of the Canal.
It was the same neatness, the same cleanliness, the same
flatness and the same baby house prettiness of scenery the
whole way. We were in two carriages: a large, long caravan
sort of concern for ourselves; the servants, the luggage and
Dowran in a smaller queer shaped machine behind us.
Dowran, disliking his position cooped up at Ward's feet,
took an opportunity to jump out, against all rules, no dogs
allowed to be at large during the hot months. A frightful
hubbub ensued. Men running, yelling, screaming, bran-
dishing sticks, throwing stones. The terrified animal flying
over the burning pavement, till with one thing and another
he was very nearly driven mad. William, jumping from the
carriage, had just time to save his favourite from an uplifted
club, but in what a condition was the poor creature! A
respectable bystander advised his being plunged and re-
plunged into the canal till he was nearly insensible; he was
then replaced at Ward's feet, and she and the courier turning
round, retraced the road to Rotterdam, my father giving
them a few pencil lines to deliver with the Dog to Mr Ferrier.
So long as the poor beast lived we were content, for that he
had not gone really mad we were certain. We reached the
Hague in good time to order dinner in a private room, and to
invite Sir James Gambier to partake of it.

The Hague is a beautiful town, a perfect contrast to
Rotterdam, built on a plain of course, scattered over it, space
being every where; large squares, wide streets, even gardens,
and very little water. There were buildings to see, of course,
of which I only remember the Stadt house, left with all its
splendid furniture as Louis and Hortense[1] had lived in it. It
contains one hall of Audience, said to be the largest room ever
a flat roof had been ventured to be stretched over. The
present King and Queen, though bound to live occasionally
in Holland, were supposed by the jealous Dutch to prefer

1. Hortense, daughter of Napoleon's first wife by a
    former marriage, Josephine de Beauharnais, married
    his brother Louis.

Flanders, and when they did come to their ancient dominions they preferred the privacy of the House in the Wood to the grander Stadt house in the 'village.' We went out to see the House in the Wood, an extremely pretty, country gentleman's residence, interesting to us on account of our own Queen Mary, who lived there so long with her cross but adored Prince William in days when the Stadtholder was not allowed to affect much splendour. They could hardly have had a simpler household than the King William of this age. The apartments were all comfortable, but none of them too fine for daily use; there was quite an air of domestick repose about them. The little Princess Marianne's cribbed, poor thing, stood beside her mother's, and little chairs and little tables suited to her childish size were in the business like sitting room the queen always lived in. There were good paintings in both these Royal residences, and a great many valuable curiosities scattered about. An ormolu clock in every room, abundance of chandeliers and sconces, and the beds were all set upon platforms, raised a step, or even two, from the floor, it had a good effect— imposing.

Amsterdam, twenty miles on, was a regular town again, none of the free, villa like look of the Hague; high houses with quaint gable ends, narrow streets and canals through them, bridges innumerable, ships and bustle. Plenty of sights for travellers, just the very things I care least to see. A fine picture, a few fine pictures, I can enjoy, give me time to study them one by one when I'm in the humour to look at them, but a Collection of pictures weighs me down with the headache, and to run about from one gallery of paintings to another, then to a Museum, after that to a church or two to see monuments here and carvings there, is all, to my peculiar feelings, utterly wearisome. I would walk about all day with pleasure in a strange country, keep my senses awake, and take my leisure to examine any object that interested me as it met me; but to run about looking for lions was to me intolerable. I had, however, in general to follow the lead, and so have a confused idea of a Statue to Erasmus, a pulpit and skreen, perfect marvels of carving, a whole string of ships commemorating Van Tromp, no *broom* though, some fine marble momuments to the murdered Prince of Orange, and what remains with me beyond them all, the painting of the death of Abel in the Museum of Amsterdam.

Far more than all this sightseeing I enjoyed an excursion to North Holland across the Zuyder Zee. We went to see Brock and Saardam, and on the way, as there was nothing very remarkable in the surrounding scenery, my attention was drawn to some of the passengers in the boat; they were of all degrees, market people, traders, pleasure seekers and travellers, and less noise I suppose was never made by any such number of persons who had nothing else to do but talk and smoke. The smoking was incessant, but as for talking, a word was hardly spoken by any but ourselves.

Another of my peculiarities being the total want of discernment of any brilliant qualities in that lunatick barbarian Peter the Great, Saardam with his little hut, still existing, made small impression. Brock was enchanting, a perfect curiosity, really the fit capital of a Lilliputian fairy tale. It seemed unnatural to see human beings of the usual dimensions moving about this toy of a village. No carriage was allowed to pass through its tiny streets; indeed there would hardly have been room for any much wider than a wheelbarrow. The roads or paths rather, were all paved with coloured stones in patterns. No one ever entered the little, baby houses by the front door but a Bride, or left them thro' this honoured entrance till a corpse; the family only made use of the back door, opening on a little yard as scrupulously clean as our best kept kitchens. We were permitted to enter several of the houses; the people seemed to be accustomed to shew them, and to have the greatest pride in the display of their quantities of heavy handsome furniture, polished up by hard labour to rival the best French varnish. The parlours were never lived in, that was plain, and that any family labours ever went on in the kitchen almost seemed impossible; one could hardly fancy slop pails, dirty dishes, rubbers, brick bats and scrubbing brushes could have profaned for a moment precincts apparently just burnished up for an Exhibition. The inhabitants, though too big for their dwellings, were all as spotlessly clean. Whether any dirt ever made its way to Holland looked problematical. Cooking with stoves is certainly a means of cleanliness, pipkins [1] can be used instead of black pots, and there is no burning to coat the outsides of them with soot.

The great man of the village lived in a much larger baby house than any other person possessed; he had a larger court yard too, and more than an Acre of ground behind, which he had laid out as an English garden in the following style. A wood, a meadow, a labyrinth, a river, a lake, a shady lane, a grove, and a cottage residence. Meandering walks led to all these various beauties, and at different points, in appropriate attitudes, were placed stuffed figures of men, all supposed to be busy about different rural pursuits. At the edge of the wood was a stuffed image of a sportsman properly equipped with belts and bags and a real gun, accompanied by a stuffed dog pointing at a small covey of wooden partridges nestled under a shrub. On a pretty bridge that crossed the river, a stuffed fisher with a basket under his arm held a rod over the stream, while another image on the banks was taking a painted trout off the hook at the end of his line. Under a tree sat a stuffed elderly gentleman with a real book. On the lake were two large painted swans; and in the cottage down the shady lane there were seated by a fictitious kitchen fire an old couple properly dressed, the old man mending a net, the old woman spinning at her wheel, exact representations of the proprietor's parents, in their identical clothing and their own abode, for in this hut they had passed their humble lives, and were thus commemorated by their prosperous son. All the furniture was preserved as it had been left: the bed, the heavy wardrobe, table, chairs, down to the whole kitchen utensils. It was the great man's pleasure to visit this his birthplace constantly, and keep his parents and all around them in repair. The whole garden was the idol of Brock, spoke of with an exultation quite amusing; little nursery people three feet high might have had it for a play thing, but as a real honest pleasure ground to a man weighing fifteen stone, amply fitted out with broadcloth, the fact could hardly be realised.

After Amsterdam came Leyden, the same quaint style of town, where we slept in order to have time to walk over

1. Earthenware cooking pot.

ground trodden, when its University was more famous, by my Grandfather. Then we went on to Haarlem, its environs blooming in their sandy plain, the florists here being the best in all Holland, both the soil and the water particularly suiting the gardener's trade. The water of the famous mere, since partly drained, is equally prized by the laundress, the lime it contains whitening linen so perfectly trunks of clothes come from as far as Paris to undergo the good bleaching they get here. The banker, Mr Hope, has quite a noble villa near the mere, with wonderful gardens round it. Haarlem is a pretty open town, much more cheerful than the old cooped up Cities. It has a fine market place and a great Square, and a beautiful Cathedral, where we went to hear the Organ, once the boast of Europe; there are others, they say, modern ones, finer now, only I never heard them. The performing on this at Haarlem so exhausted the Organist, he requires a high bribe to play more than once a day. We thought he deserved whatever he chose to ask, his taste and his execution were so perfect, and the tones of the Organ, some of them, so exquisite. He told us the windows had been broken once when the full power of the instrument had been called out. Since then they blow more moderately, but a battle piece he gave us, and a storm, were really surprising, the trumpet stops glorious, and the vox humana actually from a Soprano chest.

We had much disturbed our host by choosing to arrive at his hôtel, English fashion, near midnight. Every one was in bed, and to have to get up, light the stove, air linen, prepare so many chambers during the hours of natural sleep, considerably deranged the establishment. Mynherr was very cross, but there were two pretty vrowleins who, though disturbed a bit, kept their tempers that night, and gave us good counsel in the morning. They came in when Jane and I were brushing our hair, and said to us with great civility that these unseasonable arrivals were not the custom of the country, that travellers arranged their movements so as least to inconvenience other parties, and that we should find ourselves more comfortable by conforming to the habits we found established; the meals were better prepared for the regular times than when a chance repast was dished up hurriedly. After this they proposed to dress our hair. Mine, which reached to my Ankles and was too thick to hold in one hand, they admired in an extasy; and when it had been plaited in strands and wound about my head in their own beautiful fashion, a few ringlets only allowed to hang low upon the cheek and fall still lower behind the ear, I admired it myself abundantly; and so becoming was it thought to be, and so much more easily manageable did I find it, that till I took to caps some years after my marriage, fashion or no fashion, I never altered this most classical arrangement of my golden hair. We very faithfully reported the good advice of our obliging attendants, and found considerable advantage in ever after abiding by it.

Somewhere here we got to Zeist, and then to Utrecht, and so by some means to Arnheim. My recollections of the order of our progress are indistinct. I remember the places we passed through and what we saw in them, and I remember the queer Cabriolets we sometimes travelled in, and the tiresomely slow *trekshuyts* we were condemned to at others, and that is all at this distance of time I can bring to mind: a sort of generalising of the journey. Zeist was pretty, fields and wood, a village, a good inn, and the curious establishment of the Herrnhuters or Moravians within a walking distance. One of the Laboucheres, with a pretty French wife, was living at the inn. The air hereabouts is thought to be particularly salubrious, and she was established here to recover her health after a long illness. We were amused at her *English* shyness about making the slightest approach to acquaintance with us till the two M.P.'s mutually recognised one another.[1] My Mother thought it was finery, as we had arrived in two extraordinary post waggons, the horses harnessed with ropes, and we ourselves very dusty. It went off, whichever it was, and we found her both pleasant and useful. She directed us to what was best worth seeing at the Moravian Mission House, namely, their very ingeniously made toys; a whole country exhibited upon a table by means of miniature facsimiles of every article used in it, and the

1. Actually, the radical Henry Labouchere (1798–1869) was not elected until 1826.

people in their national costume besides. We sent a large box
full of Dutch representations to the Freres, unknowing of the
heavy duty which made it an expensive although an amusing
present.

The establishment was a sort of Mr Owen sociable affair;[1]
all goods in common, no private property, no homes.
Buildings for all purposes were erected round spacious yards.
There was a great hall where all assembled for every meal. A
Chapel, Workshops, Storerooms, Bedrooms, Schoolrooms.
At a certain age the young people were married, at proper
time their children entered the School; they had no choice in
matrimony, nor any power to bring up their offspring by
their own sides; indeed the parents were otherwise employed
in this true commonwealth, each person being at some work
for a certain number of hours. The premises were scrupulously clean, but very plain, a sort of total abstinence system
denying the beautiful and the agreeable. The married men
had a peculiar dress all alike, so had the married women, and
the old people of each sex, and the young, and the children;
and all the private rooms were furnished alike, nothing in
them that was not absolutely requisite. I don't think the
community were happy, certainly not cheerful, merely
contented, and it was an uninteresting, unnatural whim
altogether. They would be dull enough were they not kept
constantly busy, they make every thing they use, spin, knit,
weave, bake, etc., and have a large farm in high order.

Utrecht I forget. A large town with pleasant environs, I
think. We took the boat there to Arnheim, and were amused
for some miles by the neatness of the villas thickly succeeding
each other along the level banks of the Canal. They were all
very much alike, long houses with steep roofs, very brightly
painted, tiles one colour, walls another, windows and doors a
third. They all stand in pretty gardens, with a broad gravel

1. Robert Owen (1771–1858) used his wealth as an
   industrialist to found two communities, New Lanark
   in Scotland and New Harmony in the U.S.A., based on
   the idealistic principles of his *New View of Society*; for
   the D.N.B. he was 'an intolerable bore who was the salt of
   the earth'.

walk leading to a summer house overhanging the water. In this summer house, as the day advanced, we saw many parties smoking and drinking beer out of tall glasses, with the gravity of red Indians—pictures of Dutch enjoyment. Conversation, most surely they never thought of, even a stray remark was rare among them. Words are not wasted in Holland. In our own boat a heavy looking man stood on the deck smoking; he puffed away in a comfortable, composed manner, regardless of all around. Another heavy looking man came up to him with a countenance of exactly the same stolid cast: it was as if a thought of any kind had never crossed the mind of either; he had a pipe in his hand, too, but it was not lighted. The second heavy man approached the first, stood for a moment, not a word, not a sign passed between them; the cold pipe was raised, advanced towards the hot one—they touched—puff, puff, puff at both ends in grave silence. When the cold pipe had lighted, the owner moved away without even a bow passing between the smokers. How much this pair amused us.

Arnheim is beautiful, a pretty town in a very picturesque situation. Nimeguen still more striking; the journey between the two did not strike me sufficiently to be remembered. I recalled the bridge of boats though, by means of which we crossed the Maes, and so entered Flanders. Liège was our next stage, quite a fine city, full of handsome streets and squares and buildings, shops rivalling our own, and hotels very superiour to any we had yet met with. It is the Birmingham of Belgium, a busy manufacturing town, and thriving. I should have liked much to have visited some of the iron works, and we had time enough, for my Mother had caught a feverish cold and had to stay here three days to nurse herself; but none of the rest having my turn for details, they went on as usual hunting out the Hôtel de Ville, the churches and pictures. There is an old Cathedral at Liège worth a visit, otherwise a walk about the town is all that need be attempted. We were returning home from rather a hot one when we found several Carriages crowding the yard, and were told a great English *Milor* had just arrived. It was the Duke and Duchess of Bedford on their way to one of the German Spas for his health, without any of their children, but with Upper

Servants and Under Servants, and their Doctor, good Mr
Wolridge. I had gone up to my Mother and did not see them,
but the rest were glad to meet—at least there was great
chattering.

Nothing could equal the dreariness of the drive the greater
part of the way from Liège to Aix la Chapelle. A wild, barren
heath after the first few miles, on which, at long intervals, we
saw a few poor wretched creatures gathering the manure
from the road to mix with clay and coal dust for fuel. They
formed this composition into neat enough cakes the size of
bricks, and said it made a good strong fire, but the perfume
was the reverse of agreeable. About the middle of our journey
we stopt to rest the horses at a more desolate inn than either
Freeburn or Moulinearn in their worst days. We could get
nothing for ourselves save a very greasy omelette fried in a
bacon pan with lard, and not made of very fresh eggs; there
was some horrible cake of rye flour, and schnapps, for this
was Germany—Prussian Germany. Black eagles with two
heads stuck up every where, and little round sticks girt with
the three colours to mark the boundaries. The postillions were
in long boots, queer hats, the orthodox colours, and they
cracked for ever their thick handled whips, and kept in their
mouths the amber head of the immense pipe they never
ceased smoking. They fed their horses every now and then
with slices of the same rye bread they ate themselves, and
they were fine, tall, handsome men into the bargain. The
gloom of Aix was excessive, ''twas like some vast City of the
dead,' hardly a stir in it. Well built streets, broad, with
handsome houses, all, as it were, shut up, for we never saw
either exits or entrances, and, except the old Cathedral and
the little chair in it on which the corpse of Charlemagne had
been found seated, there was hardly any object of curiosity
in the whole large town. The neighbourhood was equally
uninteresting, there was nothing to recommend the place
but the waters; they rise warm from the Springs, and are
nauseous enough to drink; to bathe in they are delightful
leaving a softness upon the skin and a suppleness among the
bones that invigorate the whole frame. My third bath told
upon my looks quite magically, and I felt so comfortably alive
and alert, that dull as this odious place was, I should have

liked to make the week out; but nobody else could have endured the monotony of fine summer days so lost behind those walls, so we moved again back to Liège, and on to Maestricht, and then to Spa, which pretty place suited us so well we remained there for ten days. It is a hilly country, not unlike Tunbridge Wells, great variety in the scenery, the town clean and cheerful, its one steep street filled with good houses, plenty of them being hotels.

We put up at the best, where we got excellent apartments, and we diverted ourselves by walking, driving, shopping, and drinking the waters, meeting very few of the numerous visitors except early in the morning at the fountains, the *ladies* and gentlemen mostly spending their day round the rouge et noir tables. It was frightful to see them, all pale and anxious except the few who were flushed from excitement, gathered for such an unholy purpose in the lovely Autumn weather. Dupes, sharpers, swindlers, all fermenting together. A son of old Blucher's was undergoing the process of being ruined, and though he had no good looks to recommend him, his youth made one incline to pity him. There were gaming rooms in our hotel. I declare I never passed the green door leading to them without a shudder. As it swung noiselessly to and fro when pushed on either side, it seemed to me to be the barrier Dante sang of, cutting off every hope from all the doomed admitted beyond it.[1] Peace brought all this vice, and how much more, to England. There was evil enough in our country before, but not the open familiarity with degrading pursuits our Continental neighbours habitually indulge. It was then such a curse; it is only perhaps another phase of the guilt of ignorance, for in ignorance we may ascribe all the errours of our imperfect nature, errours that keep us morally and physically beneath what we might be, too frequently rendering an existence miserable that was intended to be all enjoyment. Little as I had accustomed myself to reflect at this time, those dreadful fables forced thought on me. I have ever had such an horrour of swerving from the right path.

We had a much more agreeable subject of contemplation

1. *Divina Commedia:* 'Inferno' I, ii.

across the street. From our sitting room windows, a rather lofty premier, we looked down into the quiet ménage in a lower entresol of an elderly French gentleman and his much younger wife. As their curtains were generally drawn aside, their windows frequently opened, we had by good management the opportunity of investigating all details of their daily life. Madame got up first, rather early, threw on a wrapper, covered herself further with a shawl, slipt her bare feet into *shufflers*, and leaving her plain, unbordered skull night cap over her curl papers, without further ado began to prepare the coffee. When this was ready Monsieur rose, popt on a flowered robe de chambre, tossed away his night cap, stept into his slippers, and then sat down to his coffee. Madame opened the door, evidently to a knock; it was the gazette, which she received and handed to Monsieur. While he read she busied herself in clearing away the coffee tray and setting the room to rights. The beds were soon plumped up into sofas, the draperies drawn back, the chairs and tables put in order, and then the work seemed done. Another tap at the door, the gazette was handed out again, the window curtain was let down, and we were left to imagine the toilet of Monsieur. His appearance at the conclusion of his labours, in about an hour, was perfect; we knew him quite well under his metamorphosis issuing from the door of the house with shining hat, smart redingote,[1] shirt front, cane, moustache, all in high order, and we watched him sauntering off to the Café with an air of easy negligence, quite an amusing contrast to the bustle of Madame. She, after one long look at the retiring form of her beloved, we supposed that they had been but lately married, and she was very pretty, pulled back her curtain and commenced her morning works. Sometimes she sewed, sometimes she clear starched, sometimes she ironed, folded, brushed the clothes. She was never idle. Towards the dinner hour her window was darkened for a while, and when she unveiled her chamber, Monsieur was already within sight, sauntering down the street again to receive a Lady worthy of him. The neatest little figure in the prettiest half dress tripped along the floor to meet him, and away they went

1. Double-breasted French gentleman's coat.

together, as nice looking and as quiet and as happy a pair as could well be seen at the Spa. We could never detect the time of their return home in the evening. The casement, left open by Madame, was always closed at dusk by the maid of the lodging house; no light ever seemed to gleam from within, yet we never failed in the early morning to see the fair lady in her wrapper and her curl papers, looking out for a breath of fresh air before preparing her coffee.

We went from Spa to Maestricht, a large garrison town of most agreeable aspect, and there we waited a couple of days, nothing loth, for letters. The Landlady of an excellent hotel kept a capital table d'hôte. Many of the Officers dined with her, lawyers, merchants, and a few others, her husband among them; he was a notary, with an office at a little distance, and quite as much a guest in his Wife's salon as any of the rest of the company. Madame, short and fat and well dressed, and very obliging, sat at the head of the table, her pretty daughters dispersed along each side; one made the salad, another, who spoke a little English, attended to the travellers; a third, quite a child, seemed to be a pet with the acquaintance. It was quite a gay family party, and really very amusing to strangers; no very refined manners visible, but no ill breeding. Madame had been learning English from her schooltaught daughter, and had got very perfect two small words, which on every occasion she pronounced with a winning smile to my Mother—*Ros bif*—and next day we had two miserable ribs of lean beef at dinner, baked till quite black, out of compliment to our party. A Dutch naval Officer sat next to me, a very agreeable man, and so polite as to dress himself in his Uniform afterwards, because we had none of us seen what was worn by his countrymen. It was not very unlike our own, blue, but turned up, I think, with red. Two Dutch merchants I also got on with so well that the father gave my father his card with his address at Rotterdam, and begged we would let him know when we returned there, as he must give his family the advantage of an introduction to foreigners who had made two days pass so very agreeably to himself and his son. A Frenchman could not have made a neater speech.

Here we saw the last of a Mr Hare, a young Englishman

who had tormented Jane from the hour of our landing in
Holland. They had met in some passage in the Badthouse at
Rotterdam, and he had neglected no opportunity of throwing
himself, ever after, in her·way. He even addressed her, not
rudely, not at all, but humbly, laid nosegays at her feet, sent
her flowers by Ward the maid, stood in doorways and sighed,
looked up at windows in languishing despair, followed her
not only from street to street but from place to place. We
found him at the Hague the morning after our arrival, at
Amsterdam as soon as ourselves, at Liège immediately after
us. We only escaped him at Spa from some misapprehension
about our journey there, for he used to waylay Ward and try
to bribe her with large sums of money to deliver notes and
give him intelligence of our plans. He tried the courier
too, and I am pretty sure made more of him than of little
indignant Ward, who, after many minor repulses, at last
made him a long speech in the style of Mrs Nickleby to the
man with the vegetable marrow,[1] and with equal effect, for
this poor Mr Hare was insane, had escaped from his friends,
and was not recovered by them till he had reached Maestricht. Many years afterwards, when Jane was Mrs Pennington, she met him, also married, quite rational, and perfectly
oblivious of his wanderings in the Netherlands.

Whereabouts could we have seen Cleves. We certainly
passed through this most beautiful little Duchy. A little
paradise it seemed to be, with its rich fields, its wooded hills
and old Castles upon heights. All this German scenery was
very pretty, and so was the part of Flanders we next
proceeded to. We had to return to Liège, and then we
travelled up the Maese, an enchanting journey; past Huy,
such a perfect picture of beauty, to Namur, a large fortified
town. Here, though I was never noted for a painter's eye, I
recollect nothing so well as a large picture of the Crucifixion
by Vandyke, *unrolled* for us to examine. With pride the priest
told us it had never been to France. When Buonaparte
carried off all the Spoils of all countries to embellish the
Louvre, this gem was saved by being taken down from its
place over the high altar of the Cathedral, removed out of its

1. Dickens, *Nicholas Nickleby*, Chapter XXIII.

frame, rolled up, and hid in a chimney. They were just going to replace it, there being no longer any fear of French invasions. The works of Vandyke always touch me, as do the few paintings I have seen of the Italian Masters. This consists but of two figures, the Christ on the Cross, his Mother beneath it. It has never gone out of my head. For many months after seeing it, it came back to me in my dreams, or when I was sitting quietly at work alone. I can't tell what it was that attracted me. I have no knowledge of colouring, or grouping, or even of correct outline, so that all the beauties of the painting could never be described by one so ignorant. I felt them though, and I rather think that would have satisfied the Artist himself nearly as well as the panegyrick of a connoisseur! They do talk such stuff with their technical round about phrases.[1]

The next point was Gemappes, the little rather bleak village on the hill near Quatre Bras. We dined in a room the walls of which still bore the marks of Cannon balls. The girl who waited on us had been in the house during the battle, saw the Highland regiments trot up in their peculiar fashion through the town, the people crowding out of their doors to offer them a snatch of refreshments as they quickly passed. She sang to us, in a loud, shrill voice, a few bars of some tune bearing a resemblance to the White Cockade, so that it must have been the 92nd, the gallant Gordons, that every one liked so much! those charming men with petticoats, who, when billeted on the inhabitants, helped to make the soup and rock the cradle for the half frightened mistress of the family. On the table where we had sat to eat, so many wounded Officers had lain under the Surgeon's knife. In the room overhead so many had died; the garden had been destroyed, the fields had been desolated, losses of all kinds had been suffered during those dreadful days, yet for this no one blamed Napoleon. We found his great name treasured in almost every heart, every where except in Holland proper, where neither he nor any of his dynasty were popular. Here in Flanders they made no secret of preferring any Sovereign to their present Dutch

1. *Baedeker's* first English edition (1869) suggests this picture is a copy.

one. The Flemings are half Spanish, half French; there is no similitude whatever between them and the nation they have been ill advisedly joined to; *had been*, I should say, for the forced union did not last long.[1]

On reaching Brussels we put up at the Hôtel de Bellevue in the Place Royale, just for a couple of days while we looked about us, for the whole aspect of this particularly pretty town was so agreeable to my Mother, now quite tired of travelling, that it was determined to take a house here for a month, and send for our friend Amelia Ferrier. We spent two mornings, my father and I, walking about the high and new town, looking for lodgings, and all over the low and old town, admiring both, so beautiful they are in different ways. The Place Royale in the high town is the fashionable residence of the Court, some of the nobles, most of the strangers; the houses are like palaces, three fine rows enclosing a large oblong park, very agreeably laid out in shady walks. A steep street, the Montagne de la cour, leads from this to the low town, where all the publick buildings are to be found; and there are the ramparts, a broad causeway with neat houses on one side, and fine trees in a row upon the other. A good many handsome equipages rolled about during the middle of the day; there was plenty of traffick going forward, plenty of handsome well filled shops, foot passengers in constant variety, all well dressed, and the women mostly wearing very coquettishly the becoming Spanish Mantilla instead of shawl and bonnet, so disposed as by no means to conceal the features. The whole scene was gay, it was quite a place to fall in love with. Cheap, too, as we found Flanders generally; nearly half as cheap again as Holland, and about a third cheaper than the short experience we had of Germany.

The people spoke French in Brussels so well that we got on most easily with them, and very soon settled all our business. We fixed on apartments in a fine house in the Place Royale belonging to a Cotton manufacturer whose principal residence was close to his Mill in the country. He only used the ground floor of his town house during occasional visits to the

1. It ended with the outbreak of the Belgian revolution in 1830.

City and let all the upper part. We had on the first floor a dining and a drawing room and my Mother's bedroom, all communicating; on the second floor four good bedrooms, and there were rooms in a back wing for the servants. We required no additional plagues, the Courier dusting, and the porter's daughter helping Ward upstairs; for our dinner came from a traiteur in a tray on a boy's head, cheaper than we could have cooked it at home, and very much better. We ordered it for *six*, and there was always more left than the servants wanted. Breakfast and tea the Courier managed, our obliging landlord allowing us to boil our kettle on his stove. The entrance to our 'palace home' was through a *porte cochère* into a yard surrounded by low buildings used for warehouses. A staircase, broad and handsome, led up to our apartments; they were neatly finished, the drawing room indeed handsomely, and with its cheerful look out on the Parc, it was a very pleasant sitting room, particularly after we had put a harp and a pianoforte into it. Unpacking was a short business, for we travelled light, so soon felt at home in our new situation.

CHAPTER TWENTY-THREE

1819–1820

THE day we moved from the hotel, just before despatching our last truck full of luggage, my father, who had gone out alone on some errand, returned accompanied by a country man, a gentleman he had known in his youth, Mr Pryse Gordon, a good looking, busy mannered person, with whom the world had not gone altogether well whoever had been to blame for it. He had been, he said, for some time settled in Brussels, and from a perfect knowledge of the place might be of some use to us, where so many were on the alert to take every advantage of strangers.[1] He very much regretted our precipitation in taking a house so entirely on chance, and unguardedly throwing ourselves quite into our Landlord's hands by employing all his tradespeople, the Belgians being rogues from top to bottom. He would take care in future to preserve us from this race of harpies by going with us himself to all shops as a protection, these crooked traders knowing him well, and knowing, too, that he would not suffer his friends to be imposed upon. Mrs Gordon, who was ill, or she would immediately have done herself the honour of waiting on my Mother, would introduce us to respectable milliners and dress makers; they would also shew us a little of Brussels society—do their best to make our sojourn agreeable. If we

1. See *Personal Memoirs or Reminiscences of Men and Manners at Home and Abroad during the last half century, with occasional Sketches of the Author's Life—being Fragments from the Portfolio of Pryse Gordon Esquire*, which he published in 1830; four years later came his *Belgium and Holland, with a Sketch of the Revolution in the year 1830*—this included a chapter entitled 'Hints to English families settling in Brussels'.

had never read Gil Blas,[1] we might have been more grateful to him. There was something that jarred against our sympathies in some way in his many professions; that is, we young people fancied we could do just as well without him. My father and mother were quite delighted at meeting so zealous a friend. We therefore kept our own Counsel, but as far as I could manage if I prevented Mr Gordon's interference, the rather that in one or two trifling instances I found I had made better bargains for myself than he would have made for me. The black Courier detested him, I fancy their vocations clashed; neither did Monsieur François like me, as he required a watchful eye over his proceedings; he cheated us in spite of being looked after, but he would have made a much larger private purse had Mademoiselle not learned the value of the different moneys, and picked up useful words both in Dutch and German. One thing Mr Gordon certainly did well for us, he gave us the names of the best masters. Whether, poor people, he made them pay for the recommendation there is no saying. We lost not a franc, for their terms being known we paid them the customary fees, no more.

Education at Brussels was remarkably good at this time. Many English families were living there on account of the excellence and cheapness of the Masters. We took advantage of three, Henri Bertini for the pianoforte, a lesson from whom was worth at least half a dozen from an inferiour professor. His wife for the Harp, rather a so so teacher; and inimitable Monsieur Sacré for dancing. He was the Master of the Ceremonies at the palace, most particularly attentive to the *Deportment*, yet taking the greatest trouble with the most curiously minute incidents of every day life, as relating to the manners. He gave his pupils an ease of movement that very few inherited from nature. He must have been descended from Monsieur Jourdain's celebrated Teacher, for the importance of his art filled his whole understanding.[2] He used to give us long lectures upon simple elegance, act awkwardness before

1. *Histoire de Gil Blas de Santillane* by Alaine René le Sage (1734), translated by Smollet in 1761.
2. See Molière's *Le Bourgeois Gentilhomme* (1770).

us, and then triumphantly ask which style would have greatest effect on the sympathies of our neighbour in every circumstance of life. Amelia Ferrier listened to him so gravely, so with an air of fully appreciating his reasoning, that between them we could hardly keep the entertainment they gave us within the bounds of good breeding.

Mr Ferrier had not been able to accompany his daughter. He sent her with a friend, Mr Steuart, the Editor of the Courier, a most clever, amusing little man sadly in want of a few lessons from Monsieur Sacré, for he was so thoroughly vulgar as to be some times annoying, but very witty; so up to the times, too, acquainted with every thing and every body, and so shrewd in his remarks he quite enlivened us. He delighted in musick, so that every evening while he staid we had quite a Concert. Both Amelia and I were anxious to have had some singing lessons; a celebrity was therefore engaged, but my father, who superintended the first interview, took good care to preserve us from a second. My father was unable to endure the new system of the 'sons de tête', such an ease to the singer . . . all the notes must be formed in the chest, and those that could not be thus reached, had to be let alone. The chest notes certainly are fuller, more satisfactory to a musical ear than the head notes, unless these last are excellently well produced, which they were not always in the beginning from want of practice probably. In our present day, by careful study, there is really no knowing where the two voices join, or part, and our taste being now formed to this falsetto, its sweetness and its *truth*, for being easily reached, these upper notes are never flat, quite reconcile us to what was condemned as a serious fault in the days of our fathers. Even the Italians now teach in this mode.

Our early mornings being thus occupied in agreeable studies, we devoted the middle of every day to walks about the town, or drives in the environs; the evenings we occasionally spent in such society as was accessible to us, not the best by any means, Brussels being then the refuge for all the scum and dregs of Britain. It would have required a good introduction to get at all among the Belgian *noblesse*, the specimens within their view making them very difficult of access by our countrymen. The Prince of (I forget the name) alone, who laid himself out to entertain the English, invited my father and William twice or thrice to dine. The company they met they described as no way remarkable; but they both of them spoke french so badly they were quite unequal to judge of any one's conversational powers in that language. The banquet was like one in London, with two or three slight differences.

We ladies had to put up with Mr and Mrs James Conynghame and George—the married brother had been long done up and was living with his really nice wife on a small allowance granted to him by his creditors, to whom the father Sir James, made over his income. George was run out and was recruiting queer disagreeable odd pleasant ugly old Beau of mine—Mr and Mrs Wynne Aubrey, or in full as he was a younger son, Mr and Mrs Henry Harcourt Wynne Aubrey, precisely under the same delapidated circumstances. She, such a pretty woman, beautiful indeed, a great deal handsomer than Mrs Munro her sister. Two or three more there were of this same creditable description, and one very nice family who had certainly come to Brussels to economise while educating their many children; but then they had the sure prospect of a few years of prudent saving setting their affairs all right again. Mr Houlton had been building a very fine house. We may all know the cost of that amusement. Mrs Houlton, a fair specimen of a thoroughly English woman, handsome and pleasant, looked well after all under her control. The eldest son was in the Army, not with them; the second, a dear little George, was worth making a pet of. The two elder girls were beauties in different styles; the second, a Brunette, played the guitar in Spanish fashion, not picking at the strings, but sweeping them with the thumb, and she sang Spanish and Portuguese airs to this accompaniment so bewitchingly we were not at all surprised to hear afterwards that she had married well before she was 17. There was no danger of her marrying *ill* with that wide awake mother; and so the pretty Fanny never married at all. There were several clever younger sisters, but none of them possessed the remarkable good looks of the elder ones. We got extremely intimate with these Houltons, spent many walking or driving mornings, and happy musical evenings,

together. They were from the West of England, from somewhere near Bowood, Lord Lansdowne's, I visited there, I
forget the County.

All this time Mrs Gordon never came to call. He was with
us daily, and had managed to carry us to his hairdresser and
his shoemaker and his dressmaker, etc. I really believe they
were all the best in their line, and they may not have charged
us with the *douceur* given to our obliging friend—or they
may; there was no knowing. At this period of our acquaintance suspicion of the cause of all the trouble taken for us had
not entered into the heads of the most influential among us. A
stray word of Mr Steuart of the Courier first enlightened us.
Speaking of him once after his regular daily visit, when he
had been as usual all kindness and very cheerful and
agreeable, 'Ah,' said Mr Steuart, 'poor devil! I wonder how
the deuce the fellow gets on; never did a man throw
opportunities away as did that poor Pryse Gordon, clever,
very gentlemanly man, quite cleared out long before he had
to run for it, how on earth does he manage to live here? On
his countrymen? eh? a per centage on all wares perhaps
supplied by *his* tradesmen. He had not a penny left, nor has
he any way of earning one. Who was the wife? had *she*
money?' That bit of news it seemed as if we were not likely to
know. Mr Gordon made the civilest apologies for her non
appearance, but she never came; her cold remained so very
oppressive that she, being a delicate person, could not
venture out so late in the year, September or October, while
any cough continued. At length, the day after Mr Steuart
departed to resume his editorial duties in London, Mrs
Gordon's cough had sufficiently moderated and Mr Gordon
brought her to see us, literally brought her, for she was
evidently unwilling to come. She was very awkward, very
reserved in manner, extremely silent, and instead of the
slight delicate looking woman we expected, she was a great
rawboned giantess with a scorbutick face. She must have had
a fortune; that we were persuaded of. We found from George
Conyngham that it was a *jointure*, and that she had been
married for her beauty in very early youth.

The call was returned, and then came an invitation to an
Evening party; neither Mary nor I inclined to go, nor Amelia

Ferrier, most luckily as the affair turned out. The rest accepted this civility, and Jane gave us the following account of the entertainment. In a very handsome room, scantily furnished, about twenty of the British inhabitants of Brussels were assembled, tea and cakes and lemonade were the refreshments, cards the amusement—a whist table, and a party at Stop Commerce. Every one who played Commerce had a franc in the Pool. Jane won, and was preparing to receive from George Conyngham the contents of the Cup, when the large hand of Mr Pryse Gordon arrested the movement. 'Pardon me, my dear young lady, I thought I had mentioned it; in this house we always play for the poor.' So saying, he poured the money, fifteen or sixteen francs, into a bag he took from a table drawer. We commented among ourselves upon this charitable transaction, and our eyes opening wider by the help of Ward, who got her knowledge from the Courier, we began to make out the true character of our new acquaintance; the depth to which had fallen a man equal by birth and education to the best of the society into which he had been early introduced. We did not find out his whole delinquencies, *her* history, till we were on the point of leaving Brussels. John Ferrier and his young wife, who had been travelling on the Rhine, came to pick up his sister Amelia and carry her home; and he told my brother William that Mrs Gordon had more than one jointure although she had never been a wife before, and that Mr Gordon went twice a year to England to receive for her these different annuities. Fancy the family horrour. 'Such an ugly creature too,' said my Mother. It was a most disagreeable adventure, though in reality no harm came of it. It was worth something in the way of experience, teaching a prudent caution as to the admittance of our travelling compatriots to intimacy.

A much pleasanter visit was paid by us to the country house of our Landlord. We did not all go, being now, with the John Ferriers, a large party; but I was one of the selected, having become through the medium of our housekeeping transactions quite on the most friendly terms with our Landlady. Monsieur frequently remained in town a week or more at a time, when business was lively. Madame seldom staid above a day or two at a time, much preferring her very

pretty house at the Factory, where we were very kindly
pressed to pass a day. I was in hopes we should have gone out
early enough to have had time to go all over the Mills, where
the whole process of cotton cleaning, spinning, weaving,
dyeing, printing, was carried on by the largest number of
hands employed in one concern in Belgium. However, we
were only ready for the early dinner, the Master keeping the
Workmen's hours as he superintended all matters himself.
The family consisted of the round headed, plain mannered,
thoroughly business like father; a mother infinitely more
alive—a good, homely, managing housewife too, yet seeing
beyond the cotton; a quiet, pretty, married daughter, with
two fat children and a silent husband, the Manager of the
Factory; two unmarried daughters likely to turn out as well
as their elder sister; and one son, College bred, a little
inclined to keep the spinning jennies out of sight while
making abundant use of their produce. He was particularly
well dressed, spoke French well, aped the Frenchman
indeed, and not badly at all, which 'youthful extravagances'
the good mother smiled, assuring mine that this would all
subside by and bye, and that he would become reasonable as
years passed, and become as respectable a manufacturer as
his ancestors; for the Mill had been for some generations the
patrimony of the family. She was a dear sensible old lady,
looked up to by her whole household. The dinner she gave us
was quite in the old Fleming style, very long, oddly served,
dish by dish, not in the order we are accustomed to; soup
first, some sweet things, the bouilli, different dressed meats,
fish, more sweets, game and larks, and other little birds—mere
mouthfuls, some no bigger than a walnut—fruit and cheese
together, plenty of beer and wine handed round, and coffee
directly after in another room. A walk in the pleasure
grounds, and then the drive home before dark, in full time
for our own tea. Next morning Madame came in with her
husband in his gig, to make her marketings while he loaded
waggons with bales of his finished goods, a good store of
which he always kept steady in the spacious warerooms
round the yard. I quite liked these good people and they were
so obliging. I found her recommendations to tradespeople
much more effective than Mr Gordon's. Her silk mercer gave

us infinitely better bargains than were offered us by his. My father gave us each a silk dress to remember Brussels by, and my Mother got three, all of them neatly made up by a French mantua maker, and exceedingly admired after our return home, though really I could not see that they were any way superiour either in make or fabrick to what we could have procured in Edinburgh. They were certainly cheaper though.

One of the pleasures of Brussels was walking about the pretty, clean town. Besides the shopping, there was a great deal to see in the old low town, ancient buildings and other monuments, numerous fountains in open areas amongst the rest, always surrounded by amusing groups, for there was no supply of water through pipes to every house. Perhaps this was one cause of the indelicate manners of the people; nothing near so bad as the Dutch in this respect, who are positively indecent, openly so, unpleasantly so to strangers unaccustomed to the simplicity or the coarseness of such habits. The Flemings are a degree or two more refined, still there is room for great improvement. One fountain I never could pass in any comfort; it really was only fit for playing at a Hindù festival, and strange to say, Hindostanée virtues were ascribed to the use of it. A turn on the Ramparts of a fine afternoon was delightful. Any day, rain or no rain, we could stroll in the parc, the gravel there being kept in exact order. There we constantly met the two nice little boys of the Prince of Orange, who played out half the day with their balls and hoops and bats, etc., attended by a single footman in livery. The children were plainly dressed in nankin trowsers, round blue jackets, and white hats, and they kept quite aloof from the servant, though he managed to have them always in his eye. The Abbé Sieyès, too, walked regularly in these gardens, a small, thin, thoughtful man with gray hair, a grave smile, and courteous manner; he reminded us of Belleville, wearing his stick in the same style, held out from his hands crossed behind him.[1] Another 'silent Monitor,' as some one

1. Abbé Emmanuel Joseph Sieyès (1748-1836), who helped to draft no less than three constitutions during the Revolution, was exiled to Brussels as a regicide and only returned to France in 1830.

calls these marked objects on the stream of time, was the balcony before the windows of the Hôtel de Ville whence the Duke of Alva leaned to witness his massacres of the Huguenots.[1] We are better than our fathers. Somewhat less cruel at any rate.

We had a pleasant drive one morning to Louvaine, where the sight lovers inspected the curious Hôtel de Ville. I forget how many storeys of atticks it has in its steep roof, rows of storm windows one over the other. And then we went to Lacken, the country palace of the King, only a few miles out of town and hardly a very healthy situation, lying low, a great deal of water and too much wood near the house, but very pretty and very enjoyable as a private residence, every thing that is most agreeable to rural life being in profusion— gardens, a farm, a park, a lake, and a most convenient abode fitted up with taste quite unostentatiously. The Palace in the Place Royale, on the contrary, was furnished magnificently. If I remember right, felt slippers were put on over our shoes before any of us, ladies or gentlemen, were allowed to step over the highly polished inlaid floors, and where our eyes were quite dazzled with gold, silver, chrystal, velvet, and bijouterie.

And then we went to Waterloo. Oh, will there ever be another war! At first sight there was nothing, as it seemed, to look at. A wide plain under crop, a few rising grounds wooded, a hamlet or two, and the forest of Soigny. An old man of the name of Lacoste—an old cheat, I believe—in a blouse, striped night cap, and immense shoes, came up as a guide to all the different points of interest, and did his part well, although his pretension to having been the attendant of Buonaparte during the Battle and his director in his flight was a fable. He took us up to the ruins of Houguemont, to La Haie Sainte, to the hollow with the *paved* road in the bottom of it where the Guards felt themselves so at home, to the wide

1. The Duke of Alva, Governor of the Netherlands for Philip II of Spain between 1567 and 1573, tried to quell rebellion by executing twenty-five nobles (not *Huguenots*, who were French protestants) on 5 June 1568 in the market place in front of the Hôtel de Ville.

mound raised by the heaps of the slain, to the truncated column of black marble erected to the memory of an hero. At this distance of time I do not remember all we saw, and I did not attend to all he told, mistrusting his veracity. The scene was impressive enough gazed on silently; and then to think of the terrour in Brussels, of the despair in the neighbouring villages, of the two armies individually and collectively, of the two Commanders and all that hung upon the strife so lately ended! This was but the fourth year after the victory, the world was still full of the theme, but there was little trace of the struggle left upon the ground it had been fought on. Fine crops of corn had been this very Autumn waving there, though the plough still turned up relicks of the eventful day. Monsieur Lacoste had a sack full of trophies he said had been found upon the field.[1] The feeling of the people most certainly did not go with the victors. They hated the Union with the Dutch, they hated the Dutch King ruling over them; the habits and manners of the two ill cemented nations were totally dissimilar, and with the French they amalgamated readily. The Emperour really lived in their hearts, spite of the Conscription, spite of his defeat, spite of his crimes, as we may call the consequences of his ambition.

One day my father and I, walking out a good mile into the country, we came to a tidy looking farmhouse, which, as we stopt to examine, the owner of civilly asked us to enter. We crossed a yard and were ushered at once into the Cow stable, where at the Upper end, in a space separated by a latticed-partition from the long row of milch cattle, the family lived. The place was clean, all the dairy utensils hanging round the walls were bright, and the cows were very comfortably stalled, a neat pavement running up the whole length of the building with a drain between it and the animals. After we had made what observations we chose here, the farmer opened a door into the best room, where, French fashion,

1. *Baedeker* first edition in English (1869 but the eleventh in German) comments 'Genuine relics are still occasionally turned up by the plough, but it need hardly be observed that most of those which the traveller is importuned to purchase are spurious'.

was a bed with a canopy over it and all the good furniture:
massive, highly polished and well carved presses, chests,
chairs and tables. In one corner was the treasure of the
family, a crucifix as large as life, the figure glaringly painted,
always a distressing object to me and a sort of shock when
represented thus coarsely. On the wall close to this hung not a
bad print of Napoleon. I don't know which the old Fleming
regarded with most veneration.

A Flemish farm is small generally, the fields small, dull
looking from the absence of living beings, the cattle being
mostly kept in the house. Their agriculture rather disappointed my father. A great many mouths are certainly fed
for the acres, but no fortunes are made by the farmers, who
are all mere peasants living in the most homely way on the
produce of their industry, providing themselves with all
necessaries as in more primitive times, going to market with
what they can spare, giving a fixed proportion of the profits to
the Landlord when the cultivators do not themselves own
their little domains, and buying nothing that can by any
possibility be made at home. They all seemed contented;
there were few poor, no beggars, no rags. Notwithstanding
the under current of discontent, the surface betrayed no
approaching danger; it would have been difficult to suppose
another revolution so near at hand as it proved to be. Very
likely the priests had something to do with the deposition of
the Presbyterian House of Orange.[1] The Flemings are much
attached to their own superstitions. Little Virgins and other
saints in Boxes stand in many conspicuous places; the Altars
in all the churches were gaily decorated and seldom without
kneeling figures round them; and shows went about of
Mount Calvary and the holy family and the martyrs, etc., all
figures on stages, as large as life, dressed up in real garments,
before which unpleasant appearances crowds kneeled in
mute devotion. There were quantities of images in the
Churches, all very fine, silks, velvets, jewels, and some in
wigs truly ridiculous. The worshippers as much in earnest as

1. The Belgian revolt broke out in 1830; E.G. (by then the
   wife of a protestant Irish landowner of Orange sympathies) was writing thirty years after this visit.

the Hindùs with their horrible figures. More so than many of us who from the heights of our spiritual simplicity pity what we think a mockery, and what is certainly a strange remains of barbarity to linger on for eighteen centuries after the truth was preached.

We were very sorry to leave Brussels. We had passed a very pleasant month there one way or another but the Autumn was advancing and we had the sea to cross and so we must begin our journey home. We returned by Valenciennes and Malines and gloomy Ghent, where of course we were shewn the house of Philip von Artevelde.[1] Other Friesland heroes were recalled many a time during our pleasant journey and then we rested a few days at Antwerp, John Ferrier having business there, and we besides the publick sight seeing, having a whole morning's work in viewing a private collection of paintings belonging to a Banker or a Merchant, who had spent a life time and a fortune very happily in forming this gallery. Mr Steuart had got tickets of admission for us, the *chapeau de paille* being the attraction, but many fine pictures deserved as much notice to the full. A few years after the Banker died, the Collection was dispersed, sold, and we saw the fair third wife of Rubens in a small room in Pall Mall, by herself, just before she became the property of Sir Robert Peel.[2]

Antwerp might be a noble town, perhaps it was once. Now, the wide streets are empty, the destruction of its harbour put an end to its commerce. All the fine buildings looked deserted, no new houses were rising anywhere. Very few vessels were in the river and those were of a small size. Buonaparte filled up the bed of the Scheldt in order to ruin the City and yet they like his memory. The docks are splendid but empty. It really was a melancholy place,

1. An authoritarian ruler who seized power in 1381 but died in battle two years later against Charles VI of France.
2. This famous portrait of Susanna Fourment (elder sister of Hélène, Ruben's second wife) was auctioned in Antwerp in 1822 and shown in London the following year when it was bought by Peel for the unprecedented sum of £3000.

although still there is a great deal to be seen in it. Pictures of course in plenty—the Descent from the Cross, with its two accessary wings over the high altar in the Cathedral being the *gem*. The Magdalen kneeling quite in front, her back to the Spectator, her long fair hair streaming down upon a peculiar coloured leghorn tinted gown,[1] was like a regality. Some where I saw a Madre dolorosa, whether it was here or not I cannot say. She was seated on the ground, with her son's body on her knees, there were no other figures in the picture.[2] I could have worshipped her myself, almost, her expression forbade piety. No wonder these creations added to the imposing effect of ceremonial processions and other means of exciting the imagination, take such hold of the feelings of sensitive and ignorant people, whose reasoning powers are of the weakest.

At the hôtel at Antwerp, an exceedingly comfortable one, we were waited on entirely by men. They called us in the mornings, entered our bedrooms with the jugs of hot water etc., made the beds even. We saw no maid servants—in any department. We went to Vespers in the Cathedral on the Sunday Evening, quite an Opera. An orchestra of all instruments and excellent choir, and next morning resumed our journey and soon found ourselves in an open boat on Holland's deep with a cold gale blowing and a good stiff shower meeting us when half way over. We passed Dort, saw piles of common crockery ware in stalls, on the pavements, in barges, and gladly resumed our pleasant quarters in the Badthouse at Rotterdam. Here we had a great deal to do. Every evening was spent at the Ferriers. All the mornings my father was packing his old China, quantities of which he had picked up here and there in the course of our wanderings, always despatching his purchases to Rotterdam to await our arrival. So heavy was then the duty upon foreign porcelaine, it would have cost a fortune to have sent all this Collection

1. Straw-coloured (straw-plaiting for hats came from Livorno in Tuscany).
2. This masterpiece was painted by Rubens between 1611 and 1614; it had only been returned to the Cathedral in 1814 after twenty years in Paris during the war.

home through the Custom House—it was therefore to reach us by degrees, a barrel of butter or herring or such commodities as these plates and dishes could be packed amongst was to be entrusted to our old friend the skipper of the Van Egmont every return journey he made, and positively most of these treasures in time reached us, the skipper not always taking the trouble to put them up as directed. There were private holes and corners in the Van Egmont, as the Master and Mate well knew, the mate *too* well knew, for on occasion of a quarrel between the two, the little merry mate who had been quite a favourite with us, imparted the secrets of the old tub to the Leith Custom house Officers and so half ruined his Captain. Dowran had been returned home in the same way. Mr Ferrier kept the unhappy creature till the moment for embarking, when he was taken on board in a sack and tied upon deck during the first part of his voyage. On his release he took possession of William's old bed and kept his chamber till he landed!

It was a sad leavetaking when we parted from the Ferriers. We embarked from their house for Harwich, not in the regular packet but in one which on this occasion carried the Mail. We had a stormy passage, a *pitchy* sea, the result of a storm just lulling, with a wind ahead. Even I who never suffer at sea, was ill enough for an hour or two. There were few passengers, only one at all remarkable, a little old Jew, very much frightened at the heaving of the troubled waters. He was a queer sort of dealer in odd knick knacks, pulling out quantities of valuable old fashioned jewellery from every part of his dress, for he had tucked it all away, here and there about his clothing, much after the fashion of Filch.[1] We could not help suspecting that, squally as it was, he had more to do than the wind with the difficulty of our little packet making the proper harbour. Instead of landing at Harwich, we were put ashore some few miles up the coast at a small village, where the Custom House Officer seldom expecting strangers, was certainly far from vigilant. Our inn was village like—clean beds its greatest luxury. After the palace hotels we had been accustomed to of late, the little ill furnished

1. A character in John Gay's *Beggar's Opera* (1728).

parlours, the closet bedrooms, and the inferiour style of establishment altogether in these English Country inns, made an unfavourable first impression. The hack post chaises were no worse than our cabriolets, and the horses were better, but then they were not open—there was the want of air. We saved the trouble of changing much luggage by having sent all we could spare by the Van Egmont.

It was an ugly journey all through the flats and the fens of the East Coast on to Newcastle, with but one remarkable object on the route, the Cathedral at Lincoln. The first church I saw abroad struck me as bare, so cold, with so much white washed wall and so very little ornament. The first I saw again at home seemed only like an aisle of the others, rich enough in carvings, pillars, stained glass, and so on, but so confined, so narrow, so small, all stuffed up with seats for dignatories. I missed the grand space that to the unaccustomed eye had seemed desolate. Has habit much to do with taste, after all. Do foreigners admire our florid gothick. I felt as if there were not room to move in the Cathedral, Lincoln, after being but a mite in the one at Antwerp.

At Newcastle we met Lord Grey[1] carrying some of his daughters home in a handsome travelling barouche, beside which our two hack chaises drew up, much to the annoyance of some of our party. Explanations, however, set all right, and we proceeded in our humble equipages with minds more at peace than under the circumstances could have been expected. We had all through travelled in two divisions. My father, my Mother and I and Ward. And William, Jane, Mary and the Courier. With him, however, we had parted at Brussels, where he had got a good engagement, to our relief. The people every where had taken us at first for two distinct families. My father and I they supposed to be man and wife, and my Mother was his Mother in law. William and Mary were the Monsieur and Madame of the other carriage, and Jane the sister in law; not bad guesses. My father looked like my Mother's son, and I looked far too old to be his daughter. William infinitely too old to be his son and Jane and William

1. Charles, second Earl Grey (1764–1845), was one of the leaders of her father's Whig party.

were so alike they could not be mistaken for brother and sister. We were quite amused at all these erroneous impress- ions, and the younger ones eager still further to mystify our hosts and hostesses and my father in the front of the fun, but we saw soon that it seriously annoyed my Mother. She had no idea of acting *Madame* mère to the whole party, so we had to restrain our mirth when she was by.

We reached Edinburgh late in the evening of the very last day in the month of October, welcomed back by the two highland maids, Mr Caw and poor old Dowran; the poor dog had been faithfully delivered over to Peggy and seemed glad to be at home and took kindly to his old quarters, generally lying contented by the kitchen fire, after having made a regular survey of every room in the house to satisfy himself there was really no one in it. He had once or twice set out for a walk but had never gone far, nor ever minded who came in or who went out or heeded the door bell. The night we arrived he was sleeping on the hearth. When the chaises stopt, he roused himself, pricked up his ears, got upon his feet and when the bell rang, he flew up the stairs, bounded along the passage, darted out of the door like a mad thing and passing our carriage, threw himself panting and barking up into William's arms as he was stepping out of his. There was combination in that dog's head, something far beyond instinct, quite akin to reason. *Fright* herself, clever as she is, is not more intelligent than was poor Dowran.

The length of time that has passed away since we made this pleasant little tour in the Netherlands has caused forgetful- ness of a thousand details which always add so much to the interest of any account of the first impressions of a foreign country. In talking over our travels with our good friend Miss Bessy Clerk, we used to keep her laughing by the hour at several of our adventures, none of which can I now recall. My father discouraged much conversation on the subject, he having a great objection to any egotistical display of whatever kind; the less people obtruded themselves upon the rest of the world, the better, he thought, the world liked them; besides the check to individual vanity where a prudent reserve regarding the actions, feelings, and intentions of dear self was exercised. So we soon fell back upon local topicks.

It was our last winter in Edinburgh and a gloomy one. The Law point between my father and Ballindaloch concerning the navigation of the Spey, had been appealed to the House of Lords and was a very breathless anxiety—it was a very costly suit, had we lost it ruin would have overwhelmed us some years the sooner. It was gained but at great cost and while it was pending my Mother neither liked going out nor letting us go. Jane went sometimes to our intimate friends, with all of whom she was very popular and her lively descriptions much diverted us stay at homes. When she set off on her gaieties, my Mother read aloud to Mary and me as we sat at work beside her.

There were great riots in the West Country[1] during this winter, and the yeomanry called out to keep the quarrelsome in order. Our friend and neighbour, William Gibson, quite vain of his appearance in the handsome uniform, took several occasions of running in when dressed, as if accidentally, in order we supposed to be admired. He and I had fallen out before we went abroad and we never rightly fell in again, for there was an under current of ill breeding, which sometimes broke through the artificial manner that imposed on most persons, and shocked my 'gentle' highland blood. He was a little spoiled, known to be the heir of his wealthy father and still wealthier Cousin, Mr Craig of Riccarton; the idea, therefore, of his studying for the Bar struck us all as absurd. Of course he did not spend much time over his law books, and having besides a curious habit of falling in love with every girl, no, but women he met with, even plain, stupid, elderly women if none more attractive were at hand, his father determined to send him to travel. My father and mother were sorry to see him go; he was a favourite, and has turned out so as fully to justify their early partiality. Probably the going laid the foundation of that better style of manner and feeling which have made his middle age so every way superiour to his youth.[2]

1. Strikes and riots in Glasgow culminated in the *Radical War* of April 1820 when radical weavers were dispersed in a skirmish at Bonnymuir.
2. E.G.'s sister Jane married him as her second husband.

Uncle Ralph had brought his family to Edinburgh, let Tennochside, and taken an excellent house in the most out of the way part of the town, getting it for a trifle on account of its situation in St John's Street—a blind lane off the Cannongate. James Hamilton was with them, he and Edmund having a Tutor between them to prepare them for College. They came a very short time before we left, otherwise our winter would have been pleasanter. There were many publick rejoicings although private affairs had been gathering gloom. The old Queen Charlotte had died and George the 3rd ditto. The Princess Charlotte had married and had died in childbirth with her baby, and this had set all her royal Uncles upon marrying to provide heirs to the throne. One after the other German Princesses came over to them, and in this year began the births, to the supposed delight of a grateful country. We had long tiresome mournings and then the joy bells—the old tale. But there were other losses more felt. Madame de Staël died, to the regret of Europe.[1] We had heard so much of her through the Mackintoshs that we almost fancied her an acquaintance. I think the Duke of York must have died too, and Mrs Cumming—but may be this was later. I am confused about dates, having never made any memoranda to guide me. Altogether my recollection of these few last months in Edinburgh are rather confused and far from pleasant.

One morning my mother sent Jane and Mary with a message to the poor Carrs in the Abbey; William was out elsewhere; most of the servants were despatched on errands; and then, poor woman, she told me there was to be an Execution in the house, and that I must help her to ticket a few books and drawings as belonging to the friends that had lent them to us. We had hardly finished when two startling rings announced the arrival of a string of rude looking men, who proceeded at once to business however with perfect civility, although their visit could not have been satisfactory, inasmuch as nothing almost was personal property. The

1. (1776–1817) French author, essayist, critic and famous
   conversationalist, this brilliant lady was widely fêted in
   England during her visit in 1813.

furniture was all hired, there was no cellar, very little plate. The Law library and the pianoforte were the most valuable items of the short catalogue. I attended them with the keys, and certainly they were very courteous, not going up to the bedrooms at all, nor scrutinising any where closely. When they were gone we had a good fit of crying, my mother and I, and then she told me for the first time of our difficulties as far as she herself knew them, adding that her whole wish now was to retire to the highlands; for, disappointed as she had been in every way, she had no wish to remain before the publick eye nor to continue an expensive way of living evidently beyond their circumstances. How severely I reflected on myself for having added to her griefs, for I had considerably distressed her by my heartless flirtations, entered on purposely to end in disappointment. The guilt of such conduct now came upon me as a blow, meriting just as cruel punishment as my awakening conscience was giving me; for there was no help, no cure for the past, all remaining was a better line of conduct for the future, on which I fully determined, and, thank God, lived to carry out, and so in some small degree atone for that vile flippancy which had hurt my own character and my own reputation while it tortured my poor Mother. I don't now take all the blame upon myself; I had never been rightly guided. The relations between Mother and daughter were very different then from what they are now. Our mother was very reserved with us, not watchful of us, nor considerate, nor consistent. The Governess was an affliction. We had no rule of right and so deserve excuse for our many errours. Thought would have schooled us but I never thought till this sad day. Then it seemed as if a veil fell from between my giddy spirits and real life, and the lesson I read began my education.

Mary had also grieved my poor mother a little by refusing Uncle Edward's invitation to India; Jane, by declining what were called good marriages; William, by neglecting his Law studies. A little more openness with kindness might have done good to all; tart speeches and undue fault finding will put nothing straight, ever. We had all suffered from the fretful without knowing what had caused the ill humour. It was easy to bear and easy to soothe once it was understood.

We were all the happier after we knew more of the truth of our position.

It was easy to get leave to spend the summer in Rothiemurchus; it was impossible to persuade my father that he had lost his chance of succeeding at the Scotch Bar. He took another house in Great King Street, removing all the furniture and his law books into it, as our Lease of No. 8 Picardy Place was out. My Mother, who had charge of the packing, put up and carried north every atom that was our own. She had made up her mind to return no more, though she said nothing after the new house was taken. Had she been as resolute earlier it would have been better; perhaps she did not know the necessity of the case; and then she and we looked on the forest as inexhaustible, a growth of wealth that would last for ever and retrieve any passing difficulties, with proper management. This was our sunny gleam, always.

On reading over my travels, I find I have left out a good many little incidents that in their due place would have materially lightened the rather meagre narrative, but they are in themselves too trifling to stand alone in a list of omissions—excepting indeed two incidents which really should not be forgotten. Our dinner at the Dutch merchant's at Rotterdam, for he kept his word that chance acquaintance of ours of the table d'hôte at Maestricht, and the singular behaviour of two people who, one or the other of them, crossed our path in almost every direction, the queen of Sweden and the Duc de Richelieu.

She was the Wife of Bernadotte, once Mademoiselle Le Clerk of Marseilles. Monsieur de Richelieu had, 'twas said, been her lover and *she* was constant still, age though detracting from her charms not having chilled her heart. *He* had tired of the business and he was now intent on flying, while she pursued. He had a light carriage and travelled post with small attendance and he must have had a staff of intelligence Agents all along the road besides, for frequently when he seemed quite settled comfortably in the same hotel with ourselves at different places, Aix, Liège, Spa, he would suddenly interrupt all his quiet arrangements, pack up and be off without leaving a trace behind and just get out of sight before the queen arrived in her more stately equipage, a well loaded Berline.[1] Her stay was always short, her manners hurried, the many imperials were no sooner unpacked and carried up to her apartment than they were down again and replaced upon the carriage, and her Majesty and suite hastening after them, when away they rolled upon their fruitless search. While we were in the habit of encountering them, he had always the start of her, always escaped her. She was a pretty little woman, no longer young but well preserved, beautifully dressed and had something attractive about her air though she was not in the least dignified. It was odd altogether such proceedings in a queen, for there seemed to be no attempt at any concealment of the object of her cross journeyings, the enquiries concerning the pursued being quite open and most minute. We set the whole affair down to the account of foreign manners.[2]

The dinner at the Dutch merchant's was very pleasant. He came with his wife, a very thin woman, to remind us of our promise and told us it would be quite a family party, his sons and their wives, his daughters and their husbands, and other near relations, in all we found about twenty. The hour was three and while we were waiting in the heavily furnished Drawing room, the ladies amused themselves in the windows looking at the passengers in the street below by means of small mirrours hung against the shutters for the purpose of reflecting the objects outside. The gentlemen drank madeira handed about in tall glasses on a tray. The first dish at dinner was oysters, a great quantity of which were eaten and more madeira was taken after them. Then a great number of dishes were set on the table together—the soup and the bouilli with pickles like France; several sorts of fish variously dressed; roast meat and baked meat and ragouts with vegetables.

1. A four-wheeled covered carriage, with a seat behind covered with a hood.
2. Jean Baptiste Jules Bernadotte, Napoleon's Marshal, was chosen King of Sweden in 1810 and reigned for thirty-four years. His wife, Desirée Clary, daughter of a wealthy Marseilles merchant, had been Napoleon's first fiancée and was the sister of Joseph Buonaparte's wife, Julie. The Duc de Richelieu (1766–1822) became Prime Minister in February of this same year, 1820.

Wine, excellent wine, constantly going about and Bier. A course of pastry, game and sweet dishes, came next, then red herrings raw, dressed with oil and vinegar and cut in small pieces, then a very fine dessert and cheese of two or three kinds. We had coffee in the Drawing room and so came away. They were very friendly, mannered people, not particularly bright but they had plenty to say in their bad french. The naval officer, who turned out to be a nephew, was there and a great addition to the cheerfulness of the company. It was very civil of these perfect strangers to introduce us into their home circle, the thing of all other foreigners most wish for and so seldom accomplished.

We often talked over amongst ourselves all that befell us in our short wanderings—it was conversation for many an evening that might otherwise have been dull, as little was happening that we cared for. A marriage or two took place in our Circle, the most interesting of which to us was Jane Hunter's to Charles Guthrie, a London Russian Merchant, well to do and the son of a Fifeshire Laird. Some of the relations thought she might have done better, trade not being much in favour where Highland blood flows. She chose for herself, however, and never repented though she had to live for many years in Idol Lane in a set of rooms over the Warehouse. Lady Hunter was quite pleased with the connexion, wrote long notes to my Mother on the subject and coming to dine with us to meet Uncle Bartle, who was travelling for his health, she gave him such an overdose of Guthrie-ism that he declared nothing should tempt him within a hundred miles of her till the other daughter was safe off, married, and all over for months and the affair half forgotten. Uncle Bartle had lost the Spanish Wife whom he never married! and he really believed he was sorry for her.

CHAPTER TWENTY-FOUR

1820–1823

IN July then, 1820, we returned to the highlands, which for seven years remained the only home of the family. My Mother resisted all arguments for a return to Edinburgh this first winter, and they were never again employed. She had begun to lose her brave heart, to find out how much more serious than she had ever dreamed of had become the difficulties in which my father was involved, though the full extent of his debts was concealed for some time longer from her and the world. Some sort of a Trust Deed was executed this summer, to which I know our Cousin lame James Grant, Glenmoriston's Uncle, was a party. William was to give up the Bar, and devote himself to the management of the property. Take the forest affairs into his own hands, Duncan McIntosh being quite invalided, and turn farmer as well, having qualified himself by a residence of some months in East Lothian at a first rate practical farmer's, for the care of the comparatively few acres round the Doune. My father was to proceed as usual; London and the House in Spring, and such improvements as amused him when at home.

My Mother did not enjoy a country life; she had therefore the more merit in suiting herself to it. She had no pleasure in gardening or in wandering through all that beautiful scenery, neither had she any turn for Schools, or 'cottage comforts,' or the general care of her husband's people, though in particular instances she was very kind; nor was she an active house-keeper. She ordered very good dinners, but as general overseer of expenditure she failed. She liked seeing her hanks of yarn come in and her webs come home; but whether she got back all she ought from what she sent, she never thought of. She had no extravagant habits, not one; yet for want of supervision the waste in all departments of the household was excessive. Indolently content with her book, her newspaper, or her work, late up and very late to bed, a walk to her poultry yard which was her only diversion was almost a bore to her, and a drive with my father in her pretty pony carriage quite a sacrifice. Her health was beginning to give way and her spirits with it.

William was quite pleased with the change in his destiny; he was extremely fond of commanding, very active in his habits, by no means studious, and he had never much fancied the Law. Farming he took to eagerly, and what a farmer he made. They were changed times to the highland idlers. The whole yard astir at five o'clock in the morning, himself perhaps the first to pull the bell, a certain task allotted to every one, hours fixed for this work, days set apart for that, method pursued, order enforced. It was hard, up hill work, but even to tidiness and cleanliness it was accomplished in time. He overturned the old system a little too quickly, a woman would have gone about the requisite changes with more delicacy; the result, however, justified the means. There was one stumbling block in his way, a clever rogue of a grieve, by name Aitchieson, a handsome well mannered man, a great favourite, who blinded even William by his adroit flatteries. He came from Ayrshire, highly recommended by I forget who, and having married Donald Maclean the Carpenter's pretty daughter, called Jane after my Mother, he had a strong back of connexions all disposed to be favourable to him. He was gardener as well as grieve, for George Ross was dead, and he was really skilful in both capacities, when properly guided.

The forest affairs were at least equally improved by such active superintendence, although the alterations came more by degrees. I must try and remember all that was done there, and in due order if possible. First, the general felling of timber at whatever spot the men so employed found it most convenient to them to use their axe on a marked tree, was put a stop to. William made a plan of the forest,[1] divided it into sections, and as far as was practicable allotted one portion to

1. These meticulous plans are in the possession of the
    present generation of the Grant family.

be cleared immediately, enclosed by a stout fencing, and then left to nature, not to be touched again for fifty or sixty years. The ground was so rich in seed that no other care was requisite. By the following Spring a carpet of inch high plants would be struggling to rise above the heather, in a season or two more a thicket of young fir trees would be found there, thinning themselves as they grew, the larger destroying all the weaker. Had this plan been pursued from the beginning there would never have been an end to the wood of Rothiemurchus.

The dragging of the felled timber was next systematised. The horses required were kept at the Doune, sent out regularly to their work during the time of year they were wanted, and when their business was done employed in carting deals to Forres, returning with meal sufficient for the consumption of the whole place, or to Inverness to bring back coals and other stores for the house. The little bodies and idle boys with ponies were got rid of. The Mills also disappeared. One by one these picturesque objects fell into disuse. A large building was erected on the Druie near its junction with the Spey, where all the sawing was effected. A coarse upright saw for slabbing, that is, slicing off the outsides or backs of the logs, and several packs of saws which cut the whole log up at once into deals, were all arranged in the larger division of the Mill. A wide reservoir of water held all the wood floated or dragged to the inclined plane up which the logs were rolled as wanted. When cut up, the backs were thrown out through one window, the deals through another, into a yard at the back of the Mill, where the wood was all sorted and stacked. Very few men and as many boys got easily through the work of the day. It was always a busy scene and a very exciting one, the great Lion of the place, strangers delighting in a visit to it. The noise was frightful, but there was no confusion, no bustle, no hurry. Every one employed had his own particular task, and plenty of time and space to do it in.

The smaller compartment of the great Mill was fitted up with circular saws for the purpose of preparing the thinnings of the birch woods for herring barrel staves. It was a mere toy beside its gigantick neighbour, but a very pretty one and a very profitable one, above £1000 a year profit being cleared by this manufacture of what had hitherto been valueless except as fuel. This circular saw Mill had been the first erected. It was planned by my father and William the summer they went north with my Mother and left us girls in Edinburgh. The large Mill followed, and was but just finished as we arrived, so that it was not in the good working order I have described till some months later. An Urquhart Gale, an oddity imported a few years before, had entire charge of it, and Sandy McIntosh gave all his attention to the woods. He lived with his father at the Dell, and Urquhart Gale lived on one of the islands in the Druie, where he had built himself a wooden house surrounded by a strip of garden bounded by the water.

Having set the staple business of the place in more regular order than it ever had been conducted in before, William turned his attention to the farm, with less success however for a year or two. More work was done and all work was better done, but the management remained expensive till we got rid of Aitchieson. In time he was replaced by a head ploughman from the Lothians, when all the others having learnt their places required less supervision. William indeed was himself always at his post, this new profession of his being his passion. The order he got that farm into, the crops it yielded afterwards, the beauty of his fields, the improvement of the Stock, were the wonder of the Country. This first year I did not so much attend to his doings as I did the next, having little or nothing to do with his operations. Jane and I rode as usual. We all wandered about in the woods and spent long days in the garden, and then we had the usual Autumn Company to entertain at home and in the neighbourhood.

Our first guest was John. Our young brother John whom we had not seen since he went first to Eton. My Mother, whose anxiety to meet her pet was fully equal to my sisters' and mine, proposed our driving to Pitmain, thirteen miles off, where the Coach then stopt to dine. The Barouche and four was ordered accordingly and away we went. We had nearly reached Kingussie when we espied upon the road a tall figure walking with long strides, his hat on the back of his head, his hair blowing about in the wind, very short trowsers, and arms beyond his coat sleeves—in fact an object! and this was John! grown five inches! or indeed I believe six! for he had been sixteen months away. He had carried up very creditable breadth with all this height, looking strong enough, but so altered, so unlike our little plaything of a brother, we were rather discomfited. However, we found that the ways of old had lost no charms for the Eton boy; he was more our companion than ever, promoting and enjoying fun in his quiet way, and so long as no sort of trouble fell to him, objecting to none of our many schemes of amusement. Old as we elder ones were, we used to join in cat concerts after breakfast in the dining room. My mother always breakfasted in her room, my father frequently had a tray sent to him in the Study, or if he came to us, he ate hurriedly and soon departed. We each pretended we were playing on some instrument, the sound of which we endeavoured to imitate with the voice, taking parts as in a real orchestra, generally contriving to make harmony, and going through all our favourite overtures as well as innumerable melodies. Then we would act Scenes from different plays, substituting our own words when memory failed us, or sing bits of Operas in the same *improvisatori* style. Then we would rush out of doors, be off to fish, or to visit our thousand friends, or to the forest or to the Mill, or to take a row upon the lake, unmooring the boat ourselves, and Jane and I handling the oars just as well as our brothers. Sometimes we stopt short in the garden or went no further than the hill of the Doune, or may be would lounge on to the farm yard if any work we liked was going on there. Jane had taken to sketching from nature and to gardening. I had my green house plants indoors, and the linen press, made over to my case by my mother, as were the wardrobes of my brothers. We were so happy, so busy, we felt it an interruption when there came visitors, Jane excepted. She was only in her element when in company. She very soon took the whole charge of receiving and entertaining the guests. She quite shone in this capacity and certainly made the gay meetings of friends henceforward very different from the formal parties of former times. Our guests this autumn of 1820 were Charles and Robert Grant (names ever dear to me), Sir David and Lady Brewster, and Mrs Marcet the clever authoress,[1] brought to us by the Bellevilles. We gave her a luncheon in our Cottage at Loch an Eilein, which much pleased her. This cottage had been built by General Grant of the diamond ring for his old mother—on her death it had remained untenanted till it was bestowed on us. Our kind father repaired and improved it and built us a back kitchen and made us a flower garden and my mother gave us some furniture. Our cousin Edmund was with us this summer; he helped us to fit it up, whitewashing, staining, painting, etc. One of the woodmen's wives lived in it and kept it tidy. We had a pantry and a store room, well furnished both of them, and many a party we gave there, sometimes a boating and fishing party with a luncheon, sometimes a tea with cakes of our own making, and a merry walk home by moonlight. Doctor Hooker[2] also came to botanise and the Sportsmen to shoot. Kinrara filled, and Uncle Ralph and Eliza passed the whole summer with us. Mrs Ironside was at Oxford, watching with aunt Mary the last days of Dr Griffith. Uncle Ralph was the most delightful companion that ever dwelt in a country house. Never in the way, always up to every thing, the promoter of all enjoyment, full of fun, full of anecdote, charming by the fire on a wet day, charming out of doors in the sunshine, enthusiastick about scenery, unrivalled in weaving garlands of natural flowers for the hair, altogether such a prose poet as one almost never meets with; hardly handsome, yet very fine looking, tall and with the air and the manners of a prince of the blood. He had lived much in the best society and had adorned it. Eliza was clever, very obliging, and her playing on the pianoforte was delightful. She had an everlasting collection of old simple airs belonging to all countries, which she strung together with skill, and played with expression. We had great fun this Autumn;

1. Mrs Jane Marcet (1769–1858) wrote for the young; one of her most recent works had been *Conversations on Chemistry, intended more specifically for the Female Sex* (1816).
2. Sir William Jackson Hooker (1785–1868) was to become Director of Kew Gardens in 1841.

poney races at Kingussie and a ball at the cattle tryst, picnics
in the woods, quantities of fine people at Kinrara, Lord
Tweeddale and his beautiful Marchioness (Lady Susan
Montague), the Ladies Cornwallis, kind merry girls, one of
them, Lady Louisa, nearly killing uncle Ralph by making
him dance twice down the Haymakers with her; Mrs
Rawdon and her clever daughter, Lady William Russell, who
I do not think much liked her little shabby looking Lord;
Lord Lynedoch at 80 shooting with the young men; Colonel
Ponsonby, who had gambled away a fine fortune or two and
Lady Harriet Bathurst's heart, and being supposed to be
killed at Waterloo, had had his body, when he had swooned,
built up in a wall of corpses, as a breastwork before some
regiment to shoot over. Mrs Rawdon, rather a handsome
flirting widow, taking Uncle Ralph for a widower, paid him
very tender attentions and invited Eliza to visit her in
London.

This was the summer of Queen Caroline's trial;[1] the
newspapers were of course forbidden to all us young people;
a useless prohibition, for while we sat working or drawing,
my Uncle and my Mother favoured us with full comments on
these disgusting proceedings. 'Good God, Jane', said my
Uncle, 'the woman must be a beast, just listen . . . did you
ever hear of any thing so utterly abominable . . .'; 'Not near
so bad Ralph as her exhibition before the Banker at . . .'; and
so they would go on skimming the rich filth of the dirt the
papers were polluted with. In September the poor creature
died. None of the grandees in our neighbourhood would
wear mourning for her. We had to put on black for our Uncle
Griffith, and the good natured world said that my father, in
his violent Whiggery, had dressed us in sables, when, in
truth, he had always supported the king's right to exercise his

1. When George IV became King in June 1820, he was
   determined to exclude his wife, Caroline of Brunswick-
   Wolfenbättel (whom he had bigamously married 25
   years before) from the throne. Unsavoury parliamen-
   tary inquiries were accordingly held, and for many
   Whigs Caroline was seen as a symbol of resistance to
   tyranny. Conveniently for the King, she died a month
   after his coronation, in August 1821.

own authority in his own family. So tales rise and spread. Mrs Ralph remained at Oxford to assist Aunt Mary in selecting furniture, packing up some, selling the rest, and giving up the lodgings to the new Master, Dr Rowley, our old friend of the pear tree days. The two ladies then set out for Tennochside, where Aunt Mary was to pass her year of Widowhood, Uncle Ralph and Eliza hurrying back to meet them as soon as we had returned from the Northern Meeting in October. We enjoyed it much, and brought Duncan Davidson back with us in his kilt, still a fine boy though much spoiled. He was quite in love with Jane, and she seemed for a while to respond, but they fell out one rainy day and he departed. We never could make out exactly what the disagreement had been, perhaps some historical subject—a failure as to dates or facts or something had caused her to dismiss a bold dragoon, Tom Walker of the Scots Greys, a nephew of General Need's, an excellent young man, good looking, rich and gentlemanly but not literary. She was hard to please, for Mr Crawfurd (*Archipelago*) was as learned as a professor, but sticking a fork into the potatoes, lost by his ill manners all that his learning had gained him.[1]

At the end of this year my sisters and I had to manage amongst us to replace wasteful servants and attend to my Mother's simple wants. The housekeeper went, in bad health, to the Spa at Strathpeffer, where she died; the fine cook married the Butler, and took the Inn at Dalwhinnie, which they partly furnished out of our lumber room! My Mother placed me in authority, and by patience, regularity, tact and resolution, the necessary reforms were silently made without annoying any one. It was the beginning of troubles the full extent of which I had indeed little idea of then, nor had I thought much of what I did know till one bright day, on one of our forest excursions, my rough pony was led through the moss above Auchnahartenich by honest old John Bain. We were looking over a wide, bare plain, which the last time I had seen it had been all wood. I believe I started. The good old man shook his gray head, and then, with more respect than usual in his affectionate highland manner, he told me all

1. See II, p. 78.

that was said, all that he feared, all that some one of us should know, and that he saw 'it was fixed' that Miss Lizzie should hear, for though she was 'lightsome' she would come to sense when it was wanted to keep her Mama easy, try to get her brothers on and not refuse a good match for herself, or her sisters should it come their way. Good, wise John Bain—'A match for me!' that was over, but the rest was easy, could at least be tried. 'A stout heart to a stiff brae' gets up the hill. I was ignorant of household matters. My kind friend the Lady Belleville was an admirable economist, she taught me much. Dairy and farmkitchen matters were picked up at the Dell and the Croft, and with books of reference, honest intentions, and untiring activity, less mistakes were made in this season of apprenticeship than could have been expected. And so passed the year of 1821. Few visitors that season, no Northern Meeting, a dinner or two at Kinrara, and a good many visits at Belleville. William busy with the forest and the farm.

1822 was more lively; William and I had got our departments into fair working order. Whether he had diminished expenses, I know not; I had, beyond my slightest idea, and we were fully more comfortable than we had ever been under the reign of the housekeepers. Sir David and Lady Brewster were with us for a while, and Dr Hooker, and the Grants of course, with their quaint fun and their oddities and their extra piety, which, I think, was wearing away. In the early part of the year 1822 Aunt Mary came to us from Tennochside, escorted by my father on his way home from London. She found me very ill. I had gone at Xmas on a visit to our Cousins the Roses of Holm, where I had not been since Charlotte's marriage to Sir John, then only Colonel Burgoyne. There had been no Company in the house for some time; I was put into a damp bed, which gave me such a cold, followed by such a cough that I had kept my room ever since; the dull unhealthy barrack room, very low in the roof, just under the slates, cold in winter, a furnace in summer, only one window in it. We three girls in it, my poor sisters disturbed all night with my incessant cough. Dr Smith, kind little man, took what care he could of me, and Jane, who succeeded to my 'situation,' was the best, the most untiring of nurses, but neither of them could manage my removal to a fitter apartment. Aunt Mary effected it at once. We were all brought down to the white room and its dressing room, the best in the house, so light, so very cheerful; I had the large room. The dear Miss Cumming Gordons sent up from Forres House a cuddy, whose milk, brought up to me warm every morning, soon softened the cough. Nourishing soups restored strength. In June I was on my poney; in August I was well. Weak enough, how much I owed to our dear, wise Aunt Mary. She never let us return to the barrack room. She prevailed on my father to have us settled in the old Schoolroom and the room through it, which we inhabited ever after; had we been there before I should not have been so ill, for my mother lived on the same floor, and would have been able to look after us. She was very ill herself, in the Doctor's hands, rose late, never got up the garret stairs, and was no great believer in the danger of a mere cold.

Aunt Mary amused us very much by her admiration of handsome young men. One of the Macphersons of Ralea, and the two Clarkes of Dalnavert, John and William, were very much with us; they were dangerous intimates, but they did us no harm; I do not know that they did themselves much good. Aunt Mary would have woven a romance about the Clarkes had she had time; nobodies on the father's side, but on the Mother's lineally descended from the Shawes of Rothiemurchus. It was hard on them to see their ancient foes in their inheritance. It is curious how those highland *laddies*, once introduced to the upper world, take their places in it as if born to fill them. No young man, School and College bred, could have more graceful manners than John Clarke; he entered the army from his humble home at Dalnavert, just taught a little by the kindness of Belleville. He was a first rate Officer, became A.D.C., married a Baronet's daughter, and became well the high position he won. The brother William, a gentlemanly sailor, married a woman of family and fortune, and settled in Hampshire. The sisters, after the death of their parents, went to an Aunt in South America, where most of them married well, the eldest to a nephew of the celebrated

General Greene.[1] All of them rose as no other race ever rises; there is no vulgarity for them to lose and there is the good blood and the old recollections to help them on. Then came John Dalzel, a good young man, said to be clever, known to be industrious, educated with all the care that clever parents, School, College, a good society in Lord Eldin's house, could command; who, grave, dull, awkward, looked of inferiour species to the 'gentle Celts.'

This Autumn King George the 4th, then, I think, only Regent, visited Scotland. The whole country went mad. Every body strained every point to get to Edinburgh to receive him. Sir Walter Scott and the town Council were overwhelming themselves with the preparations. My Mother did not feel well enough for the bustle, neither was I at all fit for it, so we staid at home with Aunt Mary. My father, my two sisters and William, with lace, feathers, pearls, the old landau, the old horses, and the old liveries, all went to add to the Show, which they said was delightful. The Countess of Lauderdale presented my two sisters and the two Miss Grants of Congalton, a group allowed to be the prettiest there. The Clan Grant had quite a triumph, no equipage was as handsome as that of Colonel Francis Grant, our acting Chief, in their red and green and gold. There were processions, a Review, a Levée, a Drawing room, and a Ball, at which last Jane was one of the young ladies selected to dance in the reel before the Regent, with, I think, poor Captain Murray of Abercairney, a young naval officer, for her partner.[2] A great mistake was made by the Stage Managers—one that offended all the southron Scots; the King wore at the Levée the highland dress. I daresay he

1. General Sir William Green (1725–1811), the engineer.
2. Mary and Jane Grant wrote a series of letters back to
   E.G. describing their experiences during this memorable visit. These were collected and privately printed in
   Dublin, presumably by E.G. after her marriage. They
   are an entertaining description of the King (Mary 'only
   saw a pair of thick lips, and a grave respectful-looking
   face bending towards me') and all the occasions he was
   publicly fêted.

thought the country all highland, expected no fertile plains, did not know the difference between the Saxon and the Celt.[1] However, all else went off well, this little slur on the Saxon was overlooked, and it gave occasion for a good laugh at one of lady Saltoun's witty speeches. Some one objecting to this dress, particularly on so large a man, whose nudities were no longer attractive, 'Nay,' said she, 'we should take it very kind of him; since his stay will be so short, the more we see of him the better.' Sir William Curtis was kilted too, and standing near the King, many persons mistook them, amongst others John Hamilton Dundas, who kneeled to kiss the fat Alderman's hand, when, finding out his mistake, he called out, 'Wrong, by Jove,' and rising, moved on undaunted to the larger presence.

One incident connected with this bustling time made me very cross. Lord Conyngham, the Chamberlain, was looking every where for pure *Glenlivet* whiskey—the King drank nothing else—it was not to be had out of the highlands. My father sent word to me, I was the Cellarer, to empty my pet bin, where was whiskey long in wood, long in uncorked bottles, mild as milk, and the true contraband *goût* in it. Much as I grudged this treasure it made our fortunes afterwards, shewing on what trifles great events sometimes depend. The whiskey, and fifty brace of ptarmigan all shot by one man in one day, went up to Holyrood House, and were graciously received and made much of, and a reminder of this attention at a proper moment by the gentlemanly Chamberlain ensured to my father the Indian Judgeship.

While part of the family were thus royally or loyally occupied, passing away a gay ten days in Edinburgh, my dear, kind Aunt and I were strolling through the beautiful

---

1. In a letter to Rothiemurchus (11.8.1822), E.G.'s father also criticised 'the ludicrous state of bustle and expectation of the sedate and sober citizens of the Scottish Metropolis—and the whimsical affectation of a sort of highland costume, with about as much propriety in the conception and execution as if it had taken place in Paris or Brussels'.

scenery of Rothiemurchus. She loved to revisit all the places she had so admired in her youth. When attended by the train of retainers which then accompanied her progress, she had learned from her kilted suite more of the ancient doings of our race than I with all my research had been able to pick up even from dear old Mr Cameron. She was all highland, an enthusiast in her admiration of all that fed the romance of her nature, so different from the placid comfort of her early home. Our strolls were charming; she on foot, I on my poney. We went long distances, for we often stopt to rest beside some little sparkling burnie, and seated on the heather and beside the cranberries, we ate the luncheon we had brought with us in a basket that was hung on the crutch of my saddle. I was much more fitted to understand her fine mind at this time than I should have been the year before. My long illness, which had confined me for so many months to my room, where most of the time was passed in solitude, had thrown me for amusement on the treasures of my father's library. First I took to light reading, but finding there allusions to subjects of graver import of which I was nearly ignorant, I chalked out for myself really a plan of earnest study. The history of my own country, and all connected with it, in eras, taking in a sketch of other countries, consulting the references where we had them, studying the literature of each period, comparing the past with the present. It was this course faithfully pursued till it interested me beyond idea that made me acquainted with the worth of our small collection of books. There was no subject on which sufficient information could not be got. I divided my reading time into four short sittings, varying the subjects, by advice of good Dr Smith, to avoid fatigue, and as I slept little it was surprising how many volumes even in this way I got through. It was 'the making of me,' as we Irish say. Our real mission here on earth had never been hinted to me. We had no fixed aim in life, nor even an idea of 'wasted time.' To do good, and to avoid evil, we were certainly taught, and very happy we were while all was bright around us. When sorrow came I was not fit to bear it, I had to bear it all alone. We were brought up in Spartan fashion, to let the fox bite beneath the cloke. The utmost reserve was inculcated upon us whenever a disagreeable effect would be produced by an exhibition of our feelings. In this case, too, the subject had been prohibited, so the fox bit hard and the long illness was the result, but the after-consequences were good. The mind was brightened, as well as chastened and strengthened by this wise occupation, the disposition improved by the habit of reflexion.

It was new to me to think. I had never thought before. I often lay awake in the early summer morning looking from my bed through the large south window of that pretty 'White room,' thinking of the world beyond those fine old beech trees, taking into the picture the green gate, the undulating field, the bank of birch trees, and the Ord Bain, and on the other side the height of the Polchar, and the smoke from the gardener's cottage; wondering, dreaming, and not omitting self accusation, for discipline had been necessary to me, and I had not borne my cross meekly. My foolish, frivolous, careless career and its punishment came back upon me painfully, but no longer angrily; I learned to excuse as well as to submit, so kissed the rod in a brave spirit which met its reward. Poor, poor Lizzy Glass, my name sake, the very pretty under dairy maid, used to come to my bedside every morning with a frothy cup of Ass's milk, which I owed to the kindness of Jane and Emilia Cumming, and she always said in presenting it with her sweet, innocent smile—for she was innocent then, poor thing—in the only English she knew, 'Sleep well'; which I generally did for an hour or two. I was still confined to my room, but being able now to write and to work, no longer found the time so weary and my wise Aunt found me a new and most pleasant employment. She set me upon writing essays, short tales, and at length a novel. I don't suppose they were intrinsically worth much, and I am sure I do not know what has become of them, but the venture was invaluable. I tried higher flights afterwards with success when help was more wanted.

All this while, who was very near us, within a thought of coming on to find us out, had he more accurately known our whereabouts. He who hardly seven years after became my husband. He was an Officer of the Indian Army at home on furlough,[1] diverting his leisure by a tour through part of Scotland; he was sleeping quietly at Dunkeld while I was waking during the long night at the Doune. Uncle Edward, his particular friend, had so often talked of us to him that he knew us almost individually, but for want of a letter of introduction would not volunteer a better acquaintance. It was better for me as it was. I know well, had he come to Rothiemurchus, Jane would have won his heart. So handsome she was, so lively, so kind, a sickly invalid would have had no chance with her. Major Smith and Miss Jane would have ridden enthusiastically through the woods together, and I should have been unnoticed. All happens well, could we but think so; and so my future husband returned alone to India, and I had to go there after him!

At the close of this Autumn my Aunt was to leave us to spend the winter with her old friend Miss Lawrence at Studley. I was to go with her, Doctor Smith not thinking it would be safe for me to risk the cold frosts of the highlands. Miss Lawrence so very kindly wished me to remain with her during my Aunt's visit, but Annie Need had arranged with my father that I was to be her guest during this winter; it was a long promised treat, so I could only give a month to Studley on my way to Sherwood forest.

Before we left the Doune there had been a family Council held on Weighty affairs. Our cousin Kate Ironside, the eldest of the Houghton family, who had been sent for to Bombay by Uncle Edward in the year 1819, had married well; her husband, Colonel Barnewall, an excellent man, was then Resident at Kaira, much considered in the Service; he had permitted Kate to send for her two next sisters, Eliza and Mary, and Uncle Edward wished my sister Mary to accompany them. She had been his pet in her babyhood. My father and Mother were rather offended by the proposal, but left

1. An extended leave. Born in 1780, the second son of a Co. Wicklow landowner, Henry Smith had been admitted to King's Inn, after which he enrolled as a Cadet in the East India Company Cavalry. He was promoted Major in 1820 and was to be Lieutenant Colonel four years later.

the decision to Mary herself. She declined of course for the present, leaving the matter open for future consideration, with the caution for which she was so remarkable. 'There is no saying,' said she, 'but what Bombay might some day prove a Godsend. Life is dull enough here.' At this same time a Writership offered by old Charles Grant to my brother John was refused, to my Mother's grief, for she had set her heart upon it. She had a craze for India, and would have despatched every individual boy or girl over whom she had any influence to that land of the sun. My father and William, indeed our Aunt Mary too, thought that John's great abilities would ensure him employment at home. So this matter was postponed.

Towards the end of October my Aunt and I set out upon our travels, escorted by my brother William. We went in the travelling chariot with our own horses, sleeping two nights upon the road, and we staid a week in Edinburgh in our own house in King Street, which my father had lent to Uncle Ralph. His son Edmund, his nephew James Hamilton, and John Dundas were living with him and attending College. Very few people were in town, but Aunt Judy kindly brought these few of our old friends who were remaining there to see us, and gave two very pleasant little dinners to us. Miss Clerk, and Mary Dalzel of course, with her beautiful pianoforte musick, only equalled by poor Eliza's own, and William Clerk, the clever oddity who, it was said, read up in the mornings for conversational purposes, and at the dinners adroitly brought in the prepared subject; he made himself most agreeable any way with his shrewd mother wit. I remember one bit of sarcasm particularly well. He could not bear a pompous little man, who had married his cousin, Mr Wedderburn, the Solicitor-General. As this little body was parading the Parliament house one day with the air of a Socrates, he was thus weighed and valued by the Cynick— 'Oh, gin I could buy you at my price and sell you at your own.'

We proceeded by Coach to Carlisle, the first time I had ever set foot in a publick carriage, and very disagreeable I found it, so fine was the upper world in those days. The country we passed through was delightful to us who were learned in Ballad lore; Ettrick Shawes and Galla water, the braes of Yarrow and the Cowdenknowes, all spoke to us though from a distance, as we passed on to merry Carlisle, which we reached too late and too sleepy to look at. Next day we passed on over the Wolds to Greta Bridge and Kirby, and so on to Studley, where I remained till close on Xmas. William found the life too dull, so he set off to Annie Need, with whom he remained visiting about till it was time to return for me.

At that season of the year old Miss Lawrence lived nearly alone; her open house style ended with the autumn. We found only a few intimate friends with her. Two middle aged Miss Johnstones, who seemed to make regular tours among rich acquaintances. A very underbred and very flirting Miss Glaister the old lady's goddaughter, the child of her Land Steward; Mr Charnock, her chaplain, a good kind of man in an humble way; his pupil, Mr Nares; Sir Tristram Ricketts, who romped with the younger Miss Johnstone and occasionally a Mr Newsam, a young clergyman to whom Miss Lawrence had given a good living, in expectation of his marriage with Miss Glaister.

Breakfast was early; the post, needle work, and musick occupied the morning, and a ride or a walk before luncheon; a drive in the afternoon, or another walk. Dinner, which was served in the small dining room, and was always pleasant, and then duetts on the pianoforte in the evenings. Miss Lawrence always played the bass, Miss Johnstone and I in turn the treble. I daresay the old lady had been a good musician in her day, according to the style of musick and limited execution then in fashion. It was rather a melancholy performance now. She was quite unaware of this, for when she went out to dinner she always took musick and Miss Johnstone with her. Poor Miss Johnstone, she used to look up with such a peculiar smile while selecting the pieces.

Miss Lawrence was very kind to me. She sent a pianoforte to my room that I might practise in quiet. She gave me a key to the bookcases in the library, and generally chose me as her companion in her morning rides. We rode two donkeys, she on Johnny, I on Jack. She rode first in a very old duffle cloke of a grey colour and a black gypsey hat, encouraging her somewhat slothful steed by a brisk 'Johnny, get on' every now and then. Jack required no stimulus, and thus we wandered for hours through the beautiful grounds of Studley Royal. It was one of the Lions of Harrogate, and certainly its extensive old fashioned gardens deserved a visit. There were lawns, thickets, laurel banks, lakes, grottoes, temples, statues, the beautiful old ruins of Fountains Abbey, kept most incorrectly clean and tidy as if washed and trimmed daily, and one old manor house near it—a gem—now the residence of the game keeper. The fruit gardens were large, the offices good, the house itself, though convenient, with many fine rooms in it, was hardly worthy of its surroundings. The pretty village of Ripon was within a couple of miles, a fine old Cathedral in it, which I was always to be sent to visit, but somehow never managed to get there. I did go one fine, sunny, frosty day on my donkey to Kirby Lonsdale, a pretty little bit of scenery in a tame country. It was Miss Lawrence's original inheritance, she was very fond of it. She succeeded to Studley and the large Leicestershire estates on the death of her only brother, and had passed an uneasy life since, lived on by a host of parasites who knew well how to make their own use of her. She would have been happier had she married, but she had early determined to remain single. Very plain in person, very awkward in manner, no man had ever found out her real worth during her brother's life. After his death proposals of marriage were showered on her, which so disgusted her that she made a resolution to refuse all. A sensible husband, though he could not have been a lover, would have been a true friend and would have managed her immense property, political interests and all, and kept the mean crew off.

Her chaplain, good Mr Charnock, did his best to prevent her being too shamelessly imposed upon, but he could not save her altogether; neither could her Auditor, Sir Launcelot Shadwell, whose visits were rare. She did not particularly like her heir, Lord Grantham, and she particularly disliked his very handsome Irish wife, whom she thought with reason to be rather worldly.

At this time the kind old lady was quite occupied with Miss Glaister's marriage. She had made the young pair many handsome presents, and had been deceived all through, both she and poor Mr Newsam, by this artful girl; for one fine day the young lady set out for the Border with that mere boy Mr Nares, Mr Charnock's pupil, and such a fuss ensued as never was—Doctor Nares accused Mr Charnock of inattention; Lady Charlotte accused Mrs Lawrence with connivance, and the Bride being of humble birth, only the Land Steward's daughter, the *respectable* Churchill blood never could forgive the misalliance. I never heard what became of the pair.

It was very cold during my stay at Studley, frost and snow equal to the highlands. William and I had a very chilly journey after being set down, I forget where, out of Miss Lawrence's comfortable chariot. Dear Annie Need was waiting for us at Doncaster, where poor William and I parted; he went back to Edinburgh. Annie took me to the pleasant jointure house of one of the Mrs Walkers, where we spent the night, and were amused and amazed at the Xmas Storeroom; it was as full as Mrs Lawrence's. Blankets, flannels, great coats, clokes, petticoats, stockings, all the warmth that the poor could want in the wintry season. I was unused to such wholesale charity; neither do I think it wise; there can be no spirit either of independance or economy where the expectation of relief unearned is a habit. Next day we reached Fountain Dale to dinner. It was a neat, small house, with tiny grounds, well kept, planted out from a wide stretch of heath that had once been an oak forest. A chain of fish ponds, full of well preserved fish, carp, tench and such like, enlivened the scene, but though all was very tidy, there was no beauty either there or in the neighbourhood. The remains of Sherwood forest were not near this bleak and scantily populated district. There were one or two dull villages, the ugly little town of Mansfield, very few gentlemen's seats, none with any pretensions, and a general want of wood. Perhaps if I were to see the country now I should wonder at these impressions—every body was planting busily, and thirty years gives a wonderful growth to well preserved timber.

Berry hill, belonging to Mr Thomas Walker, was the nearest house to Fountain Dale, just about three miles off over the heath, a climb the whole way. Mr and Mrs Walker were hospitable people, very kind, childless, so they surrounded themselves with relations. Their connexions were all among the mercantile aristocracy of England, a new phase of life to me with my old highland blood, and one at which I opened my eyes with wonder. The profusion of money among all these people amazed *poor* me. Guineas were thrown about, as *we* would not have dreamed to deal with shillings. There was no ostentation, no great show any where, but such plenty, such an affluence of comfort. Servants well dressed, well fed; eating, indeed, went on all day upstairs and downstairs, six meals a day the rule. Well appointed stables, delightful gardens, lights every where, fires every where, nothing wanting, every thing wished for was got; yet, though good humoured and very kindly, they were not really happier one bit than those who had to count their pennies and could only rarely gratify their tastes. Generally speaking, the generation which had made the money in the mills was more agreeable than the generation which had left the mills and was spending the well earned money. The younger people were well educated—so-called—the men were School and College bred, gentlemanly, up to the times; but there was a something wanting, and there was too much vivacity! too much noise, no repose. The young women were inferiour to the young men; they were very accomplished, in the boarding school acceptation of the word, but mind there was not, and manners were defective—no ease. They were good, charitable, and highly pleased with their surroundings and with one another, and extremely proud of their brothers. They had all well filled purses. I do not remember hearing the amount of their regular allowances, but I do remember well the new year's gift at one Walker house. There were four young people of the family, and on lifting the breakfast plate each found a fifty pound note underneath it. William left with me Five pounds for my winter's pocket money. This cut a sorry figure by comparison.

General and Mrs Need were not rich; they lived quietly, had a small establishment, and, to the credit of the rich relations, lived amongst them, apparently on equal terms. Annie, indeed, was the great lady every where, and extremely beloved. Four, I think, of the County gentlemen visited at

Berry hill and Fountain Dale: Mr Coke, a bookworm, with an odd wife; Major Bilby and Captain Cope, cadets of good families, in the militia; and Mr Hallowes, a regular country squire, fit for a novel—short, chubby, goodlooking, shooting, fishing, hunting, hospitable, kindly, a magistrate, and not an ounce of brains. The beautiful old manor house he lived in stood almost alone. In all our drives I never recollect passing a gentleman's seat; it was a very isolated part of Nottinghamshire, up in the moors. To say the truth, it was rather sleepy work this life in the Forest, and yet the time passed happily. Annie was so bright, so kind, her four boys fine little fellows, and once a fortnight there was an Oyster ploy; the particular friends were invited to meet a barrel of natives and Mr Need, the General's elder brother; by the bye, his wife was a nice, clever woman, unfortunately very deaf. At Berry hill I once met Mr and Mrs Lempriere—he was a fat little lively man, the son of the 'Classical Dictionary.'[1]

One visit I did enjoy; it was to the Strutts of Belper and Derby. General Need's father, his friend Mr Strutt, and old Arkwright—a barber, I believe—originated the cotton manufacture of England. Arkwright was the Head, Strutt the Hands, and Need the Sinews, for *he* had had the purse.[2] He was a Nottingham Stocking weaver. Of his two sons, one became a country gentleman, land to the value of £4000 a year having been purchased for him about Mansfield. This was John Need. The other, Sam Need, went into the Army with his younger son's portion, £20,000, into the Cavalry, to India, rose to high command, bore a good name, and married Annie Grant. The four daughters had £100,000 between them. Three of them married in their own Station, and very happily three brothers Walker, all in trade; the fourth, a beauty, won the heart of Mr Abney, a man of family and fortune, which alliance rather separated her from her kindred.

1. John Lemprière (1765?–1824) published his
   Bibliotheca Classica in 1788.
2. This historic partnership, 1771 to 1782, developed
   the water frame that powered the early Industrial
   Revolution.

The Strutts were silk weavers. The principal establishment was at Belper, near Derby; such a pretty place, wooded banks and a river, and a model village, the abode of the workmen. Jediah Strutt, who had married a Walker, niece of the General's, was the manager and part Owner of the Belper mills. He had an extremely pretty house in the village, with gardens behind it down to the river, and such a range of glass houses. There were Schools, an hospital, an infirmary, a Library, a chapel, and a Chaplain of their own persuasion (they were unitarians), all so liberally provided, Mrs Strutt and her young daughters all so busy in all these departments, assisted by the dear old Chaplain, who was really the soul of his flock. Then there was the Mill. It was the first of the sort I had ever seen, and it made a great impression on me. I forget now whether the moving power was steam or the pure water of the little river, but the movements produced by either are not easily forgotten. It all seemed to me like magick. Immense rooms full of countless rows of teetotums[1] twirling away by themselves, or sets of cards in hundreds of hands tearing away at cotton wool of their own accord; smoothing irons in long rows running out of the walls and sliding over quantities of stockings; hands without any bodies rubbing as if for the bare life over wash tubs, and when people wanted to reach another storey, instead of stairs they stept upon a tray, pulled a string, and up they went, or down, as suited them.

One huge iron foundry was really frightful; the Strutts manufactured their own machinery, and in this Cyclops den huge hammers were always descending on huge blocks of iron red hot, some of them, and the heat, and the din, and the wretched looking smiths at work there made a very disagreeable impression. It was a pleasant change to enter the packing house. At this time large bales were being prepared for the Russian market; the goods were built up neatly in large piles, high above our head—a string was pulled, a weight came down, and the big bale shrunk into a comfortable seat!

One of the Strutt family, an old uncle, a bachelour and an oddity, was so enamoured of his machinery that he had as much *magick* as possible introduced into his own house;

1. Light tops, spun with the fingers, originally a toy.

roasting, boiling, baking, ironing, all that it was practicable so to manage was done by turning pegs; and being rather a heavy sleeper, a hand came out of the wall in the morning at a certain hour and pulled the bed clothes off him. The whole place was amusing; Jediah and Mrs Strutt very nice, and John Strutt, a younger brother, very nice. We went to a Ball in Derby from Belper, and who should I meet there but our old Edinburgh friend Mary Balfour, now Mrs Meynell. What an ugly man she had married, but he was of high degree; and how very plain she had grown, but she had had a long purse. She was delighted to see me, and, I believe, supposed I had moved into Derbyshire for good, she was so very congratulatory; a second look showed me on the arm of the head of the Strutt family, old Mr Strutt of Derby, so she faded quietly away. This old Mr Strutt was charming, very simple, very clever, very artistick in all his tastes; he had lived a great deal abroad, and at the close of those dreadful Napoleon wars had picked up gems of price of all kinds. His house was a museum; paintings, sculpture, china, inlaid woods, not too many, and all suitably arranged.

We went from this house next day on our way home to lunch in Dovedale at Mr Arkwright's,[1] a beautiful little place in a beautiful valley. Such a luncheon of hothouse fruits. The old gentleman came out of his Mill in his miller's dress and did the honours gracefully. The upper Ten thousand had better look to themselves or they will be shoved from the high places. We paid another visit a little before this time to my old friend Tom Walker of the Scots Greys. He had married a very pretty Irish wife, Constantia Beresford, left the Army, and lived in rather a pretty place not far from Derby. At his house I met two rather agreeable young men, an Irish Mr Bowan, a dragoon, and Count Lapature, an oddity, but a clever one, though a little fine. I was glad to meet them again at the Derby Ball, where I did not know many people. Another very pleasant acquaintance was Colonel Pennington, an old Indian friend of the General's. He spent a couple of months at

1. Sir Richard Arkwright had died in 1792; this was his
   son (1755–1843), who was reported to be the richest
   commoner in England.

Fountain Dale, and left it to return to Bengal to make out the two years required to complete the 32 years of service. He was an artillery officer, had commanded the Force for some years, after indeed creating it, he was thought a great deal of by military men, and was a clever, agreeable companion, but very plain, old, little, shabby. We made him some marmalade, Annie and I, to remind him of his Scotch lady friends, and he wrote for us some amusing verses in return. He was a furious hunter, and regretted nothing in England so much as his stud.

It is strange that during my long stay in Sherwood I never went but once into Nottingham, though only 15 miles from it. My cousin, the rich Miss Launder, lived there, and Doctor Charles Pennington. It is a fine old city with its Castle upon the hill, from which the town slopes to the green plains all round. I rode once or twice to Newstead with Colonel Pennington. Colonel Wildman was not then settled there; it was undergoing repairs, having only just been bought from Lord Byron,[1] and was a fine place certainly, well wooded, with a lake, gardens and shrubberies, but flat, too flat. The house was very fine. One long gallery was divided by skreens into three large rooms, and when filled by the pleasant guests the Wildmans brought there, Annie Need found herself in her right place. When my sister Mary paid her visit to Fountain Dale she and Annie spent half their time at Newstead. Colonel Wildman was West Indian and very rich. He had made one of those queer marriages some queer men make—educated a child for his wife. She turned out neither pretty nor clever, but she satisfied him, and was liked. Haddon Hall was more interesting than Newstead, less attractive, a large high, ugly house. All the reception rooms on the 3rd storey; they were small, low, and scantily furnished; nobody ever lived there, and the Duke of Devonshire's visits were far apart. One thing touched me. The Duke was childless, unmarried; beside the bed on which

1. Byron sold his family home to Colonel Thomas
   Wildman, a Harrow contemporary, for £94,500
   in December 1817. E.G.'s sister Mary was much
   impressed by her visit shortly afterwards.

he lay when at Haddon was a small cot in which slept the little Cavendish boy who was to be his heir. I can't recollect any other incidents of my life in Nottinghamshire.

In May I went up to London with the General. We travelled all night, and about 6 o'clock in the morning I was met on Hampstead heath by my dear little Aunt Frere in her demi-fortune.

Uncle Frere had given up his London house, and lived now in a villa on Hampstead heath, a comfortable house, but ugly, standing in a small square of pleasure ground enclosed by high Walls, shutting out all view of very pretty scenery; London in the distance with its towers and its steeples, and its wide spreading streets, and the four or five miles between the great City and Hampstead Hill a perfect confusion of so called country residences. Life in the forest had been sleepy though enlivened by changes and by the hunter's horn and the bark of dogs, as the horses dashed into the yard on a hunting afternoon, the riders clamouring for bread and cheese and ale, when Annie and I would look out of the back window at what was really a pretty sight. Life at Hampstead was very sleepy, enlivened by nothing, but it was pleasant in a sleepy way, every body was so kind. It was a hot house full of children who did little and servants who did less.

We got up early, as my Uncle had to go to chambers after breakfast. We drove into London nearly every day. We had Freres without end to dinner, such miserable dinners, worse than the breakfasts, for at them we had Twyford sweet brown bread and good butter. We went to bed late, for we were often out at dinner or at plays and Concerts, and twice at the Opera, that was a treat, only no one near me felt the worth of the musick and then we had to drive the four or five miles back, which was very tiring. We always seemed to be busy, yet we did little, there was always a fuss, a quiet fuss, and I was very weary, for we heard nothing, the world was very dead to us, though we were so near the heart of it. And there was no repose, no one was ever left alone. My Uncle and Aunt were all kindness, the children were little things, good and clever, but they were only half alive. I have never since wondered at the wretched health of all that family, the wonder is that any of them lived to grow up after such an

exhausting process as was their rearing, no nourishment for
either soul or body. No young body could thrive on the
unpalatable provisions presented to not very hungry appe-
tites—and no mind could expand where there was so little
interest felt in all the improvements of this improving age.
They were mostly unnoticed and there was a sort of a
religious *bar* which closed the door against all that was bright
and beautiful. Yet these religious feelings were not morose,
there was no Calvinism in their creed. As far as their lights
allowed, they enjoyed the blessings of their lot. I don't know
that any of my Uncle's brothers were clever men. Some
had got up high but all fell down again. Uncle John made a
mill of his Spanish Ambassadorship, Uncle Bartle, who was
charming, was outwitted by a woman when acting as Uncle
John's Secretary. Between them they caused the retreat to
Corunna and the death of Sir John Moore.[1] Excepting these
two, they had all the wit to marry rich wives and really only
Hatley Frere was below par. My Uncle was a good man of
business and a man of good sense, he never seemed to be
quite awake enough even to speak distinctly; he drawled his
words and through his closed teeth, leaning back in his chair
with half closed up eyes, as if quite wearied, as perhaps he
was after a hot day's work in chambers. He was a kind,
straight forward man, with a great reputation as a man of
business, always intent upon giving pleasure to every one
around him. My dear, little Aunt was one of the 'blessed who
are pure in heart,' and if any of us are ever to 'see God' she
will be of them, for her whole life on earth was a continued
preparation for heaven. Not a praying, stern, faquir like life
of self imposed miseries, hardening the heart and closing it
against all the gentle and beautiful influences created to be
enjoyed by us; her Christian creed was 'to do good and sin

1. Sir John Frere (the recently appointed Madrid Ambassador) used every method in his power to persuade
   Moore to advance from his 1808 winter quarters to
   attack the French; Sir Charles Oman's *A History of the
   Peninsular War* argues that Frere was correct in his
   judgement but his 'uncontrolled expressions showed
   he was entirely unfit for a diplomatic post'.

not'; self she never thought of except as a means of rejoicing others. She was in truth the minister of comfort to her circle, the sun of her sphere. She yielded to the habits she found, but had she been thrown among a higher order of minds, her naturally great abilities would have developed themselves still more worthily, cramped as they were. She and all belonging to her were happy. What can we wish for more. She had eight children at this time; John and George at School, fine boys, and two little men at School too, a day School, the lessons for which they prepared with me while I was with them. The two elder girls were nearly grown up, pretty, both of them, the two younger ones were nice little bodies very fond of play. Anne was clever, so was poor Willie who did not live.

Uncle William Frere, we called them all Uncles, had married the most accomplished amateur singer in England. At this time she was taking lessons from Velluti; she missed no opportunity of improving herself. He was delighted with her voice and her style, said there were few professional singers superiour to her. She often rode out to Hampstead with her husband, sang to us the whole evening, and rode back again. I often rode in the mornings to her on my cousin Lizzie's quiet pony, and she would sing to me alone as readily as to an admiring crowd. I remembered well what she taught me. I frequently rode into town, frightened a little at first by the noise and bustle of the streets, but I got used to it. Sometimes we cantered over the heath and on to Harrow, which was a great deal pleasanter.

I must try and recollect the names of the few remarkable people I met with. I was twice at the Opera and heard Curioni, Pasta, De Begnis, Camporesi, Madame Vestris and Velluti.[1] The Messiah was admirably given at the Hanover Square Rooms, and Cramer, who was giving lessons to Miss

1. These were amongst the most celebrated contemporary
   singers of Italian opera, especially Rossini; Giuditta
   Pasta (1797–1865) was 'the greatest soprano in Europe
   for more than a decade,' while Giovanni Velluti
   (1781–1861) was 'the last of the great castrati singers'
   (*Groves*).

Richards, called, at her request, to hear the little highland girl sing 'Hanouer,' took his violin out of the case, caught up the air, and then played lovely musick of his own as a return for the gaelick Crochallan, and Castle Airley. Sir Robert Ainslie came often to hear the old Scotch ballads, and George Rose to get a listener to his translation of Ariosto, which proceeded but slowly, and never, I believe, was published. Mr William Rose occasionally came to dinner, and that poor, mad poet, Coleridge, who never held his tongue—stood pouring out a deluge of words meaning nothing, with eyes on fire, and his silver hair streaming down to his waist.[1] His family had placed him with a young doctor at Highgate, where he was well taken care of. A nephew of his, a fine young man, a great favourite with my Uncle, often came to us on a holiday; he was a great lawyer afterwards. Miss Joanna Baillie[2] was a frequent visitor; a nice old lady. Then we had Mr Irving of the unknown tongues, the most wonderful orator, eloquent beyond reason, but leading captive wiser heads. Men went to hear him and wondered. Women adored him, for he was handsome in the pulpit, tall and dark, with long black hair hanging down, a pale face set off with teeth superb, and such a pair of flashing eyes. The little chapel he served was crammed with all the titles in London. It was like a birthday procession of carriages, and such a crush on entering as to cause screaming and fainting, torn dresses, etc. Hatley Frere firmly believed this man's rhapsodies, kept him and his wife and their child in his house for ever so long, and brought them up to us for a day. We thought them very dirty; tried the translations I believe, and was busy at this very time calculating the year for the world to end. Happily the period fixed on passed away, to the exceeding relief of

1. Samuel Taylor Coleridge (1772–1834) had been a confirmed opium addict by this time for twenty years; in any case his method of conducting a conversation led M. de Staël to comment he was great in monologue but bad in dialogue.
2. Joanna Baillie (1762–1851), a prolific Scottish author-ess, made her home in Hampstead from 1806 the centre of her literary circle.

many worthy persons.[1] At a Concert of ancient musick to which my Uncle and Aunt kindly took me I saw another celebrity—the Duke of Wellington. He was standing talking with Rogers the poet, who seized on my Uncle as he was passing to appeal to him on some subject they were discussing, and for five minutes I stood next the great Duke.

My father had pleasant lodgings in Duke Street, where I went when he wished me to see some of his own friends. He took me to the Mackintosh's, where I dined. Sir James was not at home; Lady Mackintosh was kind and agreeable, her daughter Fanny was a nice girl, and Mrs Rich, Sir James's daughter by his first wife, both pleasant and clever. One subject we avoided all allusion to, unfortunate Lady Wiseman, whom we had known so well. Fanny Mackintosh spent most of her time at Holland House with Mary Fox, who was her particular friend; an intimacy my mother would have disapproved of.[2] My father took me also to the Vines; he was a rich merchant, very underbred I thought; she, a quiet little woman, very kind to me. She took me to the grand Review at Hounslow, where we went in Sir Willoughby Gordon's carriage. He was Quarter Master General, and very intimate with Mr and Mrs Vine; they were his neighbours in the Isle of Wight. Of course we were well placed, in the reserve space for the great next to the Duchess of Kent, a plain, colourless woman, ill dressed, whose little shabby daughter, wrapped in a shawl, gave no promise of turning out our pretty queen. Lady Gordon was not with us. She was keeping herself and her young daughters quiet, as they were engaged to a

1. Edward Irving (1792–1834), was a hugely successful popular preacher. His handsome features may have been marred by 'a slight obliquity of vigor' . . . but 'frivolous society in London was provided with a new sensation'. (D.N.B.) E.G.'s mention of his attempted translations of the unknown tongues refers to his belief that the obscure mouthings of a girl, Mary Campbell from Gairlochhead in his native Scotland, revealed the second advent.

2. The Hon. Mary Fox (1806–91) was related to Charles James Fox, who kept the Whig interest alive in these years of Tory domination.

children's ball in the evening at Carleton house, for these were the days of the regency. She was so obliging as to offer me a ticket for Almack's,[1] which Mrs Vine accepted for me, as she said her sister, Lady Bury, would have great pleasure in being my chaperon; but I had no mind to go. I did not like putting my father to the expense of the dress, and I should have known no body, so the matter was not thought more of, and my little cousins played with the ticket.

My time for leaving these kind relations was drawing near. I had not learned much in that sleepy house, although one way or another I had seen a good deal, and my Uncle had been so good as to take me into his Latin Class with the little boys, whose lessons I was thus able to help. I liked this much, and afterwards found my Latin very useful. George and Willy did not think so.

The Eton holidays were at hand. John Frere and my brother John were to spend them at the Doune. They were to travel with my father and me. How happy they were. We started by coach again, I was getting quite used to this vulgarity, passed through Oxford and thought of my Aunt Mary. On to Liverpool to a good hotel, in the yard of which the boys, to their great delight, discovered a tank full of live turtle; a disgusting sight I thought it, such hideous, apathetick creatures. We walked a good deal about the town; the new streets are handsome, the villas in the neighbourhood very pretty, well kept grounds to most of them. There was no Birkenhead then, but the higher part of the town was sufficient at that time for the retreat of the busy inhabitants. The quays and the squalid lanes in the lower part of the town were as dirty as Glasgow, Bristol or Dublin.

Next day we went on board the steamer for Glasgow.

1. Almacks Assembly Rooms was a fashionable meeting place in St James London; it was celebrated because of an occasion when the Duke of Wellington was refused entry for failing to wear the obligatory knee breeches and white cravat.

CHAPTER TWENTY-FIVE

1823–1827

MY Mother and my sisters left the highlands soon after Christmas, and had been ever since staying with poor Aunt Leitch, who was dying. My mother never left her, but she let my sisters visit about among the many friends and relations, Charlotte Ironside with them, and a very pleasant time they spent. Mary Ironside had gone to India with her sister Eliza, a step on her part Mrs Leitch never forgave. Uncle Ralph was at that time living at Tennochside; he used to come in once a week at least to cheer my mother. My father staid only two days in Glasgow. My sister Mary and I and the two boys accompanied him home, leaving Jane as a help to my mother and Charlotte. We went by a fast Coach that beautiful road past Stirling, Crieff, and Blair Drummond to Perth, where we got into the Caledonian Coach, and so on by the old familiar road to our own gate, where a cart was waiting for our luggage. We walked the mile down the heathery brae to the boat at the Doune, and crossed our own clear, rapid Spey at our own ferry.

I was very glad to get home; I was ill, quite exhausted by the life at Hampstead. I had left the forest perfectly well. Week by week, I lost strength while with the Freres; so little sleep, so much worry without much pleasure. My mother was shocked at my appearance. Dr Smith and the highland air and the quiet life soon restored me. Of course during my Mother's absence for such a cause we saw no company beyond the Bellevilles or a stray traveller; but while the boys were with us we were very happy, fishing, shooting, boating, riding, out of doors all day, and I had my flowers to set in order. Mary regretted Glasgow. It was a life of variety much more to her mind than that we led at home. She regretted her young friends too. Still she managed to amuse herself. I forget exactly when my Mother and Jane returned to us, not before winter, I think. There were many things for her and uncle Ralph to settle after poor Mrs Leitch's death. Charlotte was the heiress. She went to Houghton immediately, leaving Mr Shortridge to sell the house and furniture. Some legacies were left very wisely to the younger Houghton nieces, at least the interest of a certain sum, which on their marriage or death was to revert to their brother William, and so ended the year 1824.

The year 1825 was spent very happily at the Doune in the usual way, William busy, John a season at College in Edinburgh boarded with the Espinasses, and then off to Hartford or Haileybury, I forget which, the Indian College for Civil appointments, where he made a great name. Robert Grant got him the appointment, and there was no demur about it this time. We three girls were a great deal in Morayshire paying long visits, two of us at a time, to our many friends there. We were at Altyre, Relugas, Burgie, Forres House, etc. Altyre was very pleasant, so very easy. It was impossible not to like Lady Cumming, equally impossible not to disapprove of her conduct. She spent her days gardening and fishing—no man could play or land a salmon more dexterously. She was always surrounded by a suite of young men, devoted admirers, some of whose hearts she nearly broke, Sir William looking apparently satisfied. He gave us a Ball, which was extremely well managed, for they had very amusing people staying with them, and they invited all the neighbourhood besides. Poor Rawdon Clavering was there, so much in love with Jenny Dunbar. They married afterwards on nothing, went to the West Indies, lost their health, and she died. And we had those strange brothers whose real name I can't remember, but they one day announced that they were Steuarts, lineally descended from Prince Charles, out of respect to whose wife, who never had a child, the elder brother assumed the name of John Sobieski,[1] the younger brother was Charles. Nobody was more astonished

1. Charles Edward Stuart's mother was Maria Clementina Sobieska. John (c1795–1872) and Charles (c1799–1880) Sobieska claimed to be his legitimate heir.

at this assumption than their own father, a decent man who held some small situation in the Tower of London. The mother was Scotch in some way; her people had been in the service of the unfortunate Steuarts in Italy, and who can tell that she had not some right to call herself connected with them. Her two sons were very handsome men, particularly John Sobieski, who, however, had not a trace of the Steuart in his far finer face. They always wore the Highland dress, kilt and belted plaid, looked melancholy, spoke at times mysteriously. The effect their pantomime produced was astonishing; they were *fêted* to their heart's content; half the Clans in the Highlands believed in them; for several years they actually *reigned* in the north country. At last they made a mistake which finished the farce. Lovat, Fraser of Lovat, had taken them up enthusiastically, built them a villa on an island in the Beauly firth, in the pretty garden of which was a small waterfall. Here Mrs Charles Steuart sat and played the harp like Flora MacIvor, and crowds went to visit them. They turned Roman Catholicks to please their benefactor I suppose, and so lost caste with the publick. Poor Mrs Charles was a meek little woman, a widow with a small jointure whom the Prince, her husband, had met in Ireland. I don't know what took him there, for nobody ever knew what his employment had originally been. Prince Sobieski had been a coach painter, not the panel painter, the Heraldick painter, and most beautifully he finished the coat of arms.

Jane paid a very long visit to Relugas, lovely little place on a wooded bank between the Divie and the Findhorn, and then Sir Thomas and Lady Lauder, who were going to Edinburgh to a grand musical Festival, took her with them, afterwards they went a tour along the Borders, a new country to Jane. One visit they paid was to Abbotsford. Jane was in an extasy the whole time. Sir Walter Scott took to her, as who would not; they rode together all day on two rough ponies with the Ettrick Shepherd and all the dogs. Sir Walter gave her all the border legends, and she corrected his mistakes about the highlands.[1] At parting he hoped she would come

1. For this visit see *Scott's Letters*, Vol. VIII, edited by Sir Herbert Grierson, p. 278.

again, and he gave her a small ring he had picked up among the ruins of Iona, with a device on it no one ever could make out. Mrs Hemans was at Abbotsford, a nice, quiet, little woman, her two sons with her, fine little boys, quite surprised to find there was another lion in the world beside their mother.[1]

The Lauders brought Jane home in great glee and staid a week or more, during which time they held mysterious conferences and went rambles alone, and went on very queerly. I was sure that some secret business was in train, but could not make it out, as I was evidently not to be let into it. At last the discovery came—Sir Thomas was writing his first novel.[2] The hero was McIntosh of Borlam, and the scenes of his exploits were most of them laid in the woods of Rothiemurchus and the plains of Badenoch. 'Lochandhu' really was not bad; there were pretty bits of writing in it, but it was just an imitation of Walter Scott. I believe the book sold, and it certainly made the Authour and his wife completely happy during its composition. Lord Jeffrey, his wife, and Charlotte all came to see us, and Lord Moncrieff, who won my heart, charming little old man. Lord Gillies and Mrs Gillies always came for a few days, and Jane and Emilia Cumming, and the Lady Logie and May Anne and many more, for those two summers were gay. We all went to the Northern Meeting, all five of us; but without my father and mother. Glenmoriston took charge of us and his sister Harriet Fraser, and we went in a very *fast* style, escorted by Duncan Davidson, who unexpectedly arrived for the purpose. Mary was the beauty of the Meeting. She had grown up very handsome, and never lost her looks; she had become lively, and, to the amazement of the family, outshone us all. She was in fact a genius and a fine creature—poor Mary.

In the autumn of 1826, besides our usual visitors, we had Alexander Cumming to bid us good bye before returning to India, a fine, very handsome man, who on account of the

1. Mrs Felicia Hemans, the poetess (1793–1835), visited Abbotsford July 1829.
2. This novel, about one of the leaders of the Jacobite rising of 1715, was published in 1825.

Entail it was intended to marry to Mary, but they did not take to one another, and the Espinasses came, she very absurd, he a clever Frenchman; and Lord Macdonald, 6 feet 4; and then Annie Need. What a happy summer we spent with her, and all the people so delighted to see the Colonel's daughter. Later came her husband the General, and his friend Colonel Pennington, who had been to India and back since he and I parted in Sherwood Forest. He was a very clever man, and a very good man and very agreeable, but old and ugly. How could a young, brilliant creature like my sister Jane, so formed to be a first rate young man's pride, fall to be this old man's darling. But so it was; she did it of her own free will, and I don't believe she ever regretted the step she was determined to take. It was an utterly unsuitable marriage, distasteful to all of us, yet it turned out well; she was content.

The Needs left us in October 1825 taking Mary with them, who was to spend the winter at Fountain Dale. They originally intended to steam from Inverness to Glasgow and Liverpool; luckily this plan was given up. The Steamer was wrecked and nearly all on board were drowned. I don't remember any cabin passenger saved except John Peter Grant of Laggan, the only remaining child of nineteen born to the minister and his celebrated wife, and young Glengarry. Among the lost was one of the pretty Miss Duffs of Muirtown, just married to her handsome soldier husband, and on their way to join his regiment; their bodies were found clasped together, poor things, beside many others unknown. Colonel Pennington had outstaid his friends; he and Jane wandered all over Rothiemurchus, apparently delighted with each other. At last he went, leaving us to prepare for his return at Christmas.

I am not quite sure that my recollections of these two years are quite correct, writing at this distance of time without any notes to guide me; I don't think I have forgotten any thing of consequence, but the dates of these family events are confused. It must have been in September 1825 that the Needs and Colonel Pennington left us. Johnny had gone back to Haileybury, and our diminished party felt dull enough; a weight was over all our minds. We were sitting at dinner on a chill Autumn evening, enlivened by a bright wood fire, and some of the cheerful sallies of poor William, who ever did his best to keep the ball up. The post came in; I gave the key; Robert Allan opened the bag and proceeded to distribute its contents, dropping first one thick double letter into a silver flagon on the sideboard, as William's quick eye noted, though he said nothing. When we all seemed occupied with our own peculiar despatches he carried this hidden treasure to Jane. It was the proposal from her Colonel. She expected it, turned very pale, but kept her secret for two days, even from me, who shared her room. She then mentioned her *engagement* to my father first, my mother next, and left it to them to inform William and me. There never was such astonishment. I could not believe it; William laughed; my father made no objection. My mother would not listen to the subject. More letters arrived, to Jane daily, to William and me full of kind expressions, to my father and mother, hoping for their consent. My father replied for all; my mother would not write; William and I put it off. Annie Need wrote to dissuade Jane, Lord Jeffrey and Miss Clerk to approve, the lover to announce his preparations. My father and William proceeded to Edinburgh to draw up the Settlements. It was found that the fortune was very much smaller than had been expected, and from another source we heard my father would have been glad to have offended the bridegroom, but he was not to be offended; his firm intention was to secure his wife, and he would have thought the world well lost to gain her. Her interests were well cared for. Why not. If old men will marry young women, young widows should be left quite independant as some return for the sacrifice, the full extent of which they are not aware of till too late. Well! the Settlements were made by Sir James Gibson Craig, who well knew how to second my father in arranging them. After all, the young Couple were not badly off—the retiring pay of a full Colonel with the off reckonings, £25,000 in the Indian funds, and a prospect! of Deccan prize-money—some few hundred pounds which he did not get till the year before he died. My Mother wrote many letters to Edinburgh; she certainly did not wish to forward matters, but this spirited pair wanted no help. The Bride asked whether she could be provided with some additions to a rather scanty wardrobe, the best things belonging to Mother and daughter having been settled up for May for her English visit, or whether she should apply to her intended. The Bridegroom set out for the Highlands and had the banns published in *Edinburgh* on his way; a mistake of his man of business which was very annoying to all and caused a good deal of irritation—however, all got right. Jane was determined. She had argued the point in her own strong mind, decided it, and it was to be. Perhaps she was not wrong; the circumstances of the family were deplorable, there did not appear to be any hope of better days, for the girls at any rate, and we were no longer very young. So a very handsome trousseau was ordered, our great Uncle the Captain, kind old man, having left each of us £100 for the purpose, spent long before, I suppose, but Jane said she was entitled to it and so she got more than the worth of it, it added but a small sum to the vast amount of debt.

Colonel Pennington announced that he was engaged to dine with his brother in London on Christmas Day, so the wedding was fixed for the 20th of December 1825.

It was a cold, dull morning. I had been up all night preparing the breakfast, for our upper servants were gone, had been gone since the spring. Miss Elphick, poor soul, had come to be present at the first marriage amongst us. She left us when we left Edinburgh, she had been with the Kirkman Finlays in Glasgow. She assisted my labours by torrents of tears. The Bellevilles were the only guests, Mrs Macpherson so sad. The ceremony was performed in the Library by Mr Fyvie, the young episcopal clergyman from Inverness. My Mother's whole face was swelled from weeping; I was a ghost; William very grave; my poor father, the unhappy cause of our sorrow, did look heart broken when he gave that bright child of his away. The Bridegroom wore his Artillery uniform, which became his slight figure well; he did not look near his age, and he was so happy though so ugly. The Bride stood beside him in her beauty, tall, fresh, calm, composed. It was to be done, and she was doing it without one visible regret. 'I will' was so firmly said, I started. What happened after I never felt. Mrs Macpherson just whispered to me, 'Help them, Eliza,' and I believe I did. I tried I know; dear, kind Mrs Macpherson, what a friend she was, never tiring, always ready, so wise too. The breakfast went off well. The Colonel was so gay, he made his little speeches so prettily, his wife looked quite proud of him. He took leave of the humbler friends in the hall so kindly, and of us so affectionately, that we all relented to him before we parted. We all went down to the boat; the gentlemen crossed the water. On the gravelly shingle beyond was the London built chariot and four horses, the man and the maid, and the two postillions with large favours, a mob of our people round the carriage raising such a shout as their pride—ay, and their blessing—was driven away. She never forgot the home of her fathers, never lost sight of her Duchus; her protecting hand has been the one faithfully held over 'the great plain of the fir trees' from that hour to the day of her death. She has been the nursing mother to all our people, in weal or woe their prop. Beloved every where, she was worshipped there. Doing her duty every where, she has taken the duties of others on herself there. She departed on that wintry day the only unmoved person in the throng; home, to me at least, never seemed like home since.

Colonel Pennington had a hunting box in Leicestershire near the village of Normanton, where they lived till the spring. He then took a pretty, old fashioned place called Trunkwell, near Reading, which they were very sorry to be obliged to leave in a year after, when they fixed themselves at Malshanger for the rest of *his* life, near Basingstoke, in the higher part of Hampshire. It was an ugly house, but very roomy, very comfortable. The garden was good, the grounds pretty, plenty of fine trees, the scenery of the neighbourhood interesting and the place interesting. They improved it much during their time in it; both of them had good taste and delighted in a country life. She liked her garden, her horses, her new acquaintance, and was really very happy, though her husband was not a good tempered man, and certainly often forgot that he had married a girl who might almost have been his granddaughter, so that at first they rather hobbled on at times; but with so really good and clever a man, and so admirable a character as hers, these little points soon wore smooth. They were not at first appreciated; the disparity between them made people suppose all could not be right, that she was either mercenary, or the victim of mercenary relations, but as they were better known they were better understood. Few have left a fairer fame in any neighbour-hood, respected, loved, regretted, this is how they are spoken of to this day. Annie Need said a bit of bitter fun about Jane's choice, which she much disapproved. 'It was his mind,' said some of us apologetically; 'she married him for his mind.' 'She could not well have had less body then,' she said tartly enough. Slight as he was, and far from young, he led the Pytchley hunt for many years, he had a fine stud. I think that was the Hunt he belonged to; at any rate Newton Fellowes was the Master.

When the marriage was over. Bride and bridegroom gone, cake cut, guests departed, and my father, my Mother and I were left to spend the remainder of the stern highland winter together, for William went to Edinburgh on business and could not return. Alas! he was imprisoned for debt in the gaol on the Caltonhill. The debt was of his own contracting, for in his College days he had been extravagant; he believed himself to be the heir of wealth, the son of a rich man, and he had the name of a handsome allowance which was never paid him. At the time of the execution of the Trust Deed, he had taken all my father's debts upon himself, bound himself to pay them, and they were upwards of £60,000. Had he been arrested for one of them, I think it would have killed my father; I never saw him so much affected by any thing that ever happened to him; and my poor Mother, who had so gloried in the noble sacrifice of self her son had made, she sank under this; they were very miserable. The debt could not be paid, even by degrees; the sum allowed for the maintenance of the family and the expenses of the forest work was very small, and there were other creditors who would have come forward with their claims had we been able to satisfy this one. Now I saw the wisdom of Jane's marriage, her kind husband sent William money. She wrote pleasant letters; the post was our sunlight; it came but three times a week, but such a full bag; the franks permitted a frequent correspondence.[1] Jane at Normanton, Mary at Fountain

1. This was still her father's privilege as M.P. for
   Tavistock.

Dale, frequently meeting at the various houses they visited, Aunt Mary from Oxford where she was now established in a small house she had furnished. Other letters and the newspapers, all helped to brighten the long evenings. Mr Caw always came in on the post nights with his little bits of gossip for my mother. He lived at Polchar in his capacity of book keeper, which office he filled remarkably well.

My Mother never went out; my father and I were never kept in, for though cold, it was sunny; hard frost gave us power to walk miles without fatigue. Yes—twice there were heavy falls of snow, which blocked up the hill road; the mail coach could not run, it and the unfortunate passengers were dug out of deep wreaths, and we had no post. So my father took to reading aloud while my mother and I worked. We had given up crossing the hall to the dining room; dinner was laid on a narrow table in the lobby, and wheeled into the Library, my Mother being unfit for the change of apartments. She was well cloked and shawled when she went to bed.

Our establishment consisted of poor Robert Allan, who was butler and footman and gamekeeper, and never could be persuaded to leave a falling house. He had a fault, a serious one, he tippled; but the man was so good, so worthy, it had to be overlooked and he was borne with to the end. Whiskey and all, he never left the family. The cook was Nelly, invaluable Nelly; she had been kitchen maid under Mrs Watling, and now, by the help of my *Cuisinière bourgeoisie*, the best french cookery book ever written, she and I together turned out little dinners that really gave an appetite to my poor father and mother, both of them rather dainty. I always dressed in the evening; it pleased them. We had a bright fire, and we *made* conversation, and sometimes William Cameron spent the evening with us, or rather with my father in the Study; there was always a bed ready for him. William, my brother, wrote cheerfully; his young friends all came to see him, and the Gibson Craigs provided him with any amount of luxuries from Riccarton. Before long he was released; nothing could be made of his confinement, so he was let to return home a little before my father departed for London about Easter. It was a great relief to get William back. I had done my best to carry out his orders, but the distances, the wintry weather, and the difficulty of procuring either money or food, made the position painful.

In the summer of 1826 my father brought Mary back; the fine weather revived our spirits, her cheerful gossip amused our poor mother, and the farm was selling eggs, and wool, and fruit, to the shooting lodges. We had no visitors this season, not even the Grants, but kind Aunt Mary had set us up. She had married a second time, Doctor Bourne, a rich man of great repute as a physician in Oxford.[1] She sent my Mother £60. We had, when my father went to London, three wedders for our supply of meat; we bought a score now, so with the poultry yard, the garden, and the river, we did well till the winter—such a winter, our last in the dear Duchus.

We were quite alone, my mother, my sister Mary, and myself, William off and on as business required; it was a severe winter. My mother kept her room until late in the day; Mary was her maid, and such a tender one. I had my tartan cloke, with a hood and a pair of jail boots, and trotted across the yard to the cellar, and down to the farm to act housekeeper there, then back to the kitchen to manage the dinner. Fine education this, and we were happy, though our troubles were great. We had mutton enough, thanks to dear Aunt Mary, and we sold enough of other things to buy our groceries from Robby Cumming. Inverness had refused to honour my orders; heavy bills were there unpaid. Then there were the servants' wages; William paid the outsiders, but there was nothing for the insiders; how good they were, waiting so patiently, asking for their own as if they were begging for a favour. There had been good stores in the house, but they were vanishing. It was hard to bear up amid such perplexities. In a happy hour I opened my heavy heart to the very kindest friend any one ever had, the Lady Belleville. No good could come of a sinking spirit, the back must bear its burden. Cold and harsh as the world thought Mrs Macpherson, she had a warm heart, with a cool judgment, and untiring zeal in the service of those she loved.

She proposed my writing for the press. I had tried this the

1. Richard Bourne (1761–1829) was Professor of Physic and then of Clinical Medicine at Oxford.

winter before, that heavy winter, wrote what I thought a lively little paper, 'An old story,' from hints furnished by the vanity of our poor cousin Edmund Ironside after a visit of his to the hair dresser in Inverness, copied it fair, and sent it to Blackwood in a fictitious name, desiring an answer to be sent to Mr Sidey the postmaster at Perth, where our bag was made up, there being no post office for years after at Lynwuilg. Day after day did I watch the boy who went to meet the Coach, having the key of the bag, I had no fear of discovery. No answer ever came, the Editor probably never looked at the paper and so lost a story that would have told well in his magazine, for ushered into the library world afterwards by Belleville, it was favourably received by his friend a Mr Fraser, some way connected with the press and brought me £3. It did not go alone, Mary and I between us wrote a bundle of rubbish for the 'Inspector,' and received £40 in return.[1]

We wrote at night in the Barrack room, for we had been obliged to leave our more comfortable apartments on account of the state of the roof over that end of the old house. Whenever it either rained or thawed we had five or six cascades pouring into tubs set round the walls to catch the water. The Barrack room was inconvenient too; the little crooked staircase which led up to it was lighted by a large pane of glass in the roof, a sky light not very tightly fixed. Several times during the snow storms we had to wade through a wreath of snow on the steps underneath it, pretty deep occasionally, so that we were wetted above the ankles; but we did not mind, we took off our shoes and stockings, and dried our feet by a good fire which we had provided for ourselves. Fuel being scarce, we gathered in the plantation as many fallen sticks as, assisted by a few peats taken from the large stacks at the farm, gave us a nice bright fire for our mid night labours. Bits of candle stuck in succession on a save-all, manufactured by our selves out of a nail and a piece of tin, performed the part of lamp, and thus enlightened, we wrote away.

Before Mary came home, it was rather lonely up there

1. *Blackwood's Magazine; Fraser's Magazine for Town and Country; The Inspector, a Weekly Dramatic Paper.*

away from every body, but not dull—where there is an
object, the means of attaining that object become a pleasure
and in an old patched dressing gown with an old shawl over
it, my feet on the warm hearth stone, and two or three
potatoes roasting in the ashes, I passed many a happy hour.
We worked late, for the Highland winters have very dark
mornings, so we rose late. Mary's papers were very clever,
very original, they required condensing and a few grammatical corrections, but in themselves they were well deserving
of the praise they received.

Dear old Barrack room, the scene of some sorrow, and
many pleasures. In our younger days, in John's holidays, we
used to give private entertainments there far away from
molestation. We contrived a fire, made coffee, boiled eggs,
had bread and cheese and butter and porridge. John was the
Caterer, and no body ever refused him any thing. How merry
we were, hot days or cold ones. Years after, when he was
Governour of Jamaica, in one of the few letters he wrote me
he recalled the gay doings of the Barrack room, the more
enjoyable from their mystery.

When Mrs Macpherson sent us our £40, she sent us also by
her Macpherson boy, on his shaggy pony called Rob Roy, a
Times newspaper in which was a most favourable criticism
of our contributions to the Inspector, especially of Mary's
'Country campaign of a man of fashion.' We were wild; first
we skipped, then we laughed, then we sat down and cried. In
this state our only thought was, 'We must tell mamma.'

She was alone at work in the Library. We laid our Bank
notes before her, presented the praising newspaper and Mrs
Macpherson's note. We had dreaded her anger, for she was
very proud. Poor woman! that was over; she had suffered too
much. 'Dear good children,' was all she said, and then she
cried as we did, but happiness prevailed. We had all the fun
in the world arranging how to spend our treasure. We were so
very badly off for necessaries, we had difficulty in settling
what was most wanted. We had no walking shoes. It was
amusing to see us in our house shoes—old satin slippers of all
colours patched at the sides, looking a little more respectable
after we learned to dye them with ink; shabby dress gowns,
because we had no plainer for common; the two servant

maids as shabby as our selves, saying nothing, good creatures, and very grateful for the share of wages we were now
enabled to give them. We three, my Mother, Mary and I,
faithfully keeping our secret, for had William known it he
would have borrowed some of it, he was so hard up himself,
to keep the work going. We thought it best to save a little,
have a nest egg, for the hour of need might come again; but it
never came, thank God, and the kind friends raised up for
us—but I am running on too fast, and my mother thought a
few pounds should be spent on me, to enable me to accept a
very kind invitation to Huntly Lodge in the spring. Several
pretty dresses had been sent to me as presents and never
made up, and white muslin was plenty in Robby Cumming's
shop, so I set out with the kind Bellevilles for Huntly.

I had always liked Lord Huntly; he had known us young
people from our birth and liked us and my father and mother
were as intimate with him as they had been with his Mother,
the beautiful Duchess, our pleasant neighbour for so many
summers. He had married late in life, the unfortunate habit
of too many young men of fashion. Lady Huntly was an
excellent woman. She brought him a very large fortune, a
clear business head, good temper, and high principles. She
soon set straight all that she had found crooked. She was not
handsome, though she had a good figure, a good skin, and
beautiful hands—the Brodie face is very short and very flat
and very meaningless; but she suited him, every one liked
her, and she always liked me, so the fortnight I passed with
her was very agreeable. There were several guests in the house,
a large dinner party every day, all of the Gordon name, and
staying with their Uncle and Aunt were two of the Montagues,
the Ladies Caroline and Emily, and Lord Charles Russell.
It was an ugly country, the grounds uninteresting, nothing
particular to do except the sorting of what became afterwards
a very fine collection of shells and minerals, which she
afterwards left, with all that remained of her money, to little
Brodie of Brodie, her first cousin. She had no children.

Mary had well filled my place at home. She had a genius for
management, and she amused my mother with all her forest
tales. Newstead was a never failing subject, for there she got
among the great people both of them liked. Colonel Wildman

was of the household of the Duke of Sussex, belonged to a crack Cavalry Regiment, was very nice, had married his sister to Sir Robert Gardiner, all brothers all up in high places so that the guests at Newstead were mostly of note. Mary had delighted in the sociable life she had led there. Of course she found the poor old Doune dull after it; had we not had our writings to occupy us her spirits might have got very low, for her fine mind was not sufficient for itself; with a spur and a prop she ran lightly through any life, wanting either she failed; but now at home she had both, and well she did her part. She helped me in all my works and helped our mother, and then skipped merrily up at night to the 'regions of fancy' in our barrack room.

My poor Mother just at this time received a great shock in the death of her eldest brother, my Uncle William Ironside of Houghton le Spring. He was thrown from his horse and killed on the spot. She was much attached to all her family, and she felt this much; but there is a silver lining to most clouds. My father came back in the summer, John followed, and for a few weeks we passed our time as normal. Then came the end.

The Borough of Tavistock, for which my father had sat in the last two Parliaments, was now wanted by the Duke of Bedford for his wonderful son, little vain Lord John Russell.[1] This enforced retirement closed the home world to my poor father; without this shield his person was not safe. He left us; he never returned to his Duchus. When he drove away to catch the Coach that lovely summer morning, he looked for the last time on those beautiful scenes I do believe he dearly loved, most certainly was proud and vain of, though he never valued his inheritance rightly. He went first to London and then abroad, taking John with him. Then came the news of his appointment to a judgeship in India—Bombay; Charles Grant, now Lord Glenelg, had done it,[2] and we were desired to proceed to London

1. Lord John Russell had represented Tavistock 1813-20 but it was his stepbrother Lord William who sup-planted E.G.'s father in 1826.
2. The eldest son (1778-1866) of the East India Company Director.

immediately to prepare for the voyage. It was a blessing, and a shock—to me at least; every one else was rejoicing. Letters of congratulation came by every post. My poor mother smiled once more, and set about her preparations for removal with an alacrity that surprised us.

There was a good deal to be done, for the house was to be left in a proper state to be let furnished with the shootings, a new and very profitable scheme for making money out of bare moors in the highlands. We were to take nothing with us but our wardrobes, all else was to be left for sale, and lists of the property left had to be made to prepare the way for the Auction. The stock and crop at the farm, the wine, the plate, the linen, the books, there was the rub, all and everything that was not furniture was to go, even what belonged to my sister and me, except a few pet treasures packed in a small box and left to the care of Mrs Macpherson. She sent them to me, afterwards, and I have a few still, but what belonged to the Doune I gave back to John, and my own small collection of coins I sold during our Irish famine when we were sorely pressed for money; I believe I was cheated for they only brought £50 but it was very welcome at that sad time, a time that set me writing again, and with success.

My mother upset herself by reading old letters before destroying them; she was seriously ill. She warned me not to go through such a trial, and begged of me to burn all letters. I have done so, and regret it. Memory remains, fresh ever, its recollections are often quite as painful as the words of a letter.

William would not let the creditors have the little pony carriage; I don't know that it was exactly right, but nothing was ever said about it. It was given with its two pretty ponies, Sir Peter and Lady Teazle,[1] to Lady Gibson Craig, by whom it was most fully valued. It was the last remnant of our better days. When every other luxury was parted with, that was kept for my Mother's use. She took no other exercise. When my father was at home he always drove her out in it daily. I see them now—he in his gray *woodman's* coat with leather belt holding a short axe and a saw, breeches and long leather

1. Named after the elderly husband and young, frivolous wife in Sheridan's *School for Scandal* (1777).

gaiters, and a hat lined with green and turned up behind, the shortness of his neck bringing the stiff collar of the coat too near the brim of it. She in a drab great coat with a cape, made purposely for all weathers, and a queer misshaped black straw bonnet. Away they went all alone, out for hours, the commonest object of their drive being the pretty hill of the Callert, at the end of the Cambus Mor, which had been lately planted by my mother herself with money left to her by her aunt Jane Nesham. Before Jane married, when my father was away *she* was the driver. She wore a large flap straw hat, such as they all wear now, lined with green, her spectacles on, a plaid thrown round her; standing up at difficult corners, nodding and calling out to every passerby, on she whipped, my Mother, the greatest coward in the world, quite at ease under her guidance. Dear old days, happy through all the troubles. 'Is na the heart tough that it winna break,' said the unhappy Widow Macpherson, who lost her three fine sons in the Spanish war.

The difficulty now was to provide funds for our journey. My Mother had put by £10 of Aunt Mary's money; we had £5 left of the 'Inspector.' Belleville, kind Belleville, brought us £40, part of the produce of another packet of papers already printed, part advanced by him on some more which had been accepted, and would be paid for shortly. The old landau was cleaned, the horses ordered, the heavy trunks packed and sent off to Inverness to go by sea to London, and we were to start in the evening to dine and sleep at Belleville.

It was in August, early in the month; the weather was beautiful, the country looked lovely, the Spey sparkled under the sunshine, the wooded hills on either side stood as they stand now, and we watched the sun setting behind Tor Alvie on that last day, without a tear. Mary and I had determined to be brave. We had called on every one of all degrees; we had taken leave of none, purposely avoiding any allusion to our approaching departure. We denied ourselves the sad pleasure of bidding farewell to favourite scenes. Once unnerved we feared giving way, so keeping actively busy, we went on day by day, looking forward with hope and drawing the veil of resignation over the past.

My father had been knighted, and was safe in France, with

John. William had been in London and Edinburgh and I know not where else, and had returned to take charge of us. Poor William, how broken down he looked, how wise and thoughtful he was; he said a great mercy had been vouch-safed to us, an honourable recovery was before my father, happiness and comfort secured to my mother. We should nourish but one feeling, gratitude; he said this, yet looked so serious.

On this last day, all packing being done by the help of my Mother's old maid, whom we had brought over from her inn at Aviemore to be with her during the night, the only person in or out of the house who knew how near was our departure, William and my Mother were in the Study sorting papers in the large old black cabinet; Mary and I went out for a walk to the garden for fruit—the pretty garden, all banks and braes and little dells, with hanging birch all round. It was just a step into the wood at the upper end and then on to the Milltown burn, chafing and sparkling in its rocky bed as we followed it along the path under the Ord. We crossed the wooden bridge; I had always loved that shady lane with the old woman in her chair, with her fan, perched up high above, and the blue Cairngorm at the end. We went on; we caught the lake, its dark fir skreens, the cottages near this end, the flour mill, the ruined castle on its island, our own pretty cottage with its porch and little flower garden and small green lawn sloping down to the lake, our boat tyed to the old stump, our cow grazing; we did not enter, we could not have sat down in the parlour our own hands had fitted up. We passed on into the path along the shore of the lake, Loch an Eilein, we did not go on to Loch Gaun, but turned off up the hill to the sheep cote and so round that shoulder of the Ord by our own walk, to the seat round the birch tree on the knoll above the river where we had rehearsed our plays, and where Jane took the sketch of the Doune which Robson tinted,[1] then we went down through the wood to the walk by the Spey, coming out at the gate by the church, and in again to the planting by the backwater and so to the green gate under

1. G. F. Robson (1788–1833) was well known for his Scottish mountain scenes.

the beech tree, with few words, but not a tear till we heard that green gate clasp behind us; then we gave way, dropt down on the two mushroom seats and cried so bitterly. Alas! for resolution, had we not determined to avoid this grief. Even now I hear the clasp of that gate; I have heard it all my life, since I shall hear it till I die, it seemed to end the poetry of our existence. We had not meant to take that round; we had gone on gradually, enticed by the beauty of the day, the loveliness of the scenery, the recollections of the life from which we were parting. Long after we returned to the memory of this walk, recalling views, words, thoughts, never to be forgotten, and that we spoke of at sea, in India, at Pau, and at Avranches with a tender melancholy which bound my poor sister Mary and me more firmly together. We had gone through so much, with none to help us. Every body has a life, an inner life; every body has a private history; every body, at least almost every body, has found their own lot at some particular period hard to bear. The trials of our house were severe enough, when our young cheerful spirits felt their bitterness. What must my poor Mother have felt that last sad day. She so reserved, so easily fretted, so weary of suffering, so ill, and so lonely; hers had been a thickly shadowed life, none of it that I can remember really happy.

She had slept well, Mrs McKenzie said; all through the day she was composed, particularly kept busy by William. About 5 o'clock he shewed us the carriage on the shingle on the other side of the river, and putting my Mother's arm within his own, he led her out. No one till that moment knew that we were to go that evening, there was therefore no crowd; the few servants from the farm, joined by the two maids from the house, watched us crossing in the little boat, to which Mary and I walked down alone behind the others. Crossing the hall, William had caught up an old plaid of my father's, which he used to wear when sauntering about the grounds and now was carried off to be put upon the seat of the boat; he called old John McIntosh to row us over—Robert Allan was with the carriage. When leaving the boat, my Mother threw this plaid over the bewildered old man's shoulders. He knew it was the Laird's, and I heard he was buried in it. We entered the carriage, never once looked back, never shed a tear, though the eyes sometimes filled, very gravely we made out those eight miles among those hills and woods, and heaths and lakes, and the dear Spey, all of which we had loved from childhood and which never again could be the same to any of us.

Belleville and Mrs Macpherson received us so kindly, so warmly, cheerfully as of old. The dinner was even pleasant, so skilfully did these best of friends manage the conversation. No one was with them. Mrs Macpherson sat a long while with Mary and me at night, strengthening all right feelings with all her powers of wisdom. She had had two pretty lockets made to enclose her hair, and she cut a long Trichinopoly[1] chain in two to hang them on; these were her parting gifts. Belleville gave to each of us writing cases fully furnished. My Mother, who was a beautiful needle woman, had been embroidering trimmings broad and narrow to be left as remembrances with her friend of thirty years. We avoided a parting, having arranged with William to set off early, before our hosts were up; the only deceit we ever practised on them. We travelled on thro' the bleak hill road, and posting all the way reached Perth to dinner.

Here an unexpected difficulty met us. A coachmaker, not paid for some repairs done to the carriage at various times, seized it for a debt of £40. He was inexorable; we must pay our bill or lose our carriage. William came to me; I never saw him more annoyed; all our imperials and other luggage with their contents seized, like wise. We were in despair, feeling how very little would upset our poor mother—it was the last straw. I recollected kind Belleville's £40 for my unfinished 'Painter's Progress,' very grieved to give it to such a hard man to pay him all when others, more deserving, would only get their due by degrees; but we had no choice, so after a good night's rest we entered our redeemed carriage and drove on to Edinburgh. There the carriage was seized again and allowed to go; we wanted it no longer. We were much annoyed my brother and I by hosts of unpaid tradesmen, whom it was agreed that I should see, as they were likely to be more considerate with me—I, who could do nothing. William kept

1. Famous for its silver.

out of the way and we would not allow my Mother to be worried. The only cross creditor among the crowd was old Sanderson the Lapidary; there really was not much owing to him; a few pounds for setting some of uncle Edward's agates; these few pounds he insisted on getting, and as there was no money to be had he kept a pretty set of garnets he had got to clean, which had been left to me by Miss Neale, the sister of our great Uncle Alexander's Wife; they were set in gold, and though not in fashion then, have been all the rage since. I was thankful to get rid of even one of those unfortunate men, whom I was ashamed of seeing daily at our hotel, Douglas's in Saint Andrew's Square, where we were very comfortably lodged, and where we had to stay for the sailing of the Steamer, which then went but twice a week from Leith to London, and for a remittance to provide for our expenses.

At that season very few of our friends were in town, which was a relief to all, but Lord Jeffrey and Lord Moncrieff came in from their country houses to take leave of us. They were much attached both to my sisters and to me; it was a truly Uncle's kiss and an Uncle's blessing they left with us. I never saw Lord Moncreiff again; Lord Jeffrey lived to greet me with the old warmth years afterwards. What a Society we had lived with, those clever contemporaries of my father took very kindly to his children. We had sufficient intellect to understand their superiority and to shew that our minds were capable of enlargement in such company.

One day and night we spent at Riccarton; neither house nor grounds were then finished. We thought the scale grand, quite suited to the old place and the fine fortune. They were all kind, the whole family, father, mother, sons and daughters. We had been intimate for so long, so much together. Mary was married, the rest were all at home and very sad at the parting. Even William, though he tried to affect high spirits with that strange vulgarity of feeling which he retained till very late in life till long after his marriage with that pretty, lady like Bessie Vivian, who introduced him to society, which improved his ways—he became a polished gentleman and though his father could not turn him into a politician, he made a very useful and agreeable country gentleman,—he gained great credit by the reforms he made in the Edinburgh Record office. He had a good clear head and good business habits, I was sorry to bid him goodbye; his brother, afterwards my brother in law, was I think less attractive.

We were two beautiful days and two calm nights at sea; I recollect the voyage as agreeable, and there were incidents in it of no moment in themselves, and yet that turned to account. Mr and Mrs L'Espinasse and two of their children were on board going to France. She kept out of the way; he was always beside us chattering away in French in his lively style; two foreigners were attracted and edged their way up to the merry party, a Prussian and a Swiss, travelling on business more than for pleasure, but of what sort they did not say. They had scraped acquaintance with another passenger, a very agreeable American, Dr Birkbeck, whose lately published book Mary and I had just been reading, it was lent to us by Belleville.[1] We got on so well with our learned companion that he gave me a copy of his book and a passion flower wreath made in feathers by the nuns of a convent in Canada, very pretty it was and very useful. The only lady we ventured on was a nice looking woman in an Indian shawl, a straw cottage bonnet and a green veil, who was lame and very delicate. On hearing we were bound for Bombay she told us we should find her husband there, a Doctor Eckford, and that he would be glad to hear of her from those who had so lately seen her. She wrote her name on a leaf of her pocket book, and the date, tore it out and gave it to me to show to him. It was so calm we steamed on in sight of the coast a great part of the way; the sea was alive with shipping, mostly small craft, and then we sighted the North Foreland, where the L'Espinasses left us, in a boat which conveyed them to the Boulogne Steamer. We entered the river, when I was actually startled by the sight of two large Indiamen outward bound, floating down with the tide so grandly, moving on their way, their long, long way, with such a silent dignity. There seemed to be no one on board but the crew. As we passed the huge hulls and gazed upon the open cabin windows, our own

1. Morris Birkbeck: his *Notes on a Journey through France* and *Letters from Illinois* were both published in 1818.

destiny, so little liked, seemed to come more certainly upon us, and I know I turned away and wept.

We reached London, or rather Blackwall, in the afternoon, engaged two hackney coaches for ourselves and our luggage—my poor Mother, there was a fall; she did so feel it, and on we went to Dover Street, Piccadilly, where lodgings had been taken for us in the name of General Need. He and dear Annie were there to welcome us, and so began a busy time. It is so long ago, so much was done, so very much was suffered, that I can hardly now, at the end of twenty years, recall the events of those trying days; the order of them has quite escaped me. The few friends in or near London in the month of September gathered round. Dear Aunt Lissy and all her Freres, and good old Sophy Williams, Jane and Colonel Pennington, Lord Glenelg and Robert Grant. Lastly my father and John, he had to come to see Sir Charles Forbes,[1] but it encreased our difficulties for he was watched and tracked, though we had kept very quiet. A violent ringing disturbed us one day, and a violent knocking too, by several parties all insisting on being let in, on seeing some one, on finding Sir John Grant; he was in these lodgings, they were sure he was, he had lodged here before, he certainly had during a sharp fit of illness, and it was a mistake that they had been taken for us, but he knew the old maiden land lady who had been so kind to him would be attentive to his family, and she was; he had won her heart, as he won every one's, and she stood to us well. She said she had let her rooms to General Need, whose wife's trunks with her address upon them were luckily in the hall, and so she got rid of this alarm. For fear of another, it was determined to divide our party. John went to the Freres, Mary was carried off by Jane and her Colonel to Malshanger. My father and mother went to a lodging in a distant street, the General returned to his Cat and Fiddle, leaving dear Annie with me for a little time. Margaret Couper too came now and then to help me, and Mary having left her measure with the required trades people, I got through my work well, Lord Glenelg lending his carriage, for he would

1. Sir Charles Forbes (1774–1849), wealthy Bombay
   merchant and politician.

not allow Mrs Need and me to go to the City or the Dock in a hackney coach without a footman. Our imprudent father could not keep quiet; he was so well known he was followed once or twice, and being so short sighted he might have been seized but for the cleverness of the shop people. So it was resolved therefore to send him away, and on *Sunday* he and John steamed from the Tower stairs to Boulogne. William saw them safe off and then took my Mother to Malshanger. At rest at last, I got on quickly with the necessary preparations. Most of those I had to deal with were so kind, and when Mrs Need had to go home good Mrs Gillio came daily to me; her daughter Isabella was going to Bombay under my mother's care, so that our business was the same. She went with me to the docks to see the ships and arrange the cabins. It was a new and a most wonderful sight to me—a world of shipping up and down, on every side masts and huge hulls filling all space. How any particular vessel was made out our *land* eyes could never discover. We should have been perplexed indeed to make out our *Mountstewart Elphinstone*[1] had we not had a guide. The cabins were furnished, and all the linen of our wardrobes, gentlemen and ladies, supplied by an Outfitter in the Strand, and even our ordinary dresses the few that we required. I had only to get besides, shoes, stockings, gloves, books, stationery, all the little necessaries our toilettes and our occupations needed. My Mother had herself given orders to Miss Steuart for the ornamental dresses, and a tailor had measured us for habits. I saw an Ayah too, a clever little Arab accustomed to wait on ladies. She had come home with a mistress who recommended her strongly, so I hired her to attend on Mary and me. My Mother had engaged in the highlands a pretty half cast girl, the child of a returned soldier, who was anxious to go back to the country she well remembered.

Every one was obliging except old Mr Churton, who had been the family's hosier for years. My father sent me to him with the ready money order, a good large one, as some amends, the only one in his power at present, for old unpaid debts. He refused to have any dealings with it, caught up his

1. Named after the Governor of Bombay, 1819–27.

long bills and a long story, and a grievance, with reflexions on
my father's conduct to him which it was not comfortable for
his daughter to hear. I told the old cross crab what my father
had told me, adding that this was sure money, and that we
were going where he would soon save sufficient to pay all his
creditors in full. He did not care, he wanted none of this
money, nor any orders from the family, nor any speeches
either; he wanted nothing but his rights. I had never met
with such incivility, was quite unused to be so addressed. I
got very faint and queer I fancy, for he seemed frightened and
called his sister, who appeared distressed, told the 'dear
young lady' not to mind and brought me a glass of wine. But
I had recovered, and got grand, and would not touch it,
swallowed my tears, and turning to the shopboy, desired him
to call up Lord Glenelg's carriage. I walked out à la Princesse,
leaving the ill conditioned old man making humble apologies
to the air. It was very cruel in him to taunt a young girl with
her parents' delinquencies.

As soon as all was in train, all our assistants at work, little
Christy and I went down by the coach to Basingstoke. There
Jane met us driving her basket phaeton, old Goody herself,
and on we went four miles to that most comfortable,
thoroughly English place, Malshanger, pretty, in an uninteresting country, being well wooded, the ground undulating, and the neighbourhood thickly studded with gentlemen's seats. It was a very good house, rather large indeed,
well sized rooms, cheerful bedrooms, good garden, orchard,
paddock, lawn, shrubbery. They made an extremely pretty
flower garden afterwards, opening from a Conservatory they
added to the Drawing room, and to the charming bow
windowed study there was a Verandah covered with creepers. When the flower garden bloomed in front of it, the suite
was indeed enjoyable. Jane was very well cared for and very
happy. There was a stable full of horses, and servants in
plenty. Our kitchen maid Nelly was the Cook, then and ever.
The little sister Christy was lady's maid; Robert Allan,
Butler—all the old friends established there. We spent three
most pleasant weeks at Malshanger. The Colonel seemed so
glad to have us, and he was so good natured to us. He rode
with me every second day all over those fine Hampshire

downs, miles and miles away in every direction, he on his hunters in their turn, I on the 'gentle Mortimer,' which always carried his master to covert all through the hunting season. The intervening days Jane took me off in her basket.

I had got quite out of health; I had been obliged to consult Doctor Wauchope in London, my father being a little uneasy about my altered looks. Little could be done till I got to the country—here I soon recovered and by strictly obeying a few simple rules I was 'all right' before I left these good quarters.

The Colonel and Jane dined out frequently, taking Mary with them. Jane was always handsomely dressed, though she never all her life could put her clothes on neatly. Mary wore plain white muslin and natural flowers in her hair and really she looked beautiful. She was immensely admired, and had she remained longer in this well to do neighbourhood she need never have gone to India. My Mother had gone to Oxford to stay with Aunt Mary in her new home, a very wealthy one. Doctor Bourne, a clever and an amiable man, took good care of my mother, put her into better health, and kept her till William went to bring her up to London a few days before we started for Portsmouth, for the parting had to be borne—poor Jane. Before we left her, William gave us a Deed which Mary and I were to sign. A Deed most improperly asked for, for the true nature of which was not explained to us and which, had it not been for our dear Aunt Bourne, would have left us nigh penniless. It bound us as Securitors for a debt due to Lord Lauderdale, in case of there being no funds at my father's death to acquit it, the interest in the mean while was provided for from the estate. I do not think either my father or Lord Lauderdale knew much about this transaction, it was arranged by the Trustees and the lawyers and William was charged to see the Deed executed—he trusted to Indian funds, and was thankful to get rid by any means of what might have put a stop to India. Debt, that fearful master, tyrant that one by one destroys all good principles, all good feelings, bending at the same time the victim in fetters the most galling—and all the misery caused, all the meanness engendered, all the sad retrospect, all the clouded future, it is the break up of happiness. How the £2,000 given by Government for the outfit (was spent)

I cannot tell, about £400 passed through my hands and paid the Outfitters, the lodgings, the journeys and current expenses. The passage money was of course high, three of the best cabins, and the French expenses and William's—it was little enough I believe. What little personal comforts Mary and I got were provided by good Mrs Sophy Williams. She presented us each with a few yards of lace neatly folded up, and on opening the little parcel, a £5 note was found pinned on the lace. The Freres gave us useful keepsakes and came to see us.

We were filling our carpet bags ready for our early start next morning, when a noisy visitor ran quickly up the stairs, and in bounded William Clarke, just arrived from China. He had in his hand a small case containing a beautiful ivory fishwoman, on her tiny arm a basket full of fish: the old promised wife for our ivory fruiterer. He was in a great hurry to return to clear his ship, and that puts me in mind that among our Edinburgh baggage was a case of whiskey bitters made for the long sea voyage, and a few bottles of fine old Glenlivet; it was seized at the Custom house, and though General Need took a great deal of trouble to represent the peculiar circumstances, we never saw more of our precious contrabands. One of the Clerks told the General confidentially that his Chief considered them quite a prize. I would not carry back my pretty fishwoman to her native tropicks; I sent it and a Bombay work box Uncle Edward had sent me to Fountain Dale to dear Annie. William Clarke, who expected soon to be at Dalnavert, was loaded with messages to the Bellevilles and warmly thanked for his own kind remembrance of us. So he went away.

We had finished all our business with fewer mistakes than could have been expected, considering all that had to be done and how little used to management were the doers, and at 5 o'clock next morning we were picked up by the Southampton Stage, with Lewis Grant in it as our escort. William had gone to France. Sir Charles Forbes, whose essential kindness was almost unexampled, for, without his head and without his purse, my father could never have escaped from some exasperated creditors, had sent one of his head clerks to attend my Mother on her journey. Lewis Grant of Kincorth and his twin brother had been wards of my father; there was an old connexion between us.

Was it Southampton we sailed from, or Portsmouth. I think it must have been Portsmouth, at any rate, it was the same place at which I landed three years later, when my General brought me home.[1] A small inn looking on the harbour—Mrs Gillio was already there with her daughter and her brother, Colonel Grant. He warned us that the Silver Arrow was out after my poor hunted father, scouring the sea and visiting the land. We saw some of the gentlemen bearing it, whom Lewis Grant told that Sir John Grant was not to join his family till the morrow, when they knew the Havre Steamer was expected and that the *Mountstewart Elphinstone* could not sail till the following day, the Captain said, as he was still loading. What should we have done without this friend, who to his sorrow had a part to play and well he played it, for to deception he was forced to stoop, mean deception, my Mother and Mary and I being deceived like the others. The Havre steamer came in, my father and brother not in her. My Mother's anxiety was therefore genuine, we were all three amazed, not knowing what to make of it. Colonel Alexander Grant went about the town making cautious enquiries, Lewis Grant said openly he feared my father had gone up to London and been detained. In the evening he brought us word our ship had moved out to the roads, Spithead, and tho' she would not sail till the following day, the passengers were ordered on board at once. Half bewildered we obeyed at once.

It was late in the September day—the 28th I remember it was, in the year 1827—nearly dark. We got into a good sailing boat and proceeded out to sea, Mrs Gillio, her brother, and Lewis Grant with us. In an hour we reached our huge 'ocean home'; down came the chair, we were soon upon the deck, amid such confusion, all noise, all hubbub, all a dream, but not to last long, for the rumour grew in a moment that the wind had changed. The captain ordered the anchors

1. Her husband was a Lieutenant Colonel down to his retiral in 1832; this promotion came in 1854, the year E.G. completed her *Memoirs*.

up; our kind friends must go. Mrs Gillio parted with the last of her daughters, her youngest child, and with us whom she loved almost as well. Lewis Grant came up from the cabin, where he had been comforting my Mother. He took leave of my sister and me, a quiet leave. Had he not his romance at the bottom of his honest, warm highland heart. It had laid there, I believe, ever since that Inverness meeting and a little of it lurked there for many a day, at least. I thought so when he and I met again and talked of her 'who had no parallel.' He had mentioned to my mother all his clever arrangement with Captain Henning. She was therefore watching for my father. We stood out to sea and beat about till nearly 10 o'clock, when a Jersey boat sighted our peculiar light, came alongside, and my father and both my brothers came on deck; a few moments were allowed for a few words. My father shut himself up with my Mother; John remained beside Mary and me. William, in an agony of grief I never saw equalled in any man, burst out of our Cabin. We watched the sound of the oars of the Jersey boat as it bore him from us, and then said Mary, pale as a corpse, but without a tear, 'We are done with home.' We got under weigh directly, and favoured by the wind, long before we waked from heavy slumbers, were out of reach of any silver oars.

CHAPTER TWENTY-SIX

1827–1828

I HAD £30 left of the money entrusted to me, this I handed over to poor William, who was to pay the Bill at the hotel out of it and keep the rest. It was not until long after that I heard Colonel Grant had paid the bill and would not accept repayment 'till better days,' which, alas! never in that good man's lifetime came to poor William.

William's story from that period for the next four years would be a good foundation for a novel. His struggles were very hard—he had not learned wisdom. He bore his trials well, and was helped by many friends, proving that there were kind hearts in a world some of us have felt it is a mistake to call so hard as it is reputed. I may touch on his romance again; at present I proceed with my own.

A long four months' voyage in a narrow space amid a crowd of strangers. I could not avoid believing that some of them must have become acquainted with the humiliating circumstances attending our departure; they never showed this, and the Captain, who had been an actor in the miserable scene, was the most delicate of all, apparently ignorant of all; yet in odd ways Mary and I fancied he was more interested in us than in any of the rest of his passengers. We had taken a dislike to the good little man; we had met him at a tea party given by Mrs Gillio for the purpose of introducing him to us. A Captain Gordon was there and his sister in law, Mrs Gordon, a Widow afterwards Lady Stannus, and the manners of these three Indians were so unsatisfactory that our hearts sank at the prospect of Bombay society, they were not first class, certainly. On board his ship no man could be quieter or more agreeable than Captain Henning. My father and mother were the principal people; we had the best accommodation, and we formed a large party ourselves. My

father and mother had one cabin, a poop cabin, Mary and I
had the other, Isabella's smaller one opened out of ours;
opposite to hers was Mr Gardiner; the two deck cabins were
occupied by my brother John and the captain. It was quite a
home circle apart from every body else; they were all below
on the main decks.

Lieutenant Colonel and Mrs Morse were returning to
India; a little girl with two brothers who had been at school in
England, were going back to their parents in Ceylon; a young
Cavalry Officer, a Doctor, and I don't know how many
cadets; altogether, with the three mates, between thirty and
forty at the Cuddy table,[1] not omitting Mr Caw, that clever,
good hearted oddity, who was going with us to India in the
hope of being provided for, as his long, unwearied services
deserved.

The first feeling that struck me was the absence of all fear;
alone on those wide waters, with but a plank between our
heads and death, the danger of our situation never occurred
to me. There was such a sober certainty of life apparent in the
regular routine observed: the early holy stoning, the early
cleaning, manoeuvring, arranging, the regular bells, the
busy crew, the busy cuddy servants, the regular meals, the
walks upon the deck, the quiet preparation of all in the
Cuddy, of all in our cabins, as if we were to go on thus for
ever, as if we had gone on thus for years past; all looked so
usual that the terrours which assail the spirits of those on
shore who watch the sea never once entered the heads of the
most cowardly amongst us. Storms, rocks, fogs without,
fires, leaks, want of care within, all so readily arranged before
the timid ashore, never once started up in a single mind at
sea.

On we sailed, those bright summer days, with hardly
breeze enough to fill our sails, skimming leisurely over
undulating rather than swelling waves, hardly aware that we
were crossing the Bay of Biscay. With Fatima's help our
cabin was soon set in order. It was well filled; a sofa bed, a
dressing table that closed over a washing apparatus, a writing

1. A cabin near the stern, reserved for officers and cabin
   passengers to use as a dining room.

table, a pianoforte, a bookcase, and a large trunk with trays in it, each tray containing a week's supply of linen. In the locker was a good supply of extra stores, water well bottled, in particular. A swing tray and a swing lamp hung from the roof, and two small chairs filled corners; there was a pretty mat upon the floor, and no little room could look more comfortable. The whole locker end was one large window, closed till we left the colder latitudes, open ever after, and shaded by venetians during the heat of the day. A small closet called a galley, in which Ayah kept her peculiar treasures, had a shower bath in it, readily filled by the sailors, and a most delightful and strengthening refreshment to us. Isabella, in her smaller way, was equally well lodged.

We soon learned to employ our days regularly, taught by the regularity round us. The life we led was monotonous, but far from being disagreeable, indeed after the first week it was pleasant; the quiet, the repose, the freedom from care, the delicious air, and a large party all in spirits, aided the bright sun in diffusing universal cheerfulness. Few were ill after the first weeks, the soreness of parting was over, a prosperous career was before the young, a return to friends, to business, and to pay awaited the elder; and *we* had left misery behind us and were entering on a new life free from trials that had been hard to bear.

It was some little time before I was quite restored to strength—the nervous system had been overstrained as well as the body overfatigued. There was nothing now to disturb either. I occupied myself pretty much as at home, reading, writing, working, shading my charts, and making extracts from the books I read, a habit I had indulged for some years and found to be extremely useful, the memory was so strengthened by this means and the intellect expanded as thought always accompanied this exercise. We were all well supplied with books and lent them freely to one another. Captain Henning had a very good library, and with him and one or two others we could converse pleasantly. Mr Gardiner was very agreeable and soon became a favourite with my father and with Mary. He was a Civilian, not young; he had been ten years in India, and was returning there now after a two years' leave at home. He was about thirty, had held a good appointment, and expected a better. The family was Irish; the father, Colonel Gardiner, had inherited money and made more, and on dying left £100,000 to his five children. A son died, a daughter married a very gallant soldier—Sir Edward Blakeney[1]—two sisters remained unmarried and lived with an Aunt at Twickenham, a Miss Porter, also Irish, their mother's sister. No difficulties could occur to render this intimacy undesirable, so while Isabella and I at the Cuddy door were warbling pretty Canzonettes to our light guitars, and listening in our turn to Mrs Morse, who often brought her harp upon deck in the evenings, Mr Gardiner and his lady love amused us all by the care they took never to be far asunder.

The first Sunday at sea was very impressive. The Bells were rung for prayers, the passengers were seated all round the binnacle, the crew, so trimly dressed, were further back, even the Lascars looked on. The captain read the service, shortened; when he came to 'bless the ship in which we sail,' I know my eyes filled. Our little ship, alone on the wide waters, our little world, as it were, busy with its own little plans and schemes, such a speck in a grand universe; it was very touching. I always liked the Sunday service and always felt more truly religious, more humble, more patient, than I had ever felt in a church on shore; and a funeral at sea—this I did not witness till we were coming home; it is most affecting; that splash into the water after the coffin has been slided through the porthole, shook me from tip to toe; I did not recover it for hours. Such was my father's funeral years afterwards.

So on we sped in our 'gallant ship,' the *Mountstewart Elphinstone*, 600 tons, built by Captain Henning his own self up at Surat, and a very slow sailer! he made her. As we proceeded under brightening skies we ourselves seemed to grow sunnier. We learned to vary our amusements too, I got on famously. The little Ceylon children were very nice,

1. Sir Edward Blakeney (1778–1868), later Field Marshall (and C. in C. of troops in Ireland 1836–55 when the married E.G. met him often) married Maria Gardiner.

particularly the little girl; it was a pity to see them lose what they had been learning, so I made them come to me to school for 3 hours daily, Mary, when she was well enough, helping to teach them; however, she soon gave herself something better to do. Then I liked to watch the Captain taking his observation every day at noon, and one of the Officers proposed to me to make a chart of the voyage with the ship's course traced regularly and dated; it was very interesting getting on day by day, sometimes great long runs that carried my dots on ever so many degrees, and then a little shabby move hardly observable. Once, in a calm, we went round in a circle for 3 or 4 days, quite annoyingly.

After crossing the equator we found a charming occupa-tion—a map of the Southern sky. The constellations were so beautiful. We have no idea in these cloudy climates of the exquisite brilliancy of the cloudless ones, the size of the stars too. We marked each as it rose, often staying on the poop till actually ordered away. The Cross, Sirius, Aldebaran, never were such diamonds in a sky. Captain Henning, his old mate, the young Cavalry officer and I, were the *we* who were so busy. Captain Henning was naturally clever, very obliging, but vain and uncultivated, a superiour person when one got over the little under beau manner. The young officer was somebody we should all have heard of had he lived. The Captain was extremely cross at times, but there was too much in his little knot of a head for any of us to resent this.

Besides these more private intellectual pursuits we had publick diversions. Mrs Morse played the harp well, Mr Lloyd sang; every Saturday night the captain gave us a supper; in return each guest spoke or sang, the worse the better fun, but *we* did our best. John, Mary, and I got up many pretty duetts, and glees, and one solo never palled, 'the *wet* sheet and the flowing sea,' though the captain always made me sing it '*taut*,' the '*taut* sheet and the flowing sea,' more correct a great deal but the sound unmusickal.[1]

Another day was for the sailors; they danced and they sang, and did athletick exercises, ending with a supper.

1. The best-remembered poem of the Dumfriesshire
   poet, Allan Cunningham (1784–1842).

Mrs Morse gave a Concert once a week down below in her range of cabins, and my Mother, opening our 4 *en suite*, gave another. Then we played cards in the Cuddy. Every body inclining to be agreeable, amusement was easily managed.

The Cadets killed a shark, and the Doctor dissected the head, giving quite a pretty lecture on the Eye. A nautilus, too, came under his knife, and a dolphin, and flying fish and sucking fish. One day I had been doing my map in the Cuddy, and wanting some pencil or something, went into our cabin; the locker venetians were all open, and there before me, resting on the waters beyond, was an albatross surrounded by her young. Such a beautiful sight. That 'Ancient Mariner' committed a dreadful crime. Another day a storm at a distance revealed to us as it ended a waterspout, which, had it broken on us, would have been our end. It was in hour glass form, spouting up very high. Then we had a near view of Madeira, merely villas among trees on a hill, a town on the shore. A boat or two came off with fruits and took back our letters, but we hardly slackened sail, just passed stately on, all of us absorbed in the vision of the distant peak of Teneriffe, which seemed to tower *through* the skies.

On the line we were becalmed, very hot and very tiresome. We amused several evenings by lowering the boats and taking a rowing circuit of some miles, till to me the feeling of insecurity became oppressive, the ship a speck, and we, some half dozen of us, abandoned as it were without resources on the deep. We had stormy weather near the Cape, bitterly cold; all the thick wraps we were provided with were insufficient to keep us comfortable. One really wild day I had myself lashed to the companion that I might take a steadier survey of the sea 'mountains high.' The waves rose to the mast head, apparently; we were up on top of them one minute, down in such a hollow the next, the spray falling heavy on the deck. The dinner that day little mattered, so few partook. We stouter ones were contented with one dish, a meat dumpling, our portion served to each in a bowl, and the attendant requisites either kept together by padded subdivisions strapped across the table or propt upon the swing trays overhead.

In these latitudes began the sudden showers, so heavy, so incessant, with drops so large, their rattling deafened us. In 3 or 4 minutes a wash hand basin was quite filled; the servants had a grand display of pottery, running about so eagerly to catch an additional supply of that commonest of all Nature's gifts ashore, the scarcest, the most prized at sea, pure water.

We passed very few vessels, two only near enough for hailing, one only able to receive our letters home; yet we went on journalising as if we had next door the penny post box. At length we scented, really and truly scented Ceylon; the mild elastick air which blew from it upon us literally was perfumed by the spice groves it had passed over. I never felt any thing so delicious.

Our vessel was soon surrounded by the singular shaped boats of the Cingalese, a monkey looking race, scarcely a rag upon them, chattering like as many apes, and scrambling about with the wares they had brought for us, and tried to force us all to buy. Their jewellery was false enough, but pretty, their cottons mediocre enough, as were their fruits and vegetables, but we thought these last quite excellent spite of their strangeness to our palates. We had been so long without either, except a few preserved. A whole day we enjoyed ourselves with our savage visitors, amusing ourselves with their gestures, their wares, their extraordinary appearance; the sea alive with boats, the harbour full of shipping, the shore very pretty. We had touched at Point de Galle. At first the charm of green trees, white walls, etc., was sufficient for our admiring eyes. Soon we were calm enough to discriminate, and then it only seemed the more interesting to discover no feature we were used to amid the scenery; roofless houses, closed venetians within verandah shades, no windows visible and for trees, such long, high poles with cabbage heads or wide extending wiry arms, leafless to our ideas. It was like a vision, not like the long desired land.

Poor little Mary and her brothers felt much on leaving us. She had been so happy in our cabin with her studies. Her father, a merchant, a heavy looking man, came for her about noon in a neat boat with an awning over the cushions, under which the poor child threw herself, crying bitterly. Her brothers were calmer, the father very grateful, and so that scene moved away. I never saw Mary again. I wrote to her and sent her presents, and she replied but when I left India I lost all trace of a young intelligent companion, who had beguiled many an hour 'at sea.'

In the afternoon we went on shore ourselves; the captain took us with him to the Master Attendant's house, where he had sent to say we would spend the evening. None but those who have had their limbs cramped up during a long voyage can understand the delight with which the simple movement of one foot fall after another upon firm ground is attended. The sky so bright and sea so clear would have been hot and dazzling otherwise; nothing unpleasant assailed our sensibilities just now; the breeze was cooling, we repeated for ever, and on we went till darkness tumbled down upon us, just as we entered a gate which opened on the bank at top of which was placed Mr Tyndale's bungalow, all fairy land to us, at least. An Indian dwelling consists of one long room, from which sometimes smaller open on either hand; a shaded verandah surrounds it, parts of which are frequently made into chambers as required, by merely dividing them off by a skreen. The simple way of lighting this simple dwelling is by glass cups hanging from the ceiling or stuck against the walls, filled with cocoa nut oil in which floats a cotton wick. The ceilings are mostly breadths of calico sewed together and stretched across the rafters; the floors a composition of lime covered by matting; the furniture scanty, but handsome though bare, no draperies, no covers, nor curtains nor colouring. All must look cool, clean, dark. In such a home we found a set of hospitable people, quite pleased to hear our news from England. They gave us tea, *good bread and butter* and fruit, no fuss, hardly a sound, the shoeless servants quite startling us by offering us refreshments in gentle tones at our elbows when we had never heard them enter the room. There were several men to wait on us, all dressed in close fitting white cotton dresses and red turbans, little black creatures, very ugly, but doing their parts well. The family themselves were no way remarkable, kind obliging persons, it was the surroundings which gave so agreeable an impression—the quiet, the ease, the climate, the beauty of the whole scene which so completely satisfied the feelings. We had left our shawls in a small room near the entrance. On going back to put them on we were astonished at the radiance of the walls; they shone from ceiling to floor in spots all over in a manner incomprehensible to us, till a smiling servant, bringing a tumbler and sweeping some spots into it, revealed a knot of fire flies by the light from which we easily read a book Mrs Tyndale opened. We walked away under stars as bright, and rowed back to our ship over a sea so smooth over which such a fresh, delicious, night breeze played. It was the white day of our voyage.

At day break we were off again. Coasting up within sight of land for the most part, all along the shores of Malabar, not without danger. One night Mr Gardiner, being on deck, became aware of the cause of a great commotion among the watch; a sunken rock had nearly finished our worldly affairs; the captain was called, and by energetick measures we merely saved our distance and our lives. It was cool except for the few hours of midday, very pleasant from the balmy air, the frequent sight of land, and the cheerfulness diffused among our company by the near termination of our long voyage.

We landed on the 8th of February 1828 in Bombay. We entered that most magnificent harbour at sunset, a circular basin of enormous size, filled with islands, high, rocky, wooded, surrounded by a range of mountains beautifully irregular; and to the north on the low shore spread the City, protected by the Fort, skreened by half the shipping of the world. We were standing on the deck. 'If this be exile,' said my father musingly, 'it is splendid exile.' 'Who are those bowing men?' said my mother, touching his arm and pointing to a group of natives with Coloured high crowned caps on some heads, and small red turbans on others, all in white dresses, and all with shoeless feet, who had approached us with extraordinary deference. One of the high caps held out a letter. It was from Uncle Edward, my Mother's younger brother, who had turned the corner round Sir Giffin Wilson's wall so many years ago with his hat pulled down over such tearful eyes, and these were his servants come to conduct us to his country house. All was confusion around us, friends arriving, departing, luggage shifting, each passenger being allowed to carry a bag on shore with necessaries. And it grew dark in a moment, encreasing our perplexity.

At last we were arranged, descended the side of our poor old ship, entered the bunder boat, moved, swung round to the steps of the ghaut,[1] mounted them, found carriages waiting, and away we drove some three miles or so through part of the town and then through a wooded plain, till we stopt at a shabby gate which opened on a narrow road and led us to the wide steps of a portico, reached by a good long flight, edged with two lines of turbaned servants glittering with gold adornments, reflected by the torch each third man bore. A blaze of light flashed from the long building beyond, in front of the entrance to which stood a tall figure all in white, of a most dignified presence, queenlike as a stage heroine, who gave a sign, and from her sides moved on and down the steps four persons in scarlet robes trimmed with gold and bearing in their hands gold sticks the stature of themselves. They opened our carriage doors and out we stept; and thus we were received by my Uncle's wife.

They had come down from Surat, partly to meet us, and partly for my Uncle's health, which repeated attacks of gout had much weakened. He was at this moment on his couch, incapable of leaving it, and still in pain, yet had he made every possible arrangement for our Comfort. The large house of Camballa, which he had hired to receive us in, was of the usual Indian Construction, the large, long centre hall with broad verandahs round it; but such a hall, 80 feet long, 80 feet wide, Verandahs 20 feet wide. It stood on a platform in the middle of the descent of a rocky hill, round which swept the sea, with a plain of rice fields, and a tank, a handsome tank, between the foot of it and the Breach Candi road along the beach. From the hill end of the hall rose a wide staircase in stages; each stage led off on either hand to a terrace, each terrace on the one hand was a flower garden, on the other a covered gallery leading to offices. Top of all, and very high it was, the Terraces were covered in as bedrooms, catching all the air that blew and commanding from their latticed balconies such a view as was alone worth *almost* the voyage from Europe.

1. Bunder is a harbour, hence a boat for short journeys; ghat is Anglo-Indian for hindi landing stage.

Dinner was served in one of the Verandahs to the great hall with such a display of plate, so brilliant a light, and such an array of attendants as were startling after our Cuddy reminiscences. I thought of the Arabian nights. The scenes there depicted were realised with a charm belonging to them quite beyond any description to paint and which now at this distance of time rouses the fancy again, and gives them back to memory with a freshness never to be impaired. There was light, vastness, beauty, regal pomp, and *true affection*. All was not gold, however; a better acquaintance with our palace disturbed much of our admiration. Our bedrooms were really merely barns, no ceilings, the bare rafters, bare walls, no fastenings to the doors, the bathrooms very like sculleries, the flowery terraces suspected of concealing snakes, and most certainly harbouring myriads of insects most supremely troublesome, and the tank a nuisance. Very beautiful as it seemed, with its graduated sides descending to the water, interesting from the groups of native women resorting there at all hours with those pyramids of Etruscan shaped pots upon their heads, and their draperied clothing, and winging on with such a graceful step, the tank at night became a nuisance from the multitude of frogs—the large bull frog with such a dreadful croak as deafened us. Still these were minor evils. It was all a stage play life, and we were enchanted with it.

It was some days before our goods were cleared from the Custom House. We had landed in plain white dresses, my Mother and Mary and I, and had merely brought a second of the same sort in our bags; no toilette this to receive the visits of the Presidency. Great expectations had been formed of the new great man, the great Lady his wife, and the celebrated beauties his daughters. It was a bitter disappointment to find people of no mark at all, ladies with no new fashions, the Judge busy, the lady mother ditto, the daughters in white plain dresses, and the handsomer of the two engaged to be married, for Mr Gardiner had not lost the opportunity of securing to himself about the most attractive creature that ever brightened this changing world.

As we were great people, *burra sahibs*, every attention was paid to us. The cannon fired from the Fort when my father went to take the oaths, and every body called on my Lady. It is the custom in this part of India for the older inhabitants to visit the new comers; we, therefore, had to receive a perfect crowd. Many came at the breakfast hour, nine o'clock, the sun had less power thus early, the fashionable part of the society came later, some in carriages of various descriptions, some in palanquins,[1] all the ladies appeared very much dressed, the style of toilette most agreeable in a hot climate being very much more elegant than the every day costume of colder latitudes; the gentlemen in their cool white jackets and trowsers and shirt breasts unconcealed by any waistcoat, looked all so young and so clean that these Civilians quite rivalled the military in uniform.

All these mornings of the first week we were quite busy receiving company; we could hardly find time to unpack our Wardrobes. After luncheon indeed we were free, as no one called afterwards, but then we were tired or we had notes or letters to write, or wished to lie still upon a sofa waiting for the fresh sea breeze. I have lain half dead with exhaustion watching the drops of one of the large chandeliers, as the first intimation of the advancing current was the slow movement of this glittering drop. As soon as we really felt the air, we prepared for our evening airing, and on returning dressed for a party either at home or abroad, for in spite of the heat these gay doings were incessant.

I wish I had preserved a more minute recollection of my first Bombay impressions; they were very vivid at the time, and I remember being struck with surprise that all accounts of India that had ever fallen in my way were so meagre, when materials new and strange were in such abundance. I must brush up memory a bit, try to carry myself back to all the incidents of that interesting time.

The youth of the women, and the beauty of the greater part of them, is one very distinguishing feature of the society; the cheerful spirits of all, gentlemen and ladies, is quite remarkable, to be accounted for, probably, by the easy circumstances of almost all, and the Occupation of their time. There

1. A litter, usually for one, consisting of a large box with
   wooden shutters, carried on poles by 4 or 6 men.

are no idlers in India. Every man has his employment; he may do it well or ill, but he has it there to do, a business hour recurring with every day, releasing him every afternoon, and well and regularly paid the first of every month. The women must attend to their households and their nurseries with watchful care, or they will rue it, and tho' some may neglect their duties more or less, none can avoid them. Then it is the most sociable country in the world, truly hospitable. Every body is acquainted, every door is open, literally as well as figuratively, there is an ease, a welcome, a sort of family feel among these Colonists in a strange land that knits them altogether very pleasantly. There are gradations in the scale of course, and very rigidly observed too, the ladies in particular preserving carefully their proper position. The Governour does for King, his suite for Court, the Commander in Chief and his suite almost as grand; then the 3 members of Council and their 3 wives! very grand indeed. An Admiral, or rather Head of the Navy. All the Civilians according to seniority, all the military according to their rank; the Judges of the Supreme Court, Officials pertaining thereto; barristers, Merchants—rather below par, with one or two exceptions; attorneys thought little of; Indian Navy ditto; Royal Navy in great repute when a stray vessel came in. A few French and Americans admitted. And several of the natives quite in fashion; rich Parsees, and one or two Hindus. All these elements shook up together very cordially, and there was an undergrouping of lower caste, native and foreign, all in their peculiar costumes, which, with the singular vehicles, the strange scenery, the ocean, and the cloudless sky, made a succession of pictures that would have enchanted an artist eye.

As soon as all the Dignitaries and all the undignified had paid their visits, and what a crowd collected in our Aunt Caroline's fine hall, daily, for a fortnight, my Mother and I had to return this attention. Mary was excused on account of her approaching marriage, which ceremony indeed interrupted our civilities; but we got thro' as many calls as we could, as soon as we had unpacked our finery. My father very wisely built a carriage expressly for this sunny clime, with open sides shaded by venetians and a double roof, with a space between the outer leather and the inner *cork*. It was a delightful contrivance; we never felt baked in it, tho' to say truth it was always disagreeable to me to drive out in the glare of the mid day.

People lived about in so scattered a manner it took us a long time to get thro' our *roster* of several hundreds. Very few inhabited the Fort; a few had cool dwellings on Rampart Row, but only a few. Bungalows on the Esplanade were much more in favour, oddly enough, for they were far from being cool or pretty; they were set down in a long row surrounded by dingy palisades, giving to each house of sticks and mats a bare compound—as the space we should use for garden is called. As these rickety residences cannot be lived in during the rains, they get rather rough usage twice a year, on being first set up, and then pulled down, and few people beautify them with a shrubbery for this space of time. The few tents sprinkled about look prettier, tho' they could not be so comfortable.

The pleasantest houses are those dotted all over the plain and on every rising ground and along the Breach Candi road by the sea, with gardens round them like Camballa, and some little attempt at permanence of construction. The whole scene is very beautiful, the whole style very attractive, and the life, but for the exhausting midday heat, would be very agreeable.

My sister's marriage was a grand affair. I don't remember how many people my Aunt thought it necessary to invite to the breakfast; there were above 20 present at the Ceremony in the Cathedral. We had such a Cousinhood at the Presidency, and Mr Gardiner and Uncle Edward had so many friends, and there were my father's brother judges, etc. Good Mr Carr, now the Bishop, married them.

For so very pretty a girl as Mary then was, so beautiful a woman as she became, there never was a less interesting, I was going to say a plainer, Bride. Her dress was heavy and unbecoming, and a very large veil, the gift of Mr Norris, hid all of her face except the large nose, the feature that had been best concealed. She was perfectly silent before the ceremony and equally silent after it, self possessed all through. She bowed without smiling when her health was drank and she went off with her husband in her new carriage to Salsette as if she had been going out just to take a drive with me.

I never pretended to understand Mary; what she felt, or whether she felt, nobody ever knew when she did not choose to tell them. Like Jane, and I believe like myself, what she determined on doing she did, and well, without fuss, after conviction of its propriety. One thing is certain, she married a most estimable man; and she made a most happy marriage, and whatever she felt towards him the day she became his Wife, she was afterwards truly attached to him and she valued him to the end of her days as he deserved.

We had had plenty to do, she and I, preparing for this event, for Mary, not content with her outfit, ordered considerable additions to her wardrobe, such things as she and our Aunt Caroline considered indispensible in her new position—near £100 my father had to pay. Then there were toilette requisites, a carriage, liveries, horses, servants, linen etc., on Mr Gardiner's part, all to be chosen by her. A friend, Mr Elliot, lent them or rented to them his furnished house at Bycullah, which saved them both trouble and expense, he Mr Elliot being ill and ordered to the Neilgherries; still there were many little matters to settle, and we had no help from my father and mother. They were completely absorbed in the same sort of affairs of their own. Really it was amusing to see persons of their age, who had kept house for so many years, and had full experience of such business, so completely occupied with every the minutest detail of their Bombay establishment. Their house, its situation, furniture, number of servants, etc., one could understand would require attention; but the shape of the turbans, the colour of the cumberbands, *their width*, the length of the robes of the Chobdars, all these minutiae received the greatest consideration. I declare I don't believe the Secretaries to the Government gave half so much thought to their minutes of council. Mr Gardiner and Mary made much shorter work of it, but then certainly they had not so much to do. I had no sinecure listening to both parties, and Aunt Caroline's comments besides.

A short honeymoon satisfied our lovers; they returned after a retirement of 10 days, and then began a round of entertainments to the newly married pair. Every incident was seized on by the community to give excuse for party giving. There was so little to interest any one going forward at any time, the mails being infrequent then, that we all gladly turned attention to the trifles which filled up our lives for want of better things. An Indian life is very eventless; very dull it was to me after Mary married and John left us. Uncle Edward continued so unwell after losing the gout that he was recommended to try a year at the Neilgherries; John went there with them, proceeding afterwards from there by Bangalore to Madras and so to Calcutta, his nomination being to Bengal.

My father and Mother and I removed on their departure to the Retreat, a very fine house belonging to one of the Cowajees, badly situated at the foot of a wooded hill, which intercepted the sea breeze, and on the edge of a tank that overwhelmed us with mosquitoes. We had a large and pretty garden divided into three; one part, round two sides of the house, filled with shrubs and flowers, a piece of higher ground beyond, ending in a long terrace where I liked to walk on moonlight nights, tho' I never sat in a Belvidere two storeys high over looking the road at the end of it, and a rose field of the small single Atta rose, the perfume from which was delightful. The house itself was a palace; a broad gravel terrace surrounded it, with several flights of broad steps at intervals leading down to the road or the gardens. Upon this terrace the verandah of course opened, and into the Verandah opened all the rooms of the ground floor; the centre hall was 60 or 70 feet long, and of sufficient width to allow of three square rooms being partitioned off each end of it; the three at one side we called Drawing rooms. We ate in the hall; at the other side, one room was a spare bedroom, the other my father's study with a bath room thro' it, and the middle room held a very handsome staircase leading up to my Mother's apartment and mine, both were alike composed of three pieces, bedroom, dressing room, wardrobe room which was dark, and contained the large tin cases in which we kept our dresses safe from insects. There were bath rooms and a connecting Verandah in which our Ayahs slept and our tailors worked. Over the hall and Drawing rooms there was no second storey.

Altho' the Drawing rooms were only separated by skreens from the hall, we lived in the hall mostly, on account of the current of air thro' it from its open sides. The kitchens were in a court behind; the stables near them; such of the servants as remained all night slept any where they chose to lay their mats down; they had no bedclothes, neither did they undress. Few of them ate together, the different religions and the different castes of each religion never mixing at meals. They had no settled hours for eating. I used to smell their vegetable curries at all sorts of times, and see piles of white rice, or scones of what looked like barley meal, carried here and there as wanted. The hungry sat in a circle on the ground out of reach of a contaminating presence, dipping their scones or their fingers into the one pot and making a nice mess of it. I have heard of a low caste, or a European, passing between the wind and them making it sinful to finish the polluted repast, which was of course thrown out.

Our Establishment consisted of a Head Servant, a Parsee, who managed all, hired the rest, marketted, ordered, took charge of every thing, doing it all admirably, and yet a rogue. An under steward or Butler, a Mohammedan, who waited on me; 4 Chobdars, officers of the Supreme Court who attended my father there, waited at meals on him and my mother, and always went behind the carriage; they were dressed in long scarlet gowns edged with gold lace, white turbans, gold belts, and they bore long gilt staves in their hands. The Parsee Head wore a short cotton tunick with a shawl round the waist, silk trowsers, very wide, and the high brown silk cap peculiar to the Parsees. My Mohammedan had a white turban, white tunick, red shawl, and red trowsers, tight to the leg. My father's valet was a Portuguese Xian in a white jacket and trowsers, European style. Besides these there were 4 Sepoys for going messages, who wore green and red and gold fancifully about their turbans and tunicks—the family livery; two *hammauls* to clean the house, two *bheasties* to fetch the water, two men to light the lamps, one water-cooler and butter maker (this last piece of business being done in a bottle on his knee), a gardener, a Cook with an assistant, two dhobees or washermen, and a slop-emptier, all these being

Hindus of various castes and going nearly naked, except the cook, who was a Portuguese.

The Stable establishment was on a similar scale: 2 pair of carriage horses, my father's riding horse and mine, a coachman, groom to each horse who always ran beside him whether we drove or rode, and a grass cutter for every pair. Wages had need be small in a country where such a retinue was requisite for three people; no one doing more than one particular kind of service renders this mob of idlers a necessity. My Mother had her maid and I had mine, whose daughter also lived with us and was very useful. We hired a tailour when we wanted one, either a mender, or a mantua maker[1] or a milliner as required.

Our life was monotonous. My father and I rose before the sun, an hour or more, by lamplight, groped our way downstairs, mounted our horses, and rode till heat and light, coming together, warned us to return. I then bathed and breakfasted and lay upon the sofa reading till Fatima came to dress me. I always appeared at the family breakfast, tho' but for form. My father, who had been hard at work, fasting, made a good meal, and my Mother, only just up, did the same. We had frequently visitors at this hour; after they went my Mother walked about with the *hammauls* behind her, dusting her china, of which she very soon collected a good stock—calling out to them *subhr* when she wanted them to go on, and *aste* when they had omitted a cup or vase, for she never could manage their easy language. I wrote or worked or played and sang while the weather remained tolerably cool. In the hot months I never heard of any one able to do any thing. My father went to Court. When it was not term time, my Mother and I sometimes went in the carriage to pay visits. We very often were amused by receiving presents from the natives, and by the arrival of bhorers to tempt us with the newest fashions just received by 'a ship come in last night,' shewn first to us as such great ladies! My father received no presents himself, and permitted us to receive none but fruit and flowers; very valuable ones were at first offered to us but being invariably touched and returned, they soon ceased.

1. An eighteenth-century term for a dress maker.

The flowers generally came tied up with silver twist in the hands of the gardener, but the fruits, fresh or dried, were always in silver bowls, covered with silver gauze and brought in on the head of the messenger. Lady Hood and, they say, Mrs Blair, used to keep the bowls, but we, better instructed, returned the dull looking precious part of the offering with its dirty bit of covering, quite contented with our simpler share.

The Bhorer entered more ostentatiously with a long string of naked porters, each bearing on his head a box. All were set down and opened, and the goods displayed upon the floor, very pretty and very good, and only about double as dear as at home, a rupee for a shilling, about. The native manufacturers are cheap enough, except the shawls; and, by the bye, Mr Gardiner gave me a shawl instead of himself—it cost £100. It is a very good thing to marry the last of a sisterhood, when one meets with such generous brothers in law. At two or rather sooner we had our tiffin, after which one is never disturbed. Particular friends drop in to tiffin sometimes, but they seldom stay long, every body retiring during those hot hours, undressing and sleeping.

At first we took no luncheon beyond a little fruit and bit of bread, my father having a theory that Brahmin fare was what was suited best to India. Neither would he let me take more than a glass of wine at dinner, none at luncheon, only fruit. Also I had to wait for the family breakfast. I was near dying. Luckily this experiment took place before Uncle Edward's departure for the Neilgherries and my Aunt interfered. She could not manage all she wished, so she got Dr Eckford at Barra to give a lecture upon the climate of India and European constitutions—and being rather peremptory in their advice, I got for the future rusks and coffee immediately after coming in from my ride in the morning, meat and better beer at luncheon and a glass of sherry on sitting down to dinner. I got so well, quite fat. As I could never sleep in the day without waking with a headache, I always occupied myself one way or another in my room in the afternoons, in my large and airy room with its shaded verandah—undressing, though, which was a great refreshment, wearing only one of my *unwashed* gingham wrappers, till towards sunset when I took a bath and dressed for the carriage airing, which was never omitted, except in the heaviest days of the rains. It was very pleasant, the drives were beautiful whichever way we went, on the beach, on the Breach Candy road, or the esplanade, and twice a week across the rice fields to Matoonga to listen to the Artillery band, all the Presidency collecting there or on the esplanade. We drove up and down, stopt along side another carriage, sometimes on a cool evening got out and walked to speak to our friends. We were all very sociable, and the Band was delightful, in such good order. The equipages were extraordinary, all the horses fine, but the carriages! very shabby. The smartest soon fades in such a climate; between the heat of one season, the wet of another, the red dust, the insects, the constant use and not much care, the London built carriage makes but a poor figure the second year, and as the renewal of them is not always convenient, and a daily airing is essential, they are used in bad enough condition sometimes, nobody seems to mind so it don't signify.

On the sun going down, which he does at once like a shot, there is no twilight, the crowd separates, the ladies glad enough of a warm shawl on their dark return home, for it was often very cold driving back over the flats. Then, if we were to pass a quiet evening, a very few minutes prepared us for dinner as we wore very pretty toilettes for our airings; but if, as was generally the case, we were to be in company either at home or abroad till midnight, there was great commotion among the Ayahs to have their preparations completed in time. What Servants these Indians are. My Arab, Fatima, was always ready. The very dress I should have chosen laid out, every suitable addition to it at hand—sark, flowers, gloves, pin, scent, handkerchief, all these, and the *curls*, which if worn in that hot land must be false, so brightly brushed beside them. She was so quick in her waiting, so gentle, so quiet, so noiseless. There are many drawbacks to an Indian life, but the servants in Bombay are a luxury.

The society at the time we were there was extremely agreeable. Many of those in high places we had known at home in their less prosperous days. Scotch abounded. My cousins, too, had married well, all the six who had gone out. Poor Kate was dead, the fine girl who had been with us in

Edinburgh. I got on well with them and with their husbands, and often spent a morning with them. We used to congregate at Mrs Bax's with our work in the cool season. Mary Grant and Gregor (one of the Redcastle Grants) lived with us at the Retreat for many months. They had not been good managers and were glad to give up housekeeping for a season. She was very lovely. Mrs Bax uncommonly handsome. Mrs Ward pleased me most, both as to looks and manners; she had married a clever man, and was quite able to profit by the companionship. Little Miss Barra, a good obliging little girl, was quite one of the family party. She came out with us in the *Mountstewart Elphinstone*, and being motherless, was very grateful to us for taking care of her. So indeed was her father, a queer kind of man, and a good Doctor I may say, for he certainly set me up.

When we first came out the dinners were rather appalling; too early in the afternoons, generally between five and six o'clock. Thirty guests, one attendant at least behind every chair. Two to the *Burra Sahibs*, the great people. Stray assistants at the sideboards besides, a military band, a glare of light, the repast handsomely served on silver or plated ware, but of a rather heavy kind as far as the meats went, rounds of beef, saddles of mutton, boiled and roast turkey, pickled pork, one or two hams, fishes and soups, of course, and a second course of sweet things and small birds, but from the first the table was filled up with a number of little plates containing dried fruits, confectionery, sugar plums, and such like. A good deal of wine, good wine, was drunk and some brandy pawnee, but the bitter beer, well frothed up and cold as saltpetre could make it, was the favourite beverage, especially with the ladies. It was well that in the great houses where these great banquets were given the dining halls were of such large dimensions, so open to the air, and the servants so well trained they were never heard. Their bare feet made no sound on the matting, they never spoke, they were machines divining wants, and supplying them magically.

I hear that this cumbrous style of entertainment has been modified of late years among those who were not obliged to give official dinners. My father never adopted much this fashion. His dinners were to sixteen or eighteen people, a small assemblage in that large hall—four small joints only, nicely dressed *entrées* took the places of the beef and the salt pork—the little plates of comfits were dispensed with, so was the military band. The wines excellent, the coolness without a punkah quite pleasant. After dinner small round tables were scattered about with tea and coffee, and additional guests arrived to enliven the evening. Our parties were thought very agreeable, and the style was, I believe, copied—all but the entrées. Our Portuguese cook and my old French book created them and we did not parade our knowledge. Lord Clare afterwards thoroughly reformed the dinner table and, of course, was imitated—even by the few who had laughed at my father.

The balls were the prettiest assemblies possible, the women so young, most of them so pretty, their dresses so light, their air so happy. The men to suite, many of them in such brilliant uniforms, the numerous rooms large and well lighted, open to the cool Verandahs; excellent music, and grades enough to satisfy vanity. To a stranger there could be nothing more striking than a large ball at Government house, not the house in the Fort, but at Parell, a sort of small palace in fine grounds about four or five miles from the town. There is a very large tank in these grounds, round which on one particular day in the year, occasionally at other times, fireworks are exhibited, such fireworks as we have no idea of in this quarter of the Globe, truly magnificent and truly startling, they cannot be described, only wondered at.

The Governour in my time was the well known Sir John Malcolm, a fine soldierly looking man, coarse in mind and manners, but kind and very hospitable. His wife, with whom he did not live happily, had not come out with him. His married daughter, Lady Campbell, did the honours for a while, but, poor thing, went mad and had to be sent home. She died within a year or two, never recovering her senses. Her husband was very silly. Major Burrowes was an A. de C. and private Secretary, very popular and very agreeable. We afterwards knew him at Cheltenham, a widower with three children, as agreeable as ever, not in despair at having lost a very aerified wife, plain and cross too.

The Commander in Chief was Sir Thomas Bradford,[1] celebrated for his admirable management of the Commissariat during the latter part of the Peninsular war; a very gentlemanly person, liked by those he took a fancy to, disliked by all under his command, and quite a despot in his family, but ruled in his turn by his very odd wife, a confirmed invalid and a very fanciful one. She had been married before to a Colonel Ainslie, and had a son and a daughter of that name with her, aspects of pity to every one. The son, Captain Ainslie, was one of the A. de Camps, and did not fare much worse than the rest of the Staff. The daughter was very hardly dealt with: shabbily dressed, seldom allowed to accept any invitation, nor to speak to any one while driving in the low phaeton with her mother. She was like the Princess in the faery tale, tormented from morning till night. When dressed for a party, a rare pleasure, would be sent to bed; when some grand occasion required a fresh toilette, none was forthcoming, some old faded dress was selected. She was allowed to make no acquaintance, therefore passed the long day alone. If she did get to a dance, she did not have to converse with her partners, who all moved in the melancholy quadrille as if they too were enduring punishment. Major Jameson made us feel quite sorry for her; he was the private Secretary and a favourite, but he could only pity. The single recreation the poor girl had was the evening drive. The little carriage with the four inside was always to be seen among the crowd wherever we congregated, two of the suite as outsiders. The General bowing stiffly but abundantly, the ladies motionless for they knew so few.

Lady Bradford knew nobody for she never visited, and never appeared at the dinners at home. She had been a beautiful woman, now broken down long before her time by asthma and the madeira she took to relieve it. She never dressed but in a close cap and wrapper. When she took her

1. Sir Thomas Bradfield (1777–1853) had served with the Portuguese forces in the Peninsular War, not the Commissariat.

evening drive she put over the close cap a coarse straw cottage bonnet, and over the wrapper a cloke and she held in her hand a little parasol the size of a plate, which she crooked down by a bend or a joint in the stick, not at the time fashionable. She kept this always up between her and the sun, however low he had sunk, and then between her and the moon or the stars. Poor woman, she had left her Bradford children at home, and was always longing for her letters from those in charge of them. The severe training of her Ainslie children did not turn out well. They both married some years after into the same family, Lord Gray's of Kinfauns in Perthshire. Captain Ainslie married the youngest daughter, Jane, was an unkind husband and turned out dissipated. His sister married the Master of Gray and very nearly ruined him, between expensive dress and gambling. Lady Bradford died at St Helena on her passage home; she did not live to see those little children so beloved. Her devoted husband preserved her body in spirits, and, not properly watching the cask, it was tapped by the sailors, many of whom died from the effects of the poison. I ought to have liked her; she was very fond of me. She delighted in the old Scotch ballads, particularly the Jacobite airs, which I sang to her without musick as she lay half reclining on a sofa in the verandah. She used to 'borrow me of my mother'; that is what she called these short visits and Major Jameson said she really did enjoy this simple musick.

Sir Charles Malcolm, the Governor's brother, was in command of the Navy, a merry, pleasant, rather handsome sailor. No others of the men in high places were any way remarkable, all pleasant enough to meet. To say the truth, I did not take much to the Civilians; the elderly ones were pompous, the younger ones 'upsetting,' looking so absurdly down upon the military, who really were many of them infinitely superiour to them. Mr Bax was an intelligent man, Mr Anderson a clever man; both were kind and cousinly. James Dewar, the brother of our old companion David Dewar, though no great lawyer, was very much to be liked, as was the Advocate Depute, Mr Bridgeman, whose unfortunate Christian name, 'Orlando,' was an unfailing source of fun to Aunt Caroline.

Frequently we were enlivened by chance arrivals; passengers to and from other seaports used to touch at Bombay. In this way we had a peep of Charles Marjoribanks, who was going home for his baronetcy—too late—for he died and George Gordon Glentomie, John Peter Cumming, Archie Arbuthnot, and others, the scene was ever varying.

CHAPTER TWENTY-SEVEN

1828–1829

WE had landed in February and were fairly established in the Retreat by the middle of March. Early in April the hot weather began, encreasing day by day in intensity till the first week in June, exhausting me so completely that, but for the better beer, I never could have dragged my failing powers through it. Mr Norris fairly knocked up and had to depart suddenly for the Neilgherries, a bit of good fortune for us, as Mr Gardiner, who had been acting in the Commissariat, was promoted to act for Mr Norris as one of the secretaries to Government; he got also the loan of Mr Norris's very pretty and very cool house on the top of one of the hills near us, Prospect Lodge. This was very pleasant for Mary and me, through having no palanquins, either of us, and walking being impossible, we could not very often meet. Halfway down this hill, at the Hermitage, lived Sir Charles Chambers, a brother Judge of the Supreme Court, a heavy man, related to the Charles Grants, married to a common place wife from Glen Urquhart. At the foot of this hill was Colonel Goodfellow, who commanded the Engineers, with a daughter who played admirably on the pianoforte, and just across our tank lived a Major Griffith, who had charge of the Artillery stores, from which he made most useful presents to Miss Goodfellow and to me. I got a sweeping brush, emery powder, paper of all sorts, ink etc. And besides this he gave us most delightful musick. He was most musick mad; he had organised an excellent Band of stringed instruments, most of them Portuguese, under the direction of the Artillery Bandmaster, and whether they played in his own Compound, or in our fine hall, or better still, from boats on the tank, it was really charming to listen to the well selected and well 'interpreted,' that's the term! good classick musick.

There was one great draw back to our Retreat. The hill which rose at the end of our garden between us and the sea had on its summit the Parsee burying place, a sloping building with a grating over a deep hollow, on which grating were laid the dead bodies of the Parsees; there they lay till devoured by vultures; the bones then dropt through. The condition of the deceased in the new state, or purgatory, into which death has introduced him, is determined by the part of the corpse first attacked by the vultures. An eye ensures happiness, any part of the head is comforting; an arm I suppose is useless as one was dropt in our shrubbery. The vulture is a disgusting bird with its long neck bare of feathers; the first time I saw one seated on my window sill I was really horrified.

The heat encreased, no air by day or by night. We lay on mats with no covering, not even a sheet, as little clothing as possible in the day and all loose, no bands or belts or collars, exertion of any kind exhausting, occupation too fatiguing, even thinking nearly impossible; and the thermometer was not high—94 or 96; it was the moisture of the climate that overcame us; it was completely enervating, and its effect on the skin most thoroughly disgreeable. It was the approach of the Monsoon. Most people left Bombay at this time in search of a drier atmosphere at Poonah or elsewhere. Luckily, this extreme heat did not last long.

The opening of the monsoon is one of the grandest phenomena in nature. About a week or two before the outbreak clouds began to gather over a sky that had been hitherto without relief. Day by day the gloom thickened; at last the storm broke. We were going to sit down to luncheon when a feeling of suffocation, a distant rumbling, a sudden darkness, made us all sensible of some unusual change approaching. The servants rushed to the venetians and closed one side of the hall, with the utmost expedition, the side next the storm; yet they could not save us altogether—from the wind they did, a wind, suddenly rising, burst from the plain with a violence which overwhelmed every opposing object, and while the gust lasted we could hear nothing else, not a step, nor a voice, nor a sound of any kind. It did no harm to our well secured apartment, but it brought with it a shower, a tempest rather, of sand, so fine, so impalpable, that it entered like the air through every crevice, covered the floor, the seats, the tables with a red dust which well nigh choked us. This was succeeded by a lull almost awful in its intensity, and then the first thunder growled; at a vast distance it seemed to rumble, then, strengthening, it broke suddenly right over the house with a power that was overwhelming; flash after flash of lightning glared, it was more, far more, than a gleam; then rain, such as is only known in the tropicks, poured down in flakes with the din of a cataract. On came the thunder; again and again it shook the house, rolling round in its fearful might as if the annihilation of the world were its dreadful aim.

My Mother and I were as pale as two spectres. In my life, neither before nor since, I never felt so thoroughly appalled. It lasted about two hours, after which a heavy rain set in, falling dully and equally hour upon hour until about tiffin time the following day, when we had a second thunder storm, less terrifick, however, than the first, or less to us from having had that sample. After this the heavy rain continued unceasingly for 48 hours, making such a noise it deafened us, completely, we could hear no other sound, and creating darkness and a chill damp feel equally oppressive. The roads were soon like streams, the plain a lake, the tanks overflowing. No Europeans stirred out. A party collected at the Shiltons for tiffin only, remained at this bungalow during those three first violent days—only such natives stirred beyond the shelter of a house as could not avoid going out on business, and they were dressed for the deluge in oilskin coverings that enveloped the whole person, face and all, out of which they saw thro' two glass eyes inserted at the proper place, the most hideous masquerade, but absolutely necessary. The first desperate week over, the rain fell less constantly and less heavily. We even got a drive sometimes, as it was occasionally fair for an hour or more but all thro' the rains, which lasted near 4 months, the weather was extremely disagreeable in Bombay, hot, chilly, airless, relaxing, every thing wet we touched. Pans of fire had to be placed in the rooms frequently. All our clothes had to be dried on cane skreens made like boxes, or large cases, within which were the same pans of fire, and still the damp clung to us; yet it was never an unhealthy season.

Up the country the rain was much lighter, more like showery weather at home up at Poonah and beyond. People enjoyed the freshness extremely, while we at the sea side were steaming like the pipes of a factory. The last week rivalled the first very nearly, the Monsoon departing, as it came, in a storm of thunder.

I was glad to see cloudless skies again. October was, however, a melancholy month; pools of stagnant water, decaying vegetation, unpleasant smells, and sickness, such sickness. Now was the time that small white tents filled every space upon the esplanade; the little crazy bungalows that had been hurriedly removed at the first threatening of the rains were now being leisurely replaced, and amongst them and around them was an encampment of the sick from the upcountry stations come down for advice, or for a change, or their furlough to England. The Doctors had busy times moving about in gigs or palanquins doing their best to save the invalids. One of the busiest of these was our Scotch friend, Doctor Eckford. We saw a great deal of him, for we had got very intimate. I had been very ill, an attack of liver, and he was very kindly attentive to me, and had taken quite a fancy to me, on account, I believe, of the leaf I brought him out of his Wife's pocket book. But really, old as I was, I was quite in fashion—a second season of celebrity, a coming out again! Like my father, I have all my life looked 10 years younger than my age; nobody guessed me at 30, and being handsome, lively, obliging and a great man's daughter, I reigned in good earnest over many a better queen! than myself. Of course every eligible was to be married to me, not only that but every body was busy marrying me. 'Now, don't mind them, Eliza, my dear,' said uncle Edward very early in my Indian career; 'don't fix yet, wait for Smith, my friend Smith; he'll be sure to be down here next season, and he's just the very man I have fixed on for you.' Then my Aunt, 'I don't mind your not liking old so and so and that tiresome this, and that ill humoured that, I had rather you married Colonel Smith than any body.' Then my cousins, 'Oh you will so like Colonel Smith, Eliza, every one likes Colonel

Smith, he will make such a kind husband, he is so kind to his horses.' 'My goodness, Miss Grant,' said Mrs Norris, 'is it possible you have refused —— the best match in the Presidency—will certainly be in Council. Who do you mean to marry, pray.' (Every body must marry, they can't help it here.) 'I am waiting,' said I, 'for Colonel Smith.' Great laughing this caused, of course, none laughing more than the intending Bride, to whom this Colonel Smith was no more than a bit of fun, just as likely to be her husband as her most particular admirer, a great fat Parsee.

One morning I was sitting at work; the cooler weather had restored us our needles and I was employing mine for Mary's expected baby, early in November, my Mother lying on the sofa reading, when the Chobdar in waiting announced Colonel Smith. It is customary for all new arrivals to call on the Burra Sahibs. He entered, and in spite of all the nonsense we had amused outselves with, we liked him. 'Well,' said Mary, on hearing who had called, 'will he do?' 'Better than any of your upsetting Civilians,' answered I, 'a million of times, I never liked the Military at home and here I don't like the Civilians. Colonel Smith is the most gentlemanly man I have seen in India.' Mary and Mr Gardiner laughed and neither they nor I thought more about him.

He had come down from Satara, where he commanded, for change of air, not being well. He lived with his friend Doctor Eckford, and we frequently met them in the evenings driving out together and sometimes we met them in society, but our paths did not seem to cross. He paid no particular attention to me neither do I recollect being at all occupied about him, nor did he dine once in my father's house till many months after we had become acquainted. My father and he had got on a sort of pleasant intimacy ages before he seemed to think of me. We used to meet generally in the mornings. We rode always, my father and I, on the Breach Candi road, which was close to us and agreeable from its skirting the sea, and probably the breeze and the sun rise pleased our new companion, as he came a considerable distance to enjoy them. He also seemed to like political disquisitions, for he and my father rode on before deep in Catholick claims which were then being finally discussed in Parliament,[1] while I had plenty to do, by myself, in managing that dreadful Donegal and watching the Parsees' morning adoration of the sun. I had also a certain green book to reflect on; two thick volumes, handsomely bound, lent me, as well as the horse, by Mr Bax; his travels in MS., a small illegible hand and very prosy composition in which the Czar, a grand Duchess, two Archdukes, and Princes, Sultans, and Counts palatine figured in profusion.

These rides in this guise continued all the cold weather, our party latterly reinforced by my cousin John Cumming, who was staying with us, and who sometimes got twisted out of his usual place by me to the side of my father, Colonel Smith exchanging with him for a turn or two, to my father's regret, who on these occasions observed that the Captain had inopportunely interrupted a very interesting argument on the influence of the Irish priesthood over the flocks; that poor Smith was a sad Orangeman, quite benighted, but honest and worth enlightening. It was Mr Gardiner and his radical- ism over again.

So began my happy future to gleam on me, particularly after a few, half laughing, half earnest, hints from Dr Eckford, whom my Mother about this time began to talk of as Love's messenger, and then styled roundly Cupid. Such a Cupid. Children, you have seen him, I need say no more. Cupid knew his business well. He threw shafts and bow away as unsuitable to a staid Brigadier and a maiden past her prime. His object was to touch the lady's reason, which he did, no matter how, and the parents too, a matter effected principally by the Irish acres, warranted not to be bog. Who would have thought a marriage thus systematically arranged could have turned out so well. It took a long time for India, tho', and while it was progressing, to the mystification of all lookers on who could not understand why it did not go on in Caesar fashion and be settled on the 3rd day, my Mother's 1st grandchild, dear little Janie Gardiner, was born. It was my

1. Daniel O'Connell's attempt to persuade Wellington's government to pass the Catholic Relief Act dominated the politics of this year.

brother John's birthday, the 23rd of November, and all the cousinhood were assembled at the Retreat to do him honour; Gregor and Mary Grant were indeed staying with us. Mr Gardiner and Mary were expected, but just before dinner they sent their excuse; she did not feel quite well. On leaving the hall a note from Mr Gardiner summoned my Mother, and after the Company departed, I set off myself, up to Prospect Lodge, mounting the long, long, dimly lighted flight of steps that led up the side of the hill without a thought of the snakes at other times I used to be nervous about.

The clock had struck 12; it was the 24th.; 5 minutes after my arrival my little niece was laid upon my knees, and I believe for weeks after I thought of no other existing creature. These Memoirs are but the fair outside, after all, a deal is hid, both as regards myself and others, that it would be painful to record and worse than useless to remember. We 3 sisters had gone thro' much. This blessed baby opened another view of life to all; all loved and welcomed it and leaned on it but our strange mother, who paid it very little attention, never sent for it, never asked for it, never gave it one single gift or even nursed poor Mary. Perhaps she did not like the shove back a grade; there was another generation born and she, the once beautiful wife, was a Grandmother. Somehow she never took to Mary married. She liked none of our marriages. Jane's one could understand her regretting for tho' Colonel Pennington was rich and respected, he was old and ugly. Mr Gardiner, well connected, high in the Civil Service and with £20,000 private property, good looking, gentlemanly, clever, good and six and thirty, he was really a bit of good luck for a tocherless lass, however lang her pedigree. But she never cared for him, for her or their child while they were near her. Afterwards they were highly praised, when they were gone and she felt what they had been to her.

To me I know my baby niece was a perfect delight. All the pleasant cold weather, I walked about with it in my arms whenever it was brought to the Retreat or I could contrive a visit to Prospect Lodge. Mr Gardiner and Mary went very little into company. Before the birth of the baby Mary had been for months very suffering, first the heat and then the rains incommoded her greatly. She never took to her Indian life, never could bear the climate nor suit herself to the ways nor endure the habits nor the society—*that* indeed she undervalued very absurdly and in consequence of her air, she was in turn undervalued herself, so that the spirit of discontent which pervaded the atmosphere around her, quite prevented her life from being a happy one. She never took any exercise, never rose to meet the fresh air in the mornings; the evening drive was often shirked and when the pair in their hideous landaulet did set forth in sulky looking state, they shunned the general meeting place and moved along some byepath all alone. I was a thousand times happier. Our Retreat was a little pompous in some of its arrangements and the fine coach with the Chobdars was a dignified vehicle, rather. I should have preferred Mrs Dewar's gig, for my life was dull, very lonely except just at those hours when meals, the drive or company brought my father, my Mother and myself together. So passed the months until the beginning of March brought a degree of heat again, which poor Mary felt too oppressive. I do believe the poor thing was never well, had never been well from a child and that the merest trifles affected her ill organised frame. At any rate, she was ill, and advised to try the cooler air of the higher land. So an expedition was arranged to Khandalla, a beautiful plain at the head of the pass up the Ghauts on the road to Poonah. These finely shaped, very picturesque mountains enclosed the Bay at its inner extremity, seeming to run near and round it, and to shut it in its 100 wooded islands out from the rest of the world. In reality there was a wide plain to traverse before reaching their base, and the bay to cross before reaching the plain.

As Mary would be dull alone, I was to go with her and her husband, a plan I liked. A change was pleasant, a journey in India new, life in tents! delightful.

The ugly landaulet conveyed the Gardiner *Sahibs*, their baba, and her ama or wetnurse, and a peon to the Bunder. I, escorted by my father, proceeded thither in a queer sort of old pony carriage left especially for my use by Uncle Edward; and strange to say, for an Indian lady, I carried no attendant of any sort with me.

The luggage had gone before with the other servants and the tents. We had a sail of some hours, the scenery so beautiful, varying every moment as we scudded among the islands, then on landing, we rested, while the queer pony carriage which had come over with us was prepared to take us on; it shook us famously and tired Mary, so she took a sleep at the next bungalow, where we left it, and at dusk entered our palanquins, travelling on by torch light, a goodly train, up a steep hill, as I felt from the tilt of the palanquin, tho' I could see nothing. At last it was level ground again, and then a short half hour brought us to our encampment.

I saw, on alighting, only a pretty, oblong room, floor matted, walls and ceiling white as usual, but ceiling domed which was not usual; lamps depending from it, and a well served table laid for dinner with every appendage we were used to elsewhere. We had a pleasant meal in spite of fatigue. Tea, as usual; and then, preceded by a torch bearer, and accompanied by the Head Servant, Mary, her Ayah, who was to wait on me, and Mr Gardiner, highly amused at our state of excitement, I retired to my own tent, which I was lucky enough to get into without entangling my feet in the tent cords. There all was in order like my own bed chamber, my own furniture, most of it, having been transported as if by magick for my use, even to the bath, some books, and the writing table.

After undressing her mistress the Ayah returned, and laid herself down near the door of my tent, inside; a peon stretched himself outside, between the tent and the curtain, and the guard, two or three strong, patrolling around, we all went to sleep as securely as tho' our walls had been of stone instead of canvas.

Next morning, very early, I stept out to feel the cool air and look down on a gully of exquisite verdure opening out into a vast plain of beauty, spreading far away without a limit; the scene around was flat just where we were pitched, but in the distance were rising grounds, woods, and a few shrubs dotted here and there in patches; the road stretched along at a little distance. Very fine the scene was, but it was the air that was so charming. We were just on the brow of the ravine, so that we caught the breeze at once.

Any one looking up at us must have thought the little encampment a very pretty sight, the four larger tents in a semicircle in front, the rowlies for the servants behind, the horses picketted out under the only tope of trees at hand, and beside them the fire, where breakfast was preparing under the cover of the 'cloudless sky.'

How the little baby enjoyed the morning air, sprawling almost naked on its mat after a refreshing bath. We would not let them dress it all the day, there being nobody to remark upon the simplicity of its toilette. We passed our day as usual, books and work—no healthy play, however, the middle hours being very hot, just as sultry as in Bombay, but there was not that relaxing moisture. In the evenings we drove along the road till dark. Once or twice we went as far as the wood of Lanowlie, a beautiful bit of scenery, the wood enclosing both a hill and a tank. The shade appeared to us so irresistible, the glare at our ravine being almost painful, that Mr Gardiner determined on shifting our position. So we had the diversion of moving our camp, striking our tents, packing our goods, travelling our miles, and setting all up again.

The change was delightful, the tents among the trees looked prettier than ever; the horses, in full view, so completely sheltered, were a picture; the air from the water so cool; the flowers in the wood so lovely! I went walking there as far as the creepers would let me, but their trunks and tendrils were so thick, so interlaced among the branches of the forest trees, and there were so many thorns, that in spite of the shade, and a pleasant pathway and the exquisite flowers and the verdure I could get but a little way, and I had to give up the romantick intention of a moonlight ramble therein. I therefore, spent the evening in hanging round my tent large clusters of the blue persian grape, a basket full of which I had bought from a travelling fruitseller. These grapes are extremely delicious, high flavoured, sweet, juicy, yet more of the consistency, size, and shape of a plum than we are used to in grapes. They ripen to perfection at Poonah, and if properly dried make fine raisins. Mary was busy in the same way; our work done, we went to tea, and then to bed after a visit to Janie. I thought, as I turned in to my tent, that a prettier scene had never been fancied. The bright moon-light on the water, the horses beneath the trees, the flickering fire, the white tents with the sleeping figures near them, and the watchful guard moving like dark shadows back and fore. It was gypsey life in its Sunday suit; there was something delightfully free, natural about it, and I thought to myself it would not be at all disagreeable to move thus about with a regiment, especially if one belonged to any one in high enough rank to command as many servants as my civilian brother in law.

And so, I lay me down in peace and took my rest. What waked me? A noise, which once heard can never be forgotten, a noise unlike any other sound in nature, a growl, so deep, so low, so full, so strong, that it almost paralysed sensation. It was just at my ear; there was only a bit of canvas between me and a tiger.

Mine was a single tent, the door of it was open; the moonlight streamed in and shewed me the peon standing upright, shivering with fear, and no Ayah. 'Hush, sahib,' whispered the peon, ''tis the great tiger.'

The wood of Lanowlie was known to the natives as a favourite haunt of this dreadful creature, which is worship-ped by some of native tribes of the neighbourhood, and, therefore, is held too sacred to be exterminated. Not very long before our encroachment on his haunts, the post between Bombay and Poonah, a native runner had dis-appeared, leaving no trace beyond a fragment of turban among some bushes near the road. This came into my mind at the moment—a long one as it seemed; then came the growl again, but not so near; then the scream of the horses, I never heard a horse scream before, nor since; it is a fearful sound, and then came Mr Gardiner's voice. Such a blessed relief. He told me not to fear, that the Tiger had only come to drink at the tank, that the array of human beings would frighten it, that we were all safe, while there were horses, goats and buffaloes to be had, and that the cords and pegs of the tents would ensure the safety of the inmates.

The Ayah, poor soul, had fled at the first alarm to her mistress to call attention to the baby. Mary was with her child in a moment. Next came firing, great firing, the muskets of the guard, Mr Gardiner's pistols; then all the pots and pans began. Every servant seized on one and rattled and shook and beat and thumped; then they screeched and hallooed and screamed; really the tiger must have been more than beast had he remained among such a din. He wisely turned and leaped away, nor did he shew again. Of course our watch and noise continued to make all sure; but he had had enough of us, and we had had enough of Lanowlie. Nothing would induce Mary to risk her precious baby near such a neighbour another day. So a messenger was despatched on the moment to have a boat ready, and at daybreak we broke up our camp in earnest and set out on our return to Bombay.

We drove to the top of the pass, got into palanquins there, and found breakfast ready for us in the bungalow at the foot of the Ghauts. These bungalows are wretched places. A single room unfurnished, bare walls, mud floor, plenty of insects, reptiles even, for scorpions are common in them; no comforts but such as the travellers themselves provided. We were glad enough, however, to find rest and shelter after the excitement of the descent, which in broad daylight gave me here and there a shudder. At one point, a sharp turn brought the side of the palanquin on the edge of a precipice that fell straight down 5 or 600 feet, with not even a bush to break the line till close to the bottom. We crossed the harbour in the afternoon, and just about dark we reached the Retreat, where, instead of sympathy, we were met with shouts of laughter for having quailed before the tiger.

My letters from Khandalla and my more vivid descriptions in conversation had quite bitten my father with a wish to change the relaxing air of the seaside for the freshness of the mountains; but he meditated a much more daring exploit than a visit to the Poonah Ghauts. Colonel Smith, who had been his constant riding companion in my absence, had inspired him with a wish to see more of the country, to try a few weeks of the Mahableishwa hills during the present hot season, when really Bombay was too oppressive. These charming hills were in our new friend's district; he commanded the Brigade at Satara, and Mahableishwa, tho' distant 30 miles, was included. He had been, it seems, most extremely eloquent in his descriptions of the scenery, the lights and shadows, mists, and other phenomena, and had kindly offered every assistance as to preparations, routes, encampment there, etc.

My Mother, who began to have her suspicions as to the cause of all this politeness, exhibited no wish to move. She did not feel it the least too hot where she was, nor did she like the idea of packing, moving, going in boats, in palanquins, over the sea and up precipices, to live in tents without any comforts.

My father, however, was quite taken up with the plan; Colonel Smith dined two or three days running to concoct all the plans properly, tho' they were quickly enough arranged seemingly, for he was listening to my ballads all the evenings, and then one morning he called to take leave. He was to start early next day for Mahableishwa, where he meant to remain till the rains began, would lose no time in doing—I forget what—choosing a spot for our tents, I believe, and would write full particulars of all we were to expect on our journey.

Preparations were accordingly begun. My father and his head Servant Nasserwanjee were closetted for hours for several days, and at last all was announced as ready. My Mother and I did nothing, the ayahs packed our clothes, taking more a great deal than we wished, but Fatima, who had travelled hundreds of miles, hundreds of times, with her former mistresses, Mesdames Hunter Blair and Baker, was not to be thwarted, and she was right; she understood ruralising in India a deal better than we did.

With the exception of our large tin cases, we seemed to have left every thing we generally used behind, for we missed nothing up to the very moment of our departure; yet we must have brought all with us, for I, at least, never asked for a single article afterwards that was not forthcoming. They are wonderful managers, these Indian Servants.

We drove to the Fort, on to the Harbour, descended the broad steps of the ghaut, and entered a very good boat with a neat cabin in it sheltered by an awning. The sail down the coast of Malabar was very pretty indeed, the blue sea under so brightly blue a sky, wooded shores, and a background of mountains. We had room enough to move about, for only the Upper servants were with us, the rest, with the horses, the tents and other luggage, followed in our wake. Near sunset we reached Bancoote; it was quite a pleasure to climb up on our own feet, so seldom used in that country, a rather steep path to a half ruined tower on a point of rock, which was to be our resting place for the night. The view from it was very fine, over land and sea and up a river which flowed rather swiftly round the rock.

We were still admiring it when called to dinner, and there, in the bare walled turret room, was as neatly laid a table and as nice a small repast as any people need ever wish to sit down to. It had all been prepared on board the servants' bunderboat. We had no roasts, but fish, and stews, and curry, rice, fruit, and vegetables, all as well prepared as in the good kitchen at the Retreat. A saunter afterwards, and early to bed, my room as comfortable as in a warm climate was necessary, my own furniture in it, a shawl hung up against the unshuttered window to keep the land wind out and Fatima's little cot close to the door.

Colonel Smith had begged us to get over the bar at the mouth of the river with the morning tide, which served very early, and would help us on in our course up it; we were then to make no delay on leaving the boats but to push on up the mountain to a certain place—Mowlie, I think—where we were to pitch our tents for the night; but my father preferred his own plans. The boats got over the bar, or we had others which were within the bar. I don't know which—we went down to them I know in palanquins, and it was not a short trot; we had had our breakfast first very comfortably in the ruined tower, dressing leisurely, admiring the view, and gathering branches of oleander, almond, and other beautiful flowering shrubs unknown to me.

It was all so pleasant in the cool of the morning, but the river was very far from pleasant in the heat of the noon day; part of the way it was confined by high banks, which reflected the sun's rays, and kept all air from us. We had not brought an awning, and the roof of the cabin soon heated thro'. It was really three or four hours of suffering. On landing, my Mother was so done up that the plan was again departed from, and instead of pushing on up the pass, we resolved on resting—to dine at the spot we had been warned against at the foot of the mountain, a pretty little plain facing the *west*, a rock rising behind it and enclosing it, a hot wind blowing. It was a foretaste of what awaits the doomed, rest there was none. Every stitch of clothes but a gingham wrapper I threw off me, tucked up the sleeves, opened the collar, pulled off my rings, took out my combs, which actually scorched my head, and, creeping below the table in my tent, lay there more dead than alive till the signal for moving was given; dinner was countermanded, and a little fruit welcomed instead. When we were to march my palanquin was so burning I could not breathe in it; they threw *chatties* of water over it, and up rose a steam worse than the scorching. We had to wait half an hour before I could bear its atmosphere.

At last we were off, and as the sun declined and the air cooled, and the ascending path brought the mountain breezes to us, I was able to look up and out, and enjoy the singular scene presented by our party.

A *burra Sahib* needs a large retinue when travelling in the East, or did need it years ago; all may be altered now that we hear of dawks,[1] roads and railroads. First went Nasserwanjee on a *tattoo* (a little pony) leading us all, sword in hand, for the scabbard only hung gallantly by his side, the naked blade flourished at every turn above his head; next were some Sepoys or peons, then my Mother's palanquin and her spare bearers, then mine and more peons, then my father's, then the two Ayahs'; then the upper servants on ponies, but without swords; then under servants on foot or on bullocks; the luggage, tents, canteens, trunks, all on bullocks, peons and coolies running beside them to the number altogether of 50 or 60, with the beasts besides and our horses led. It was a long train winding round among the hills, always ascending and turning corners, and when night came on, and the torches were lighted and one was placed in about every fourth man's hand—the effect was wonderfully beautiful, the flames waving as the arms moved, leaves, branches, rocks, gleaming in turn among the dusky train that wound along up the steep pathway. Daylight might not have been so picturesque, but it

1. Anglo-Indian: relays of men or horses used for trans-
   porting mail or passengers.

would have been far more suitable to the kind of journey, and the distance being considerable, many a weary step was taken before we reached our resting place.

It was near midnight when we came to three tents sent by General Robertson for our accommodation. All we wanted was soon ready, for a fire was there, burning in a furnace made of some stones, the usual travelling fire place. Our curry was reheated, I had near a bottle of beer, and my bed being ready by the time this supper was over, I was soon fast asleep in a region as wild as Glen Ennich.

My Mother was quite reconciled to our journey next morning, for a messenger arrived very early with two notes for my father, one from General Robertson, Colonel Robertson then, and one from Colonel Smith; they were notes of welcome, with directions, which warned by the sufferings of yesterday, we obeyed; very kind they were. Every body is kind in India—but it was not that that pleased my mother, it was the messenger. He was one of the irregular horse, a native, light made, handsomely dressed, in coloured trowsers, flowing robe, and yellow cap, I think, and he rode well and caracoled his little spirited horse before us for just as long as we pleased to look at him. She took it into her head that he was one of Colonel Smith's regiment, which regiment was Heaven knows where—in Gujerat, I believe, so she asked Nasserwanjee for a rupee to give to him, and did the civil with the air of a Princess. She certainly, good, dear Mother, liked the rôle of the great lady.

After breakfast we started again on our somewhat perilous road. At least I sometimes trembled a little lest the palanquin bearers should make a false step but on they went through all, and by all, and over all safely, up the steep, very steep rises, down the sharp descents, round those dreadful corners revealing depths that made one shudder. On they went, with their short quick trot that seldom slackened, giving the regular grunt which apparently relieves the chest. They generally have a jar of water slung behind the palanquin a draught of which is the only refreshment I ever saw them take. Parts of this pass were finely wooded, parts bare and rocky, and fine though without water, no roaring cataract nor gliding stream. This is a great want in the landscape throughout India. A long ascent, just as dark, and then a stretch of level road, brought us to the end of our journey. A large double poled tent of Colonel Smith's, which was to be lent to us during our stay on the hills and in which we found his servants and the table laid for dinner. He was himself dining at Colonel Robertson's, so my Mother was able to scrutinise the premises. I was really ashamed of her behaviour. She walked here and there, observed the chairs, the lights, the table linen, and much admired the plate—'Upon my word, Miss Grant, your Colonel is very handsomely supplied, there's really nothing wanting.' The words gave a sort of shock to me. It was the first time I had heard either her or my father connect the Colonel's name with mine. I knew how all these attentions would end from that moment. We had a very good dinner very well served, and retired to our sleeping tents in great good humour. The night was so piercing cold we called for blanket after blanket, the chill of the water next morning was really painful; and as Fatima chose to take the dust of the journey out of my long, long hair outside the tent before I had all my warmer clothing on, I was really shivering. A canter however warmed me and gave me also a good view of the curious place we were settled on. A wide plain on the top of a long ridge of mountains, not much wood near us, but plenty all round, no rising either close at hand, with one exception, a hillock on which stood the Governour's small bungalow, his and the Resident's a little way off, were the only houses at the Station. Everybody else including the sick soldiers sent up there lived in tents, scattered about anywhere in groups of from three to five and six according to the size of each establishment. Riding, we came on the head of beautiful gullies far below us, stretching far out under the morning mist. We looked *down* on mountain tops, stood *above* wooded ravines, which made the scenery so curious.

The air was enchanting, the sun hot in the middle of the day, yet quite bearable, the mornings and evenings delightful, the nights rather cold. The society was on the pleasantest picknicky footing; the way of life most agreeable as soon as we got into it. The first few days we kept our Bombay hours, late dinners, and so on, therefore an exchange of calls with our neighbours was the extent of our intercourse. But as soon as we shewed ourselves well bred enough to conform to the habits of the place we got on merrily : dined at the Robertsons' often, lunched here and there, gave little dinners and little luncheons, and went with parties to the only two lions that there were, the sources of some river and a hill fort. We had Mrs James Farquharson, poor Pauline, and her sister Mrs Simson. A fat man who amused us all, and a thin padre whom we must have amused, for he was always smiling; Sir Lionel Smith, and others.

One very disagreeable circumstance met us there, indeed accompanied us every where, my father's unfortunate dispute with the Government. It had begun some weeks before, and arose thus. Some native case, about Ramchander something else, I may well remember the name, for goodness knows how many times I had to write it over, I often, in any hurry or on confidential affairs, clerked for my father, which had been before the Sudder for some length of time, was removed into the Supreme Court, where the opinion of the 3 Judges on its merits was in direct opposition to that of the Company's.[1] Before my father's appointment, there had been serious misunderstandings between those two powers, each having been in some degree to blame. My father had been well 'advised' by the Board of Controul that it would be very agreeable to have these differences healed and that he could do nothing that would be better approved at home both by the Board of Controul and the Court of Directors than to put an end to these unseemly jarrings. The Bombay Government, anxious to support their own authorities, were delighted at the new Judge's connexion with one of their own servants. Uncle Edward seized on my father at once, seconded by Mr Norris, telling their own version of Sir Edward West's mistakes; but that little wasp with his King's servants and his pomposity and his flattery of similar

1. The case was Moroo Ragonath against his uncle
   Pandoorung Ramchunder; a writ was issued in February 1829. It turned on whether the court's jurisdiction extended outwith the island and factories of Bombay.
   Sir Charles Chambers was one of the other judges.

weakness, aided by the heavy weight of Sir Charles Chambers, got the upper hand of the Civil Service, and enlisted my father in right earnest on their own side. The Sudder Adawlut ordered one thing, the Supreme Court ordered another, the Governour in Council interfered, and the King's Judges ignored the Government.

Mr Norris very unluckily had gone to the Neilgherries; the only Indian my father considered to have brains, a mistake rather, but he would take advice from no other. Mr Gardiner came to me one day in real alarm, he was acting Secretary then, to say that a most intemperate paper had been sent in by the 3 judges, and that as they were most decidedly in the wrong, on some points, serious disputes having grave results would be the consequence. I could not speak; he did without effect; I tried my Mother, but she as usual was on the fighting side; these pugnacious women have much to answer for. So the quarrel spread till it became personal. All parties lost temper, all parties listened to tittle tattle, Mr Caw did mischief, poor man, as usual, chiefly by filling my Mother's head with little low whisperings of slights, and slighting words, most of them inventions, and so it went on till both parties appealed to home.

At this point Sir Edward West suddenly died, his Widow followed him in a week or so, leaving one Orphan child, a little delicate girl, to the care of Sir Charles and Lady Chambers. In a month Sir Charles died too. Lady Chambers, poor woman, waited for her confinement, my Mother and I standing Godmothers to the poor posthumous child, Anne Catherine, and then sailing with all the Orphans for England.

The overwork of the Courts quite pleased my father, who went on capitally all his own way, as busy as half a dozen; but the Bombay Government interfering again about that Ramchander business, he, in a pet, closed the Court, a step every body, including my mother, condemned; but he was thoroughly out of temper, and no one to hold him in.

I forget whether he closed the Courts before or after our visit to Mahableishwa, but the dispute was in full vigour at that time, so we were out of the range of all the Governour's civilities, never asked to meet him either—that is, collectively.

I individually was quite his friend, riding with him frequently in the mornings, particularly on the hills, at least till he fancied he might be thought in the way. He used to read me the letters he received from his wife and children, sent me their pictures, newspapers, new books, fruit, flowers, etc. And when it was known that I was soon to remove to Satara, he not only wished me joy with all his heart, and told me I was marrying one of the best fellows in the service, but he confided to me that in the contemplated changes there would no longer be a Brigadier at Satara, the Resident would command what troops were necessary, and that Colonel Smith would be moved. Where would I like to go to. Akmednugger, he called it Nugger, was a good climate and a pleasant place, quite in the way of travellers, he'd send him there if the Station suited me. Only once we got upon the quarrel; he said if I had been my father's Wife instead of his daughter it would never have gone such lengths; so he had listened to gossip too.

I took very much to Colonel and Mrs Robertson; he was delightful, he was quite a Scotchman, mostly a self educated one, and not refined but his innate goodness and long habits of command had given him the manner of a man in authority. He looked great at the head of his own *long* table, beaming his benevolent smiles all round, reading Burns aloud at some of our pleasant gatherings with the accent and the feeling of a country man. Here, too, we made the better acquaintance of Major Jameson, son of old Bailie Jameson at Inverness, connected with the Alves's, Inglis's, and other good northern bodies. Good natured man, he used to devote hours to my mother gossiping with her over all the north *countrie*. She liked him better than any person in Bombay, and was certainly a very great deal happier after he came among us. He was not in my Colonel's regiment, but in one of the other Cavalry ones, and wore the handsome french gray uniform with silver. My Colonel used to meet me most mornings just where the path from our tents joined the road; we then went on together, generally towards Satara. One day either I was earlier than usual, or he was later, at any rate I arrived at the trysting place and he was not there. I did not know that I looked disappointed, but I looked up and down the road, I suppose. 'The Colonel Sahib has gone on,' said the syce,[1] pointing to the fresh marks of a horse's feet. I am sure I blushed, like the 'rosy morn', a little at the man's sharpness, a little at my cool Colonel's easy way of taking matters. Didn't he pay for it. I should think so—he sometimes breakfasted with us, but very rarely, for sooth to say our breakfasts were not tempting to those Indian palates; toast and tea and butter, nothing more, no fish, no rice, no curry.

I had my coffee as usual after my ride, and then I often took a stroll round the tents, and then sat with a book near the curtain, which acted door, looking out on the scene around. Here I passed an hour or so before my father and mother joined me. She never rose early; he had very much given up his morning ride, not liking, perhaps, to meet the Governour. After breakfast we had our usual occupations, visitors or visiting, and then a neat toilette for an early dinner at home or elsewhere. In the evening often a saunter, and I, often a drive in Colonel Smith's gig, none of us having brought up other carriages.

One day I had a ride on an elephant, an extremely disagreeable mode of moving, like a boat heaving up the wrong way. The great beast kneeled down when desired, and I got up his side by the help of a little ladder of 6 or 8 rungs slung to his back, and entered a curricle seat with a head to it. The roll of the creature as it rose was horrid, its awkward walk ditto, I was very glad to get safe on the ground again. Our strolls in the gray of the evening were checked by the appearance of a small green serpent, whose bite was venomous; a peon of the Robertsons' died in consequence, and as we did not know where they might be, their colour concealing them too, we gave up our wanderings.

I was one morning writing at a table near the door of the tent, my toes touching a pile of books on the ground beneath it. Nasserwanjee came behind, and laying one hand on my shoulder to keep me in the chair and the other on the back of the chair, he pulled both back together, asking pardon for the liberty all the while. When I was at a safe distance, two peons moved forward and dashed a billet of wood on one of these

1. Attendant, following a horseman on foot.

little serpents, which had been lying close to the books and my toes—there's a pleasant little interlude in one's occupations. I saw only one other strange animal in these mountains—a large monkey, or an ape rather, which I took for a little old Indian hindu, gray with age, for it was walking upright with a branch in its hand.

And now our time was up, and we were to go back to Bombay, and it was necessary to acquaint Sir John and Miladi that I thought it wiser to go off instead to Satara. It was but 30 miles, every comfort was already there in my Colonel's bungalow, most of my wardrobe was with me, and some furniture. A clergyman was at hand—the smiling one—the Judge could grant the license, and the Resident do all the rest.

My father was delighted, particularly when he heard all the particulars of the Irish estate, the bachelour brother etc. He was charmed, too, at the idea of the mountain wedding, so queer, so primitive. I think he wanted to get rid of me with as little expense, too, as possible. Not so my Mother. She had no wish for any marriage, it would only throw so much more trouble on her. She did not see that either of my sisters had done much for herself by her determination to marry. Jane married to an old man who might be her grandfather, hideously ugly, and far from rich. Mary shut up with her airs and her baby, never seeing a creature, nor of any use to any one. She did not understand this craze for marrying; pray, who was to write all the notes. Colonel Smith was no great catch, just a soldier. An Irish lad who went out as a Cadet, like George McIntosh of the Dell and 50 more such, and a marriage huddled up in that sort of way, in a desert, on a mountain, without a church, or a cake, or any preparations, it would be no marriage at all, neither decent nor respectable; she, for one, should never consider people married who had been buckled together in that *couple beggar* fashion. If there were to be a marriage at all it should be a proper one, in the Cathedral at Bombay by the clergyman who there officiated, friends at the wedding, and every thing as it ought to be.

So there was no help, she was resolute. We had to travel down the ghaut, and along the plains, a 100 miles, I think, for she would have no more sea, and travel back again after the ceremony, at the loss of a month's extra pay, for the Colonel did not receive his allowances when on leave. Well, there was another dilemma. While I had been riding with Colonel Smith, Rose, my mother's pretty half caste maid, had been walking with Serjeant Herring, the officer in charge of the invalids, and when she found that I was to be married, she confided to me that she meant to marry too, that live in that large Retreat without me she would not, could not, that Serjeant Herring had a situation in the hospital department, which gave him enough to support a Wife on very well, that he was a pious young man and very good looking, and would get leave to come down to Bombay for her as soon as he had taken back his invalids. I really was quite frightened; I did not know how to tell my poor mother this bad news. Not so Rose. Strengthened by the love of Serjeant Herring, she could brave greater danger; she should tell my Lady at once and let her get used to it. People were not to live single, people of course must marry, and my Lady etc. So Rose told, and a fine storm we had. I had to bear the worst of it, for it was all thrown on me. I had known of this ridiculous affair, concealed it, encouraged it, planned both Rose's marriage and my own in an artful underhand way—and we should see what would come of it. My poor Mother. She felt deserted, desolate and her natural pride would not let her say so tenderly; there were many such tempers in the olden times.

A third mischance. On our intended line of road there were no traveller's bungalows, none but private ones of the Governour's, into not one of which would she set her foot, and our tents were to go by sea. On this subject she was peremptory, even violent. We were all at a stand still when Major Jameson undertook to manage her. He highly applauded her spirit, approved of her resoloution, and, tho' under all circumstances he thought the Governour's offer of his bungalows extremely obliging, he agreed it was impossible that she could accept it. He knew of proper resting places, having lately travelled that road with Sir Thomas Bradford, to whom he was A.D.C., and so, a goodly company, we set out, Major Jameson and the Colonel riding, my father in a palanquin like the ladies. We travelled long and wearily before reaching the first halting place, a comfortable bungalow where all was ready for a late dinner. The two gentlemen had ridden on, to have every thing ready, my mother and I were not long behind them, but we waited near an hour for my father, who, obliging his bearers to follow some directions of his own, had gone a long round. Good claret, well cooled, and some champagne, greatly enlivened the entertainment, my dear Mother hobnobbing with Major Jameson and asking no questions about the bungalow, taking the Governour's servants and furniture for that belonging to the traveller's restingplace.

So on we went along the line arriving in Bombay in high good humour. All but poor Colonel Smith, whose horse shying or stumbling at the crossing of the stony bed of a river, got so severe a fall, that he nearly fainted and was laid up for some weeks from a strain, in his friend Doctor Eckford's house. When he was able, he removed to the Hermitage, Prospect Lodge I mean, to be close to us, the Norrises having returned from the Neilgherries and resumed possession of their pretty home.

CHAPTER TWENTY-EIGHT

1829

MR GARDINER and Mary had removed to a house in the fort in Rampart row, where they were engaged in packing up their effects, having determined on going home to England. We were all very much distressed at this strange resolution, unwarranted by any real cause; he was in good health, she, never well, no worse in India than at home, and the child was thriving, so that to throw up the service when he was so near the top and return to idle life away on an income very insufficient for her expensive tastes was a piece of folly in the judgement of most others. There were reasons that made Bombay very distasteful to my poor sister, independant of her dislike to the climate, the habits and the society. Mr Gardiner, too, suffered from this mysterious annoyance and I really believe they feared for the safety of the baby—its life had been threatened and with only native servants to watch it, they could never bear it out of their own sight. They fancied, also, that owing to my father's quarrel with the Governour, they had been overlooked in some late appointments, while this was entirely owing to their having refused Tannah when, as is customary, they were passed over next time. However it all was they had determined on going—or rather, she had, for he had never much voice in any matter. They took their passage in a small Liverpool merchantman, 300 tons, and only waited to see me married. The last week of their stay, having sold all they did not mean to carry home, they removed to the Retreat, which I was very glad of for all their sakes. Our dinner party every evening was very pleasant; some of my cousins, or the Norris's, my Colonel, Major Jameson. A fine long marriage Settlement was prepared, for days before our marriage, news arrived of my Colonel's brother's death which made him possessor of the

Irish estate, then valued at about £1200 a year. As we had only been 16 months in India, my father told me he would offer me no additions to a wardrobe he presumed must still be amply provided, he would only buy from Mary her habit, which she had never worn as she never rode and give me that, as my own was growing shabby. My dresses in that climate had grown shabby too—but luckily a box arrived from the London dressmaker on chance, containing 3 very pretty new gowns for me, and a pelisse and hat and feathers for my Mother which she not fancying made over to me. My Colonel too sent me a pretty purse with 30 gold mohurs[1] in it and he ordered mourning for me as he wished me on reaching Satara to put it on for his brother.

My father gave me 20 gold mohurs on my Wedding morning, as I had not spent all Uncle Edward had given me on landing, I felt quite rich for the first time in my life; and I never felt poor again, for though circumstances reduced our future income infinitely below our expectations, we so managed our small income that we never yet have owed what we could not pay, nor ever known what it was to be pressed for money.

My Colonel was married in his Staff uniform, which we thought became him better than his Cavalry light gray. There was a large party of relations, a few friends, and the good Bishop, then only Mr Carr, married us. My Mother, who had become reconciled to my choice, outraged all propriety by going with me to the Cathedral; both she and I wished it, as I was to proceed across the bay immediately after the ceremony. So it all took place, how, I know not, for between the awfulness of the step I was taking, the separation from my father and mother, whose stay I had been so long, and the parting for an indefinite time from poor Mary, I was very much bewildered all that morning, and hardly knew what was doing till I found myself in the boat, sailing among the islands, far away from every one but him who was to be in lieu of every one to me for ever more. The first movement that occurred to me was to remember Fatima's advice—retire to the inner cabin, take off all my finery.

1. The chief gold coin of British India.

I had been married in white muslin, white satin, lace, pearls, and flowers and put on a cambrick wrapper she had sent on board and had laid ready. The next, to obey my new master's voice and return to him in the outer cabin, where, on the little table, was laid an excellent luncheon supplied privately by my mother, to which, as I had certainly eaten no breakfast, I, bride as I was, did ample justice. Indeed we both got very sociable over our luxurious repast and quite enjoyed the nice cold claret that accompanied it.

We were going to Satara, neither by sea to Bancoote and so up that end of the Ghauts, nor along the plain we had last travelled, but round by Poonah, ascending the Khandala Pass. On landing, therefore, we jogged on in palanquins to the bungalow at the foot of the first ascent, where I had rested with the Gardiners. There I put on my habit, we mounted our horses, and prepared to scale a wall! I could not believe, looking up, that any one would be mad enough to attempt such a climb on horseback; but not liking to make a fuss on such an occasion I stilled my nerves as best I might, and, shutting my eyes, committed myself to the sure feet of the troop horse that had been brought for me, and the care of his attendant who never left his head. After the first pull the ascent was easier, and, more accustomed to the seat, I ventured to look round on the beautiful scenery. Such wooding! such leaves! such creepers! hanging in festoons from tree to tree, sharp rocks around, deep gullies below, and the steep road mounting ever turning sharp corners as usual to rise to fresh grandeur. Not far from the top the tents were pitched on a cool knoll, servants waiting, dinner ready, all prepared as if in an abiding home, so used are Indians to such movings. Next day we past Lanowlie and went on to a bungalow not half so agreeable as the tents, and next day we arrived at Poonah, the most fashionable Station on our side of India.

We took up our abode in a ruinous kind of place just outside the Station, a sort of old temple or garden house or something, where, however, we had two cool rooms, a bath, and a rather untidy but spacious compound. Here I was very glad to rest a whole, quiet day, for the journey had been fatiguing, but my Colonel set off to visit quantities of friends, and, to my dismay, returned towards dusk with Henry Robertson, who was the first who ever called me by my new name, Mrs Smith. He wanted me to dine with him and Jemima, but I begged off, so while we were still at our dessert he and Jemima arrived to join us at tea, and my Cousin Fanny and Mr Ward came soon after, so the next morning I felt confidence enough to face the world, only I was not called on to do it, as we were to continue our homeward journey.

There being a considerable plain to traverse, we applied for an escort, and had a troop of irregular horse sent to us, which materially improved the picturesque of the journey. They were Lancers, and dressed in eastern style, turbans, trowsers, flowing robes, and the smart flag flying. They rode well, and contrasted with the loaded camels, the bullocks, the various attendants, the palanquins, etc.; I thought, when riding by my husband's side in the cool of the morning, that there had never been off the stage a prettier procession. Our first halt was to breakfast in another temple kind of half ruined building, sheltered by a tope of fine trees, and on the bank of a clear stream. We were to rest here all the hot day, so the camels kneeled down to be lightened of their loads, the bullocks were freed from theirs, the escort dismounted and began to feed and groom their horses beneath the trees, the servants prepared the fires for their meal, and we entered our temple to undress and bathe and put on wrappers, take our breakfast and lie on sofas with our books till time for starting in the afternoon.

The first two hours we used our palanquins, passing at one time through a perfectly deserted town—streets upon streets of really good houses tenantless, not a living creature to be seen in a place of such extent that it took the bearers quite an hour to jog trot thro' it. On the sun going down we took to our horses, and, after a pleasant ride in the dark, reached the cheerful tent, where lights were gleaming, table laid, dinner ready, and all our furniture and toilettes arranged. On the evening of the next day we rode up to Satara, passed the Resident's house, the Lines, and, mounting a gentle rise, stopt at the door of our own home—such a pretty one. Often and often the first impression of it recurs to me.

It was the usual Indian bungalow, one long building

divided into two rooms, with Verandahs all round subdi-
vided into various apartments. The peculiar feature of this
very pretty cottage was that the centre building to the front
projected in a bow, giving such a charming air of cheerfulness
to our only sitting room, besides very much encreasing its
size; the Verandah to one side held the sideboard and other
necessaries for the table, the other Verandah acted as
entrance hall and anteroom. There were no walls on either
side between the house and the Verandah, only pillars to
support the roof. The back part of the long building was the
bedroom, one side Verandah the Colonel's dressing room,
the other mine, and the one at the end was furnished in
boudoir fashion for me. The bathrooms were in a small court
adjoining, the servants' offices at a little distance, and any
strangers who came to see us slept in tents. Was there ever
any establishment more suited to the country.

We looked over the long Lines of the encampment to a
wooded country beyond. To the right were two or three small
bungalows at a little distance, the Brigade Major's, the
Doctor's, and still further off the Residency. To the left a
good way on stretched the native town of Satara, with a hill
fort towering above it; altogether a very interesting scene,
and the climate when I went there in June really quite
delightful.

We rode every morning, drove every evening, and when
the rains fell it was in gentle showers like summer rains in
England. Sentries guarded our door, and there was a guard
besides ready to run all messages. We were waked by the
reveillée, but I can't say that we went to sleep at the rappel;
our hours in the evening were rather late for an up country
station, none of us dining till 5 o'clock. The society consisted
of the Resident, Colonel Robertson, with wife and children;
his assistant, some young man I don't remember; the
Doctor, Bird, who was absent at that time; the Brigade
Major Wilson, who had with him on a visit his sister and her
husband, Captain and Mrs Law. All these lived like ourselves
in bungalows. The Officers belonging to the Brigade lived in
tents in the Lines—Major Capon, Captain and Mrs Soppitt,
and two or three married lieutenants, whose wives I did pity,
poor young things, when I went to return their calls; girls

brought up comfortably in England, one, with an ivory handled pen ornamented with turquoises, and a work box having her initials on the lid in brilliants, using her trunk as a seat, the two chairs being presented to us, and the one camp table holding the fine work box. Some seemed dull enough, others radiantly happy, and they were the wise ones. What use was there in repining. People must creep before they fly, as the Irish say, and if the poor lieutenants lived they would rise to rank and all its comforts.

The Resident had company at dinner daily; he was a hospitable man and never seemed better pleased than at the head of his well filled table. We generally dined with him thrice a week at least; once a week they regularly dined with us, the day after our Official dinner. Every Wednesday so many of the Officers, married and unmarried, dined with us, invited by Major Wilson, who kept a roster, and called the names regularly thro'. I used to have a little battle with him when sometimes I wished to have a favourite over again, or out of turn. The next day the Robertsons and other private friends came to eat up the scraps, an entertainment always very pleasant, and called on our side of India a brass knocker, I am sure I don't know why. The Soppitts were good kind people. She pretty and always tastefully dressed, none of the rest interesting, only a Mrs Goodenough played on the pianoforte splendidly. The Surgeon, Doctor Young, was a goose, his Wife a most odious woman, Mr Wilson very nice indeed. Except a stray visitor arrived, we had no relief from the small circle. It would have been stupid for a continuance but for the Robertsons, who suited us perfectly.

Once in three weeks our cousin, Mr Ward, drove over in a gig from Poonah to read prayers to us in the Robertsons' Dining room. Our life was regular enough. We generally rode early, taking the road from the Lines to the river Mowlie, a couple of miles or so thro' a grove of fine trees leading to the broad stream that flowed quietly on beneath hanging banks of wood. In the afternoon we drove through the town and round the fort of Satara, down the long, dingy street guarded about the middle by a lion and a tiger, one at each side, chained of course, but in the open air, plunging about, sometimes with a fierce tug at the chain and a low roar that made me tremble till well past them; then by a field where the Rajah's elephants were picketed out, the tame ones tied by only one leg, a savage one by three. This savage hated women, and when maddened by the sight of one made most violent efforts to release himself, so violent that I could not but fear he might succeed before we got beyond his fury. These pieces of oriental splendour were far from agreeable to me. The hill fort rose high above the town; a half ruined building covered the summit, which the Rajah had lent to the Robertsons, and thither we often repaired with them to drink tea and sleep in the cooler air up at that height, the servants of each family carrying there all requisites necessary for our separate accommodation.

It was seldom so hot as to prevent me employing myself the whole day, and I had plenty to do in my new character of housewife, mending my husband's large and very ragged wardrobe, that is, making the tailor do it instead of leaning over his work, needle and thread in hands indeed, but half asleep. And in overlooking the doings of the head servant, whom I had soon to make understand that Madame was supreme, that the way to please Madame was 'to be honest and just in all his dealings' and that if he did not please Madame, he would go. When he found that this was in earnest, that the Sahib was aware of his crooked ways, and though too indolent to reform them himself, was quite willing to have them reformed, this rogue gave in, so far, as not to exhibit his delinquencies too flagrantly. One of his dodges had been about the poultry. There was a nice poultry yard full of fine fowl, and a regular sum expended weekly in feeding them, and yet we never had any fit for the table, all that we consumed were bought in the bazaar, and were certainly excellent; ours all died of cramps or cramming, and the eggs were addled or were stolen by vermin; they did not thrive in any way. I said they must—we must have so many eggs and so many fowl per week, and I never would buy one from that hour; nor did I, nor did we ever want a fair supply of the very same description, too, that we had bought in the bazaar. In truth these had been our own, without a doubt, that we had bought for our Parsee's behoof twice over. The sheep too; one frequently died, and I announced that the next we lost he should pay for, and such a casualty never occurred again. So, all through, first with one thing, then with another; the quantities said to be given to the kitchen and the stable were more of every sort than it was possible could be consumed. I boldly diminished them by one half, leaving him quite margin enough after all, as I knew from my father's accounts, which we had regulated by the aid of Mrs Ironside. My Colonel lived for less per month after he married than he had done before, with a larger establishment of course. Batchelours are made to be fleeced very properly. It is the duty of man to have Wife and bairns and if he neglect this law of his kind, let him pay for it, certainly.

Besides these various arrangements Major Wilson helped me in a more elegant employment, the making the entrance Verandah into a perfect greenhouse, in a very short time too; plants grow so quickly in that climate.

When we first reached the Station we were very gay. Mrs Robertson gave us a grand state dinner and a Ball. Major Wilson gave us a dinner, and the Regiments gave us a Ball, which I opened with Captain Soppitt to 'St Patrick's day in the morning.' We danced in the Mess tent, which was very prettily decorated. For this very grand occasion I destined my hat and feathers; being in mourning I could only dress in white muslin, so I thought this handsome hat, which had been considered, when tried on, most particularly becoming, would elevate the plainer part of the attire, and add quite an air of dignity to the Commandant's Wife. It was a *chapeau de paille* shape, of *crêpe lisse*, and really in good taste, but the Colonel was terrified. Such a headgear had never been seen in those regions; plain Mrs Robertson and pretty Mrs Soppitt had never either of them attempted such an outrageous adornment and for *his* Wife to originate such a singularity, he could never stand it; he never had seen ladies wear hats except riding. It was no use talking to him of fashion, beauty, pictures, artists, and so forth; he really was in an agony. So there was nothing for it but to replace my mother's present in its tin case, braid up my long hair in its own peculiar fashion with a pearl comb at the back and a bunch of white roses at one ear, and look girlish instead of matronly. Frequently afterwards his extraordinary dislike to any change in dress he

had not been used to obliged me to appear very unlike the
times, and look dowdy enough for many a year. Latterly, his
eye became more accustomed to all the vagaries of fashion
and so he bore his whims with greater patience—to my great
comfort for it did annoy me more than it ought perhaps, to
wear thin arms when other women cased their in balloons, a
low head beside their towers, and other such peculiarities.
The fate of the hat made me so nervous about a cap in the
shape of a butterfly with spread wings, which had accompanied the last dresses from London, that I never produced it
before any eyes but Mrs Young's, who was poor and fond of
finery, and accepted it with gratitude. It suited her so well,
she looked almost handsome in it, as Colonel Smith remarked in chorus among other voices, wondering where she
could have got so pretty a headdress! These were light
troubles, after all. The only visitors we had were Major
Jameson and a King's Officer, I think named Bonamy,
Captain Bonamy. They came together, staid a week, causing
a round of dinners much enlivened by them. I liked the
Robertson children, poor Tilly and Elphie, ugly little things
but very intelligent. Elphinstone is now a fine young man out
somewhere in India, Matilda in her Satara grave, her mother,
unable to part with her only daughter, kept her on year after
year in that dangerous climate to infancy, and she died of
liver at 9 years old. After we left, mercifully; they had, then,
besides four boys at home.

In the month of October, asthma, to which for many years
my Colonel had been subject, attacked him very seriously.
Night after night he spent in an easy chair smoking
stramonium and appearing to suffer painfully. It is probably
a disease worse to witness than to bear, the breathlessness
seeming to be so distressing. As the fit became worse instead
of better, Doctor Bird, who had returned to his duties,
advised change of air, not to Poonah but to Bombay, to leave
the high ground at once and descend to the Coast for a while,
but not remain there. He told me privately the stomach and
liver were quite deranged from long residence in a tropical
climate and that our best plan would be to return home. This
neither of us wished, and we suggested the Neilgherries;
he said they were only a make shift, present ease, but no

remedy. He advised a consultation on reaching Bombay, after watching the effect of the journey.

As, at any rate, we were not to return to Satara, the new arrangements being to take place after Xmas, we made such preparations as were fitting for the break up there. Discharged the Parsee and all the servants but our personal attendants, packed what furniture we meant to keep in such a way as would render it easy of moving, and all perishable and unnecessary articles were left to be sold. My Grand pianoforte went back to my mother, and with all the quantity of an Indian travelling equipage surrounding us, with the addition of many extras, boxes, cases, horses, gig, servants, etc., we left my first married home, where indeed I had been very happy. Spite of some trials thro' which I think I may say I came well, for I had made a promise to myself to be patient, forbearing, accommodating wherever principle was not concerned, and even then to oppose with gentleness.

I regretted the Robertsons very much, and I regretted a promised visit from the Rajah.[1] The little fat man was coming in state on his elephant with his body guard and a whole long train of attendants to pay a visit of ceremony to the Commandant's wife, and he was bringing shawls, muslins, tissues and pearls to lay at her feet, all which would have been very acceptable; altho' in general the presents thus made are of a very inferiour description. The military are allowed on particular occasions to receive such gifts, the Civilians never; so the Rajah gained by our departure whatever I lost, for he kept his presents. This poor little man was either a most consummate hypocrite, or he was most shamefully illused by those who succeeded General Robertson. On account of political intrigues said to be brought to light, implicating his veracity, indeed his honour, on all points, he was deprived of his dominions, banished to Bengal on a small annuity and overwhelmed with indignities. In our time he was considered perfectly harmless; he had taught

1. Pratad Singh: descended from the great
   Sivaji, enthroned 1818; his rule over this small,
   semi-independent principality was little more than
   nominal.

himself English, read the newspapers, after a fashion, and the Encyclopaedia Britannica, which he had bought from the Colonel in 40 volumes, assisted by some interpreter probably little better versed in our language than himself. His principal aim seemed to be to imitate the brilliant style of representation habitual to the French. He had his *Champ de mars*, literally called so, and there he manoeuvred his troops to his own delight, and mine, for they were dressed in every variety of uniform he had been able to pick up at sales of old clothing, horse, foot, artillery of all ages, for he had some Hanoverian Jack boots and feather fringed cocked hats much admired by his Officers, who looked in them, their slight frames swallowed up inside these monstrous habiliments, like so many Tom Thumbs in pewter pots. He was too fat for horseback, he therefore directed operations from his elephant, which was very grandly painted, and hung about with brocade and tassels and gold and silver. He was improving his town too, and had his garden of roses around his palace, neatly kept.

I cannot but think he was honest, for a native, then. We must not judge of them by our standard; truth is not in them; it would be called folly. Their wisdom is cunning, underhand measures are their skill, deceiving is their sagacity; they deal with us as they deal with each other; so the poor Rajah, deprived of his true friend Colonel Robertson, with his shield of integrity, may have fallen into the tricks of his race, or may have been the victim of the intrigues of his brother and successor who bore a very bad character. I have always been sorry for our Rajah.

We required no escort on our return to Poonah, being so large a party. We made out our two days' journey well, and established ourselves in a pavilion in Henry Robertson's compound, where we only slept for we took all our meals with them. He had married, a year before, Jemima Dunlop, a remarkably pretty young woman, Scotch, niece to Mrs Glasgow, well known to my people, as was all her family. She had been a little spoiled and on coming out to India had announced the most high sounding matrimonial intentions; the handsomest, the cleverest, the best born, the best bred man alone was worthy of her name and beauty. So a year passed over, another, and a third. So, dropping a requisite each season, she contented herself with abilities, sinking the other three or outweighing them with worth, which she got into the bargain and had forgotten in her catalogue. She was a very curious woman, exceedingly disagreeable to me, so self opinionated, stingy, dirty and silly, I thought. There was one little baby, a frightful thing kept rolled up in flannel, was four months old and had never been dressed or washed, it looked like, for she did not shine in the washing way. I remember years after when they came to visit us at Baltiboys with the only two children they had left of seven, *he* bathed both boy and girl in a Tub every morning, and the youngest of the two was ten years old.

They were very kind to us at Poonah, gave a dinner party in our honour. We dined out too, at the Wards, and somewhere else, I forget the name. The Wards were living in Wogan Browne's house, a very pretty one, and Fanny had it so beautifully furnished, herself and children so beautifully dressed, and Mr Ward, who managed the Bazaar affairs, kept so good a table, it was quite a pleasure to visit them.

Poonah is a nice place, no beauty of scenery, a wide plain, a wandering town and straggling encampment, always full of people, always full of gaiety, and a delightful dry climate, the very air for me, but not fit for my asthmatick husband; so we determined to move on after a sort of military display was over which was to take place on the following evening, before all the beauty and fashion of Poonah. There was to be a preparatory series of exercises in the morning, to which the Colonel wished to go, and to take me with him, and as my horse was an old trooper bought from Captain Graham of the 4th Dragoons—Sir James' brother—I felt not a bit afraid of either trumpets or firing. It was a very pretty sight; the lines were just forming in the gray half light of the Indian very short dawn. We rode along them in the midst of a party of friends all in high spirits, to take up a good station off the field. When lo! the first bugle call. Hotspur pricked up his ears, seemed every inch of him to grow alive. The second call. Off he set, and scouring the whole plain, planted himself and me in the ranks of his old regiment. I never was so bewildered in my life, fairly *dazed*, and so unequal to resume the reins I had let fall to grasp the crutch that Major Willoughby dismounted, stept forward, took me off my excited steed and led me to somebody's carriage, where I felt much more comfortable than at the head of that troop of cavalry, altho' my abominable Colonel came up in fits of laughing to condole with me, echoed by his merry companions, none of whom were *Civilians* to a certainty. I don't suppose riding on horseback was my forte, for I was always meeting with disasters, from the day Paddle gave me a bath in the Druie, to Donegal's capers in the Paddy fields, and this pleasant Exhibition at Poonah.

As I was not quite sure what sort of figure I had cut in my habit and hat, and Major Willoughby's arms, I resolved to efface any disadvantageous impression made in the morning by an extraordinary display of feminine loveliness at the Review in the evening, and for this purpose I repaired rather early after luncheon to our summer house, and ordering a tin case to be opened, dived down for the box which held the fine hat and feathers. The box was there—but within it! a riddle of what had been crape and catgut that fell to dust on being raised, and some remains of feathers amid a swarm of heaven knows what kind of creepers; the Ayah must have left the case open at some time and so let these destructive insects in. I was wise enough to hold my tongue, the Poonah world never knew how much elegance it had lost the sight of; neither did my Colonel till long after. May be the insects saved us a scene for he might have forbidden the contemplated display—he had very backward notions about dress in those days. The only smart head tire I had with me was a cottage bonnet of white net, with a bunch of roses. It very likely suited me and the Review better than did the hat and feathers.

We went on in the evening to Dapourie, with Sir Charles and Lady Malcolm, who were staying there in the Governour's absence, to a late dinner. I rather think they were honeymooning it, at any rate they had been but a short time married. She was a very pretty, little, dark, Jewess looking woman, a Miss Shawe, and he a good sort of rough seaman. He had not done as much for himself as the other clever brothers had done for themselves.[1] He had the courage, the daring of the borderer tribe without much abilities. We staid a couple of days in this pleasant spot, a large cool house in pretty grounds, and then we proceeded on our journey to Bombay, where we took up our residence with my father and mother.

Colonel Smith felt better for a day or two, and then he got ill again. Doctor Eckford said he must really do as Doctor Bird had advised, go for 6 months to the Neilgherries; he however recommended a consultation, so Dr McAdam and Dr Penny were called in, and they decided for a voyage home. Whether they were right or wrong, who can say, but they were so uneasy about him that they asked for a private audience of me, and told me he was in serious ill health, had been too long in that climate, that another season could not but go very hard with him, that the Neilgherries was only a palliative, not a cure, and that, in short, were he not to sail for England they could not answer for the consequences.

My father was very unwilling to lose us from India, and gave his voice for the Neilgherry plan; to satisfy me he went again to Doctor McAdam, and on returning told me there was nothing for it but the voyage home. I must own I was very sorry. We had made up our minds to remain 3 years longer, and this sudden retirement from place and pay was a disappointment.

The close of the rains being a very unhealthy time on the Coast we all moved up to Khandalla for ten days, we pitching our tents directly over the deep ravine, my father and mother occupying the bungalow. Here the bracing mountain air, and the fine breeze, tempered by the near neighbourhood of the sea, made the heat of the day quite bearable and the cool nights very enjoyable. We breakfasted at home, spent the mornings as we liked, always dined with my father, and played whist in the evenings. Several travellers paid us visits in passing, all doors being open to all comers in India, which

1. There were ten brothers in this Dumfriesshire family,
   all of whom had to make their own way in the world.
   Sir Charles, the youngest, became Vice Admiral in
   Bombay, where his brother Sir John was Governor:
   another brother Sir Pulteney became an Admiral.

chance meetings made a pleasant variety, and when the stray guest could play whist I was not sorry to resign my hand to him, for these were in my early gambling days, and I fancy I was not the best of partners, for my husband and myself managed between us to lose as much to our more fortunate parents as paid their boat hire on our return; a piece of luck my father particularly enjoyed the mention of and made a boast of for many a day. He translated two odes of Horace during this visit to the Ghauts, my Mother darning table linen beside him as he wrote. We were by no means so refined in our employments in our tents as were the *burra sahibs* in the bungalow. Doctor Eckford joined us, and we played backgammon etc. And talked and laughed by the hour.

One night we had all gone early to bed; it was calm and dark, no moon, no sound, the sentries being either asleep, or as quiet as if they had been. Suddenly a roar like the roar at Lanowlie broke the stillness, roused us all—it was frightful, such a vicious tone, so near. It came again, and then thro' the ravine came the shriek of a buffalo. The guard stept up to the curtain of the tent and called the Colonel; he valiantly seized a pistol and, wrapping his gown round him, ventured out, to meet Doctor Eckford in similar guise. How I shook within. They soon satisfied themselves that we were in no danger. Our acquaintance the tiger was engaged in deadly conflict with a buffalo, too busy a great deal in the bottom of the dell to have any thoughts of ascending to our height. The poor buffalo had no chance; his moans were soon hushed, and we hoped the horrid scene was over, but another actor had arrived, some other ferocious beast, who set upon the tiger, and really the fearful yells they uttered were terrifying. For a full half hour the battle raged; then all was still. How the combatants had settled matters, which was worsted, or what each suffered, we never knew. In the morning part of the carcase of the buffalo remained on the field, but no other trace of the affray.

My mother at a greater distance had heard none of the outcries. She did not, however, admire such neighbours, and as we had a good many arrangements to make for our voyage, and the cold weather was beginning, we seconded her proposal to return to the Retreat, where I at least had a busy time.

Our preparations for the voyage home were interrupted by the arrival of the two last of the Ironside cousins, Annie and Julia, who had been living since their mother's death with their guardian, Uncle Ralph, at Rothesay, whither he had betaken himself after the sale of Tennochside. This step had been necessitated by the complete derangement of his affairs, into which he had never looked for years. His agent, *Crooky* Shortridge, so called from his hump back, received his rents and answered his calls for money, never intimating that the accounts, which were never looked at, had been very greatly overdrawn. Edmund had larger debts; it had cost much to get him into Mr Kinderley's office, where his foolish and extravagant conduct prevented his remaining. It cost more again to equip him for India, my father having got him a Cavalry Cadetship for Bengal. And lastly, my Uncle had gone security with three others for what had been required to finish the education and provide the equipment of his brother Edward. The necessary funds were furnished by the advice of my father, who was one of the Securities and was never repaid. The other two were James Grant, Corrimo, James Grant, Duke Street, having died bankrupt, and my father's part being in the hands of his Trustees, those from whom the £2,000 had been borrowed came down upon poor Uncle Ralph. The sale paid all debts and left a surplus. It had always been said that there was coal on the estate; this my uncle disbelieved, and took no trouble about it. The Glasgow merchant who bought Tennochside had capital and energy; found the coal, worked the mines, and realised a very handsome income out of them.

My Uncle bore his misfortunes well; he was easy under great trials, like many others; but his temper, never good, became very irritable. He and his wife had never agreed and he and his niece Anne were at open war. She was a saucy, ill bred girl and resented the greater favour shewn to Julia, who was quiet in manner and modest and very handsome. The one most to be pitied of this ill assorted party was my Aunt Judith. All had been hers, and most certainly she had spent none of it; frugality could not have been carried further than by her in every department. What she felt no one ever knew. She went on exactly as usual, silent, grave, stolid, unimpressible, apparently never provoked, and most surely never pleased; the poor Houghton girls were very miserable in a home so unlike their own. We liked them very much but thought Anne the better looking, she had an intelligent countenance and a fine figure, while Julia was dull and fat.

A great many parties were given in honour of the ship's cargo of young pretty girls, and as I am writing of gaieties, I may mention what I had forgotten in its proper place—Mr Bouchier's masquerade. He gave it before I married. He was the head of the post office, a fat, portly man, very good natured, very well off, and a bachelour.

It was great fun choosing our characters, the suitable dresses etc. Our host was the best himself; large, and fat, and fashionably attired, he represented a School mistress with a long sticked fan; his scholars were the tallest young Officers he could get—all in short frocks and red sashes—whom he watched most rigorously, interfering with their partners, gathering them round him and lecturing them on their behaviour by the help of the long sticked fan. The figure that made the most sensation was my Lady Bradford, she had insisted on going, the only time she was ever known to attend any assembly. She had no need for any fancy dress. Her usual attire was quite sufficiently out of the ordinary attire of her sex to pass for a fancy dress—a faded silk, very plain and very scanty gown, and the close cap, made her quite unlike any body else. No one knew her at first, she passed for Jane Shawe. There was the usual number of characters of all times, some very well supported: an Albanian whose beautiful costume was so becoming to handsome Mr Le Geyt that all fell in love with him. Mary was dressed after a print of Celia in 'As you like it.' I was a Hungarian lady of distinction with a wealth of jewels on me that would have frightened me had Mr Forbes told me their value when he sent them. He was the head of Sir Charles Forbes's house at Bombay, a particularly nice person, and able to borrow any amount of jewellery from his native acquaintance. Large, well lighted rooms, the best musick and an excellent supper sent the whole queer looking crowd away happy.

Mr and Mrs Bax at this time made a party to Elephanta, a pretty wooded island about the middle of the Bay, remarkable among all the rest for a cave cut out of the solid rock—the general hindu custom. The supports were huge elephants, by no means coarsely carved. Four of them with arches between, formed the portico, all part of the rock, cut from it like the Temple within. A very large elephant was inside. I forget now if there was any thing else remarkable except the situation and the variety of beautiful flowers, mostly creepers which hung about the stones and the trees. It took us a couple of hours to reach this famous place, where luncheon was soon prepared—the same time to return. Our boat had a good awning, and yet we were all burned nearly black by the fierce sun.

And here I may mention what I had forgotten in its proper place, that on our way to Bombay from Poonah we had stopt to visit another more celebrated excavation, the Temple of Ellora. A wooded hill rises from the plain; at one end a little search reveals a door, not any way remarkable, except that one can't but wonder what it does there. The priest in charge opens it, and reveals such a lovely little display of exquisite carving as is only equalled by Melrose or Roslin; but they were built, they and their pillars, and then ornamented by fine carving. Ellora was cut out of the solid rock, as we cut the props of our coal mines, and the carving was done at the same time with the forming. What a curious people—such patience, such industry and taste too, according to their rights. At Ellora the proportions were elegant, the dome was lofty, the pillars light, unlike Elephanta where all was cumbrous, heavy, suited to the huge animal it was supposed to shelter.

Our newly arrived cousins brought us many kind gifts from the dear ones at home. Jane never forgot us and my good little Aunt Frere well remembered me. She sent me a quantity of useful things, dear in India and sometimes not to be had. Jane had very pleasant news for us. She had become acquainted with the Duchess of Wellington soon after settling at Malshanger, which was not far from Stratfield Saye. I forget what brought them together, I think Colonel Pennington had served under the Duke for a term in India, and Lord Douro hunted with Mr Folyambe's hunt. At any rate, they had grown very intimate, and Jane interested the

Duchess so much about our fine young cousin William Ironside that he was invited to Stratfieldsaye and when Her Grace went to see some exhibition or other at Sandhurst, it was on his arm she walked about, fancy the pride of the Cadet. She got him his commission and put him into the Duke's regiment. Jane was so delighted, much more so and more interested too in that fine young man than were his sisters, who took it all very coolly, as matters of course, when I went in great joy to tell them, and never thanked Jane then, nor for her after care of this their only brother, whom they lost so early.

I had one regret on leaving Bombay; my father's unfortunate difference with the Governour. Whatever it had been in the beginning, the shutting up of the Courts had put him in the wrong at the end. In my opinion, there is a bee in the bonnet of all the Grants. As a race they are very clever, very clear headed and very hard working. Under rule and guidance, they do well, none better. Witness the numbers of the Clan who have made the name celebrated all over the world. When they make their own work, they make a mill of it—they can't sit idle and they never appear to consider the consequences of their impulsive acts. My husband and I could have done nothing had we staid. It might have been arranged perhaps had my poor Mother been in better humour. This mischief with her was that she never let herself be natural; none of us could ever find out what she really felt or what she really wished. She brooded over every occurrence all by herself, and saw every thing through prejudices not to be got rid of, because they were never named. She had taken a dislike to the Governour and Sir John Malcolm was very intimate with my Colonel; he was most anxious to end this unhappy difference, he spoke both to him and to me, and empowered him to conciliate my father. He even wrote a note to be shewn to my father, which would have let him down easy and by the aid of 'misapprehension,' 'hastiness of temper on both sides,' 'intermeddling,' he tried to soften matters. It had a good effect this kind note and Colonel Smith assuring my father of what I am quite sure was true, that the *great* Sir John had a high value for the *little* one and believed him to have been influenced by his brother judges. All was in good train when my poor Mother interfered. She never knew but the one side of any thing. She burst in with 'proper pride,' 'self respect,' 'high station of a King's Judge' on the one part and ever so many unpardonable 'impertinences' on the other, sparing neither my husband nor me for our uncalled for interference. So it became war to the knife instead of a reconciliation, a great pity.

She was irritated at our departure, which she considered unnecessary. She was good and affectionate, though she would not shew it, and she keenly felt the loss of the last of her children, the one who had stuck by her so long.

Mr Caw was much of the same style; he could not bear to lose any of us; his rudeness to Colonel Pennington was only equalled by his impertinence to Mr Gardiner, and surpassed by his spite to Colonel Smith, yet he would have laid down his life for my sisters and me, in fact, he was jealous of our husbands, he wanted no such fences between the old happy life in the old Country and himself. Never were such queer people as those people of the past age.

After several inquiries, visits to many vessels in harbour, and careful enquiries as to their commanders, we decided to sail in the *Childe Harold*, a new, swift ship, beautifully fitted up, commanded by Captain West, an old experienced lieutenant in the Royal Navy. He was to make a coasting voyage home, which was particularly recommended for Colonel Smith.

This settled, we furnished one of the poop cabins without much cost, as my father made over to us a good deal of our former cabin furniture. The small cabin next us was taken for little Willy Anderson and his maid, who was to act as mine. The Colonel also engaged a native male attendant, as when the violent fit of asthma was on him he was totally helpless and my mother did not think I should continue throughout the voyage able to wait on him alone. The small cabin opposite was taken by Doctor Eckford, who, not feeling well, had resolved to pay a short visit to the Cape. Thus we had prepared for as much comfort as a homeward voyage admits of; it is never so pleasant as a voyage out, for health and spirits are wanting, in general, to those who are leaving their occupation behind them.

We had regrets too, but we left more anxiety than it was easy to bear. The last mail from home brought out the patent for investing Mr Dewar with a knighthood and the Chief Justiceship, he a young man might have been my father's son, not clever, nor in any way qualified for such advancement save as a mark of displeasure with my poor father's folly, Mr Dewar having been acting Advocate General at the beginning of the dispute and so engaged on the side of the local government. My father was lucky not to be required to resign his puisne judgeship; he owed this to Lord Brougham.

I liked David Dewar so well, that James Dewar came in for liking too, and he deserved it from all of us; nothing could be more delicate, more respectful, more considerate than his demeanour to my father during the time they remained so strangely situated on the Bench together. I always heard my father equally commended for bearing this heavy blow so philosophically, and he was wounded on many sides, for they caricatured him as a wild elephant between two tame ones, which was a mistake and they ridiculed him in some places, animadverted on him severely in others: all to a man so sensitive as he really was under that outward stoicism, very, very annoying. It therefore did not surprise us on reaching home to find he had resigned his Bombay judgeship, and had removed to Calcutta with the intention of practising there at the Bar.[1]

My last sight of him in the cabin of the *Childe Harold*, where he and my mother left me late on the evening of the 4th of November; he lingered behind her one moment to fold me to his heart again, neither of us speaking, and then he vanished from my sight for ever. Long I sat listening to the stroke of the oars which carried them back in the darkness to their desolate home. It was a dreary parting.

Mr Anderson had put his little boy to bed in the next cabin, the child being half suffocated with weeping. Oh these

1. He resigned in September 1830 and practised at the
Calcutta Bar for three years before being again
appointed to a Puisne judgeship; he held this post until
his resignation in 1848; he died at sea on his way home
on 19 May 1848.

Indian scenes, a yearly death of the heart for every family. Poor little Willy was a great diversion to my sadness; he was going home under our care, and tho' not an engaging child, he was tractable and a source of employment for I took real charge of him, and I think improved him. He was carefully educated afterwards and has turned out extremely well; the last we heard of him was his having got his troop and married his cousin Helen Grant.

CHAPTER TWENTY-NINE

1829–1830

WE had a pleasant voyage to Colombo, down the coast the whole way, fine, cool weather, the next poop cabin empty, so Willy played there, and I often sat there late and early, our own cabin being disagreeable during the night arrangements. My Colonel slept in a hammock, a large one, which filled up nearly all our space. It was swung low, so after it was up and before it was down it was not easy to move about—it prevented the air circulating to my sofa, too, so that the empty cabin near us was a great comfort.

Doctor Eckford, always pleasant, was a nice, cheerful, clever companion; Captain West remarkably complaisant. The few other gentlemen passengers very inoffensive. There were no ladies; Captain, now Colonel Stalker and an invalid brother, Captain Bradbury, or some such name, a Widower with a little boy, a nice playfellow for Willie. Poor Archdeacon Hawtayne and his Willy, and a very foolish young man, a Mr Mills, whom we smuggled on board after leaving the harbour, or his numerous creditors would have detained him.

Captain West was going to Ceylon for cargo; coffee, spices, etc. He was also to take home invalids from thence, so expected to remain a week at Colombo. We really remained near three. The first day or two we staid in our Cabins, with most of the rest of the ship to ourselves, I sitting under the awning on the poop admiring the pretty Indian view, inhaling the really and truly fragrant air, and thinking over the 21 months that had passed in these strange lands since I had first sighted Ceylon. We then removed to the house of a merchant in the town, a friend of the Captain's, whose immense warehouses, with all the business carried on in his large Court yard, furnished me with hourly amusement.

Here we were discovered by an old Edinburgh friend of mine, Campbell Riddell, and carried off by him to his cool Bungalow on the Coast, where we remained during our stay. It was a charming place, his house hold very well appointed, and he with his Scotch welcome made us feel so quite at home. We spent our mornings in driving out, the sun never preventing exercise in Ceylon, our afternoons upon the beach where the air was delicious, our evenings in company, either at home or abroad. Sir Edward Barnes was the Governour, an old General, extremely fond of his bottle, who had married a young, *very* young and very handsome wife, and who idolised her and the two spoiled children she had brought him. It would be hard to say how the affairs of the island were carried on, the late supper parties affecting most heads next morning. The officials did sometimes appear in their offices before the clerks left them, and the troops were occasionally inspected, but it was perfectly evident that the aim and the end and the business of all the merry party at and about Government House was pleasure, and of a queer kind. A sort of child's play—all excepting the wine part, which indeed required all the strength of manly brains to bear up under, the Governour, who had made his head during a long course of campaigns, not comprehending how difficult some people found it to keep up to his high mark.

We were with their excellencies every evening except the two, when Campbell Riddell entertained them and others, himself. He was a great man, by the bye, sent out by the Home Government as Commissioner to inquire into local abuses, settle some disputed points, put much right that had gone wrong and no wonder, either! Whether he had talents for so grave a charge I should have doubted from early recollection of the rather wild young man who could never settle to business in his own country; but a conciliatory manner, with a most gentlemanly deportment and thorough honesty of purpose, he certainly did possess, and probably he carried out his instructions well, for he was afterwards sent on as Secretary to the Governour at Sydney. He and I were very happy to meet again I know, and soon becoming as intimate as in former days, he confided me his love for a very handsome girl, one of the Rodneys, whom but for her want of

education, he would have married at once. The father, Mr
Rodney, a man extremely well connected, had come out to
Ceylon years before with a wife, who died, leaving him
several children. He married again and the same events were
repeated. He took a third wife who still lived, a Dutch
woman that could scarcely read or write, and thought it
needless to give more knowledge to her step children than she
possessed herself. I think between her own and former
broods, there were altogether 21 young Rodneys, at least
they said so, and not a penny of any of them. Two girls, of
batch the first, who had had some advantage, were happily
disposed of. One had gone to Paris on a visit to her
Grandmother, Lady Aldborough, where she captivated a
Scotch nobleman, who had a little misgiving in marrying her,
and standing somewhat in awe of a naval brother, sent out to
the Station where the brother lay a sort of apologetick letter
for so rash an act. The brother's Station was Ceylon and he
had just despatched to his elder brother such another missive
as he had received to excuse his own engagement to the sister
of the Paris bride. They were beautiful young women and
amiable and both marriages as I have heard turned out well.
It did not fare so well with batch the 2nd. Caroline Rodney,
very ignorant, her temper very much chafed by her Dutch
stepmother's behaviour, brought a deal of ill humour as an
accompaniment to her extreme loveliness to poor Campbell
Riddell, his lessons in spelling and grammar and sums, in
addition, she threw in his face, disobeying also in many ways
so that for some years, at least, he had 'to rue the day he
sought her.' Whether she got wiser after her children came I
know not, but when I saw her it was in the wooing time, all
sunshine on both parts.

I found another old friend in Ceylon, Mr Anderson Blair.
What situation he filled I don't remember; he lived handsomely and appeared to be happy, and to be liked, especially
by the Governour, who found him only too ready to join in
the call for another bottle—I remember this used to be said of
him, tho' my Mother would never believe it.

The doings of Government House were certainly extraordinary. One night there was a Ball, a supper, rather riotous,
throwing about fruit at one another, making speeches, long,

rambling and *thick* enough, more dancing, or pulling and
pushing rather, from which we were glad to get away. Next
night was a Play in the pretty private theatre, 'The Honeymoon,' Lady Barnes acting the heroine. Supper of course in
the same style as before, the Governour looking on, A. de C.s
applauding. We had then a fancy Ball very well done, Lady
Barnes as Queen Elizabeth, beautifully got up and looking wonderfully handsome, her Governour rather old for
Leicester. Many characters were well dressed, several well
sustained, a few groups very grand. Colonel Churchill was
a perfect Henri IV., his Wife such a pretty, impudent
Rosalind, with a stupid Celia, but such a Touchstone! some
clever young officer. So on of all the rest—rooms large,
numerous , well lighted. A grand supper, speeches etc., great
noise towards the end. These were all grand affairs; the
intermediate evenings, the ladies and gentlemen romped
about, playing *petits jeux* with strange forfeits, hide and seek,
hunt the whistle, etc. It was all very unseemly, a perfect whirl
of riotous folly, very unlike the propriety of a Government
House, where there might be mirth and pleasure without
such a compromise of respectability.

Campbell Riddell's two quiet dinner parties were really
like a return to rational society after a turmoil of disreput-
ables. At the first of these entertainments I was taken to
dinner by a grave, particularly gentlemanly man in a
General's uniform, whose conversation was as agreeable as
his manner. He had been over half the world, knew all
celebrities, and contrived, without display, to say a great deal
one was most willing to hear. About the middle of dinner Sir
Edward Barnes called out 'Sir Hudson Lowe, a glass of wine
with you'[1]—people did such barbarisms then—to which my
companion bowed assent. Years before, with our Whig
principles and *prejudices*, we had cultivated in our highland
retirement a perfect horrour of the great, or the little!
Napoleon's gaoler. The cry of party, the feeling for the
prisoner, the book of Surgeon O'Meara, the voice from St

1. Sir Hudson Lowe (1769–1844) was Governor of
   St Helena (1815–21) until Napoleon's death ; from
   1821–31 he was second in command in Ceylon.

Helena,[1] had all worked the woman's heart to such a pitch of indignation, that this maligned name was an offence to all of us. We were to hold the owner of it in abhorrence, speak to him! never! Look at him, sit in the same room with him, never! Colcraft the Executioner would have been preferred as a companion. None were louder than I, more vehement; and here I was most comfortably beside my bugbear, and perfectly satisfied with the position too. It was a good lesson. They had sent the poor man to Ceylon because he was so miserable at home, the world judging him as we had done, tabooed him remorselessly. He was so truly sent to Coventry that he once thanked Colonel Pennington in a Coffee House for the common civility of handing over a newspaper, saying that any civility was now so new to him he must be excused for gratefully acknowledging it. The opinion of less partial times had judged more fairly of Sir Hudson, his captive, and the Surgeon. Timidity and anxiety made Sir Hudson unnecessarily vexatious, Buonaparte was not in a mood or of a mood to be placable, and Mr O'Meara wanted money and notoriety, which he gained at no expense, not having had much character to begin with, another Colonel Wardle Business.[2]

Our drives about Colombo were merely agreeable; there was no fine scenery, the sea, some wooding and fields, amongst which the frail cabins of the Cingalese were scattered. A country house of the Governour's on a rock starting out of the sea, was cool and pretty. I wondered they did not live there rather than in the dusty town; it would not have been so gay for my lady. It was odd to see the huge elephants working like smaller beasts of burden; they were employed to draw waggons, Artillery guns, etc., and seemed

1. Barry Edward O'Meara (1786–1836) was a surgeon on the *Bellerephon* taking Napoleon into exile; he was persuaded to stay by Napoleon as his physician and quarrelled bitterly with Sir Hudson, the Governor, who forced his departure in 1818. O'Meara's revenge was *Napoleon in Exile; or a voice from St Helena*, published in 1822, a copy of which was in E.G.'s father's library.
2. See I, pp. 115–6.

to be quite tractable. The climate was very enjoyable, air so balmy; altogether I know I left Ceylon with regret. And our *Childe Harold* was irksome for a day or two. Neither was it improved by the additions to its cargo; bales of cotton, coffee, spices, crowded the deck, making our walk there very confined. The invalid soldiers hung about in idle groups, and the wives and children encreased the confusion. The officers returning in charge of them were very disagreeable, Captain Floyd fine, Mr Bell fault finding; the surgeon, a boy, mischief making; and I lost my spare cabin. It was taken by Mrs Churchill and her little daughter Louisa, on whose account the mother was going home—not that the child's health required Europe, but her education could not be carried on in Ceylon with such parents, in such society, I should think not. It was impossible not to like Mrs Churchill. She was very good natured, quite unaffected, without guile, and so very handsome; but she was all wrong, poor woman, under educated, no principles, idle, frivolous, and had from her birth to the present moment been exposed to the evil influence of bad example. Her father, an Irish judge by name Finucane, had to divorce her mother on account of his own nephew. The mother always denied her guilt, but she lost her cause and her husband would never acknowledge Mrs Churchill, who was born after the separation and brought up under this cloud. When very young, and very beautiful, and very giddy, she was so much distinguished by Colonel Churchill that her character would certainly have suffered had he not married her; this extreme step he showed no intention of taking, but marched off with his regiment from whatever watering place the flirtation had been carried on at. The mother was shrewd enough; she wrote to her five Irish sons stating all circumstances. The brothers *en masse* appeared one morning pistol cases in hand, at Colonel Churchill's new quarters, and introducing themselves, begged to ask him whether he had forgot nothing at his former station.

'Gad,' said he, 'I believe I have forgotten your sister,' upon which there was a grand shaking of hands.

The marriage, thus settled, was soon concluded and then came the question how were the young and very handsome couple to live. Colonel Churchill was of the Marlborough family, his mother a Walpole, little money and less worth on either side. He lived luxuriously on such credit as he could get, helped now and then out of scrapes by various relations. Nobody, however, came forward at this time save Mrs Finucane, who gave sufficient for a fair start, and so the Bride and bridegroom began with rather a flourish at Knightsbridge. They gave the prettiest little dinners ever ordered from the French cook's shop at the corner, good wine, pleasant company, and he was the luckiest dog in the world to have found such a Wife, with such a fortune, as he gave out accompanied her. They were asked out a great deal among the 'first circles,' his connections being all in the red book.[1] She had the good sense to dress simply and to resist a hired carriage, tho' she told me in her natural way that it required all the admiration she received to the full to bear with the straw in the hackney coach, on which she set her dainty feet while bowing Adieux to the noble partners who handed her into such a vehicle. Of course this could not last, and he was fortunately ordered off to Courtray with a draft of men to encrease the Army of occupation,[2] and there he raised the wind in a way he had tried to practise on a smaller scale at Knightsbridge. The little dinners were changed to suppers, play introduced, the Wife's part being to set her bright eyes on the younger men, whom she fascinated readily, without poor thing, I do believe knowing one bit what she was doing. And so, at last some money falling to him, and some arrangement being made about it so as to assure the clearance of his debts in time, family interest got him the appointment of Secretary to the military part of the Government of Ceylon. He had grown a careless husband and she a very indifferent wife by the time we made their acquaintance. Yet they cared for one another in a way. Colonel Churchill made her over to my Colonel's care, who promised, on her landing,

1. A popular name for the *Royal Kalender, or Complete . . . Annual Register*.
2. Courtrai was the headquarters of the Allies' army of occupation in France after the war but this had been withdrawn in 1818.

to deliver her safe to old Mrs Churchill in London, while I undertook friendly offices on board. Little did either of us know the charge she was to be.

The first annoyance was to Doctor Eckford. His cabin was next to hers; part of the partition was movable, a mirrour that slipt down on a spring being touched, and so opened a communication between. Little Miss Louisa soon made this discovery, used, and abused it, bursting forth on the little Doctor at inconvenient moments, so that he never felt secure of privacy; the mother, too, soon began to follow the child, tapping first before shewing herself, but not giving much time between the tap and the apparition. I am quite sure this was all idleness, our medical friend being never attractive and at this moment livid in complexion from liver. He, however, chose to flatter himself with the idea that he was pursued, had captivated! and his serious complaints both to the Colonel and me were sufficient to overset all gravity.

She next tried my Colonel, merely a bestowal of her tedium on any one, but it was disagreeable. Dr Eckford took me every day 3 walks; so many turns upon the deck each time, for the good of my health, hereafter. The first walk was after breakfast always, while the Colonel was shaving, which he had not time for earlier in the morning. A tap at the door one day announced Mrs Churchill, who came to amuse him during the operations. She must have thought she succeeded, for next day she came again, and again, and again. 'Upon my soul,' said the Colonel, 'this is getting too bad, the woman, pretty as she is, is quite a nuisance, a man can't shave for her; Mrs Smith, you must give up your walk and stay and guard your husband.' Not a grateful office to act both guard and spy, but there was no help for it.

So after a few more days she gave up this diversion and took to one less harmless—a regular serious flirtation with Captain Floyd, whom she very nearly distracted spite of his long experience! Dr Eckford informed us he rejoiced in this for his own case but was sorry for the poor *wu*mman so exposing herself. Morning, noon, and evening the pair sat close together on the poop, in the Cuddy, or at the Cuddy door, little Louisa always with them, but busy with her doll and books. What they could find to say we used to wonder for neither shone in conversation with others. She spoke little ever and he was a real goose, only good looking. Now and then she would come and sit with me, complain of the long day, the dull voyage, the stupid life, and so on; while we three, the Colonel, the Doctor and I, were quite content, busy and happy, eyes and ears open, and inclined to be pleased, with the weather beautiful.

At length on Xmas morning we came in sight of the Isle of France,[1] and before dinner time we were at anchor in the harbour of port Louis. It was a pretty scene, plenty of shipping on the sea, plenty of wood on the shore, hills in the distance, and a long straggling town lying along the water's edge.

The sailors were all agog to bathe till the captain checked their ardour by the short word 'sharks,' which abounded all about the island; indeed, a poor fellow from a vessel alongside of us had been cut in two that very morning by one of these monsters, which actually bolted the lower part of his body while they were drawing the head and shoulders up on the deck. We saw them playing about in shoals.

The Captain having a good deal of business here we were all to go on shore for a fortnight, which, as before at Ceylon, stretched to a month. These delays must have been very inconvenient to young men with empty purses. Some of them, therefore, had to remain to live on board, merely taking a day's pleasure on land now and then, and the Captain had to provide for them as usual, which he did but scurvily they said, which affair so discontented both parties that there never was any cordial feeling between them again, and this made the remainder of our voyage extremely unpleasant. The idle soldiers got into mischief; the wives took to quarrelling; the two officers could not leave their men, even had they been invited ashore, which they were not, and the surgeon, Mr Mills, and one or two more nursed up such a crop of illhumour that it lasted them all the rest of the way home.

Mrs Churchill had a special invitation to the Governour,

1. Mauritius.

Sir Charles Colville, who sent a carriage for her next day in which she and Louisa and the penniless Mr Mills set off to his country house up among the woods, about 6 miles from the town. Captain West, who was intimately acquainted with the Secretary to the Government—now also at his country house—got the loan of his empty town house for himself and us and Dr Eckford, and this was our principal residence while we remained on the island, altho' we paid two visits, each of some days' duration, one to the Governour, and one to the Secretary, our Landlord, Mr Telfer.

We enjoyed this month extremely. It was hot sometimes at night in the town, but the breeze which came up with the tide always, refreshed the air again and the house was large and roomy, standing back from the street in a courtyard of good size, and with corridors running thro' it, which kept it as cool as could be managed without Verandahs, which luxury and ornament cannot be indulged in here on account of the hurricanes. No year passes without two or three of these destructive storms. The winds are so big, so eccentrick is their course, so overpowering that they sweep off a great deal of property, in spite of every precaution. All buildings are low, there are no projections, nothing that can be caught at, and yet no place quite escapes damage at one time or another.

The scenery is more pretty and quiet and interesting than fine. A plain of fertility beyond the town, bordered by the sea and rising to the mountains, which are some of them picturesquely peaked. 'Peter Botte' very conspicuous. The nutmeg wood belonging to Government, and beautifully kept, is one of the most interesting spots to drive thro' from the beauty of the trees; large, tall, forest trees, they are full of branches and dark leaves, so very fragrant, and the spice in all its stages bursting all around. The nutmeg, quite red when growing, peeps out from its covering of green mace, quite like a flower. The Cinnamon bushes were the underwood, their buds—the cassia buds of commerce—scenting the air. Parrot looking birds were among the branches, and monkeys skipping from tree to tree.

We often drove there, passing on our way by a good house in a large garden, called Madame La Tour's, as unlike as possible to the humble cabins of St Pierre, where stands a monument to *Paul et Virginie*[1] on the spot where her body was washed ashore! underneath which I think they said the lovers were buried! To doubt their existence in the Isle of France would be something too scandalous.

In the evenings we drove in the Champs de Mars, a rather larger space than the Rajah's, but quite as amusingly filled. All here is French, or, more properly speaking, the remains of French.

The Colonists able to remain here with their families—the climate permitting their absolute location—seldom visited the mother country, unless the men found it necessary in the way of business, or an ambitious Mama sent her children for a few years to Paris to acquire higher accomplishments. The inhabitants are therefore essentially French in race, name, language, and habits. We had had the island too short a time to make much change in it. Our few merchants and officials are just a small set of persons unlike the rest, yet all agree comfortably, all being freemen except the servants, who are slaves. Here, again, old prejudices proved deceptive. So happy a set of creatures as these same slaves never did I see in any rank in any country. From morning to night they lightened labour with their songs. I got all the airs in the *Dame Blanche*[2] by heart, hearing them one after the other during all the working hours chorussed out by the dark porters who were busy in a neighbouring store heaving up and down hogsheads of sugar. Every enquiry we made convinced us that unkind masters were rare. Out in the sugar plantations, or in the spice groves, or the Coffee grounds, in the warerooms, in the yards, house or field labour, the powers of the merry slaves were never overtaxed. They were well lodged, well fed, well cared for in sickness and old age, and had plenty to buy dress with, of which they are extravagantly fond, and make a wonderful display of on their numerous holidays. We constantly met or overtook waggon

1. Bernardin de St Pierre (1737–1814), disciple of Rous-
   seaux and novelist, visited the island (1768–70) and
   wrote this famous novel in 1787.
2. Opera (1825) by Adrien Boieldieu (1775–1834) based
   on Sir Walter Scott's two novels, *Guy Mannering* and
   The Monastery.

loads of dark beaux and belles dressed up like actors radiant
with mirth, going off a pleasuring to some *Guinguette*,[1] where
dancing would conclude the festivities, and every evening
crowds of them paraded in the Champs de Mars, the men
sometimes in sailor guise with long curls under the jauntily
set straw hat, or in more *exquisite* costume, chains and eye
glasses much in fashion, attending their ladies in full ball
dress, flowers, feathers, flounces, pink crape, blue crape,
fans, etc., all in the day light, and all so happy, only—there is
a *but* every where—trowsers and petticoats were invariably
long enough to touch the ground, for though the slaves may
do with his, or her, head what best pleases, neither shoe nor
stocking can case the feet; they must be bare, it is the mark of
caste, and they feel it, happy as their condition is made;
childish and ignorant as they are, they strive to hide the
naked feet. Yet they could not exist in freedom—not the old
slaves, used to have all provided for them.

Sir Charles Colville told us of a slave he had freed, and
made, as he thought, comfortable, with house, and field, and
work as a gardener, begging to be made a slave again; he had
not the energy to manage his own living. So, as in other cases,
we must begin with the young, let the old generations just die
away as they are.

The black fashionables were not the only amusing fre-
quenters of the evening promenade. The French, not very
particular at home as to their equipages, had certainly not
improved their taste in carriage in their colony. Such gigs and
phaetons, and post waggons, and extraordinary vehicles of
every description, with cracked leather unoiled for years,
panels over which the paintbrush could almost never have
gone, harness! horses! all so very tatterdemalion! and
within, such pretty looking women in such tasteful half
dress, so simple, so fresh; hair in such order! it really was a
contrast. The men were not so nice: the old ones little and
punchy; the younger little and dandified. We visited in one
or two merchant families; a call in the evening, a cup of
coffee, or fruit, and musick, queer singing, but good playing.
In the gay season plays, operas, concerts and balls, publick and

1. Cafés noted for dining and dancing.

private, enliven the cold weather—just now every one that could was getting thro' the heat in the country.

We lived very comfortably in Mr Telfer's house, my black maid and the Colonel's black man to wait on us; both of whom looked down with pity on the two good humoured slaves left in charge of the premises, an old Véronique very fond of a bit of finery, and a Gaspar who slept half his time away. Our breakfasts were very easily managed. Our dinners, wines and all, came from a *traiteur's* in true French style—little nice dishes admirably cooked, dressed vegetables, *plats sucrés*, and crisp biscuits. It was all so good that I wrote to my father, who was miserable with the Portuguese messes, to advise him to send to the Isle of France for a cook. Mrs Telfer was so good as to consent to assist in the business, and the *Traiteur* promised to choose a *garçon accompli*, who would expatriate himself for a bribe.

The scheme was approved and carried into effect, the cook becoming so at home in Calcutta, and I believe so truly attached to my father, and the profits of his kitchen, that he lived with him till his death, when his place was supplied by a *confrère*.

We frequently invited our castaway shipmates to partake of our shore repasts. Mrs Charles Telfer was also a frequent guest, my Colonel being perfectly well and able to enjoy our sociable ways. Our stay was varied by two country visits, one to the Governour, the other to the Secretary. The Retreat was a fine place; the gardens well laid out; the rooms large. There was a numerous suite, too, and nice children, but it was a disagreeable visit. Sir Charles was a dull man, reserved and silent, stiff to every one, but very stiff to us, for he and my Colonel had not got on altogether harmoniously during the time that he had been Commander in Chief at Bombay. His private Secretary was that gigantick Colonel Fraser, who had been such an abominable husband to poor Emmeline McLeod, and to whom therefore I could hardly contain myself to listen, particularly when he had the hardihood to speak.

Lady Colville, one of the Muirs of Caldwell, was deranged, poor thing. She had been quite frantick and had been sent home in durance, placed in a private asylum. She was restored to her husband as cured, but was unsettled in her manners, very easily excited. One evening she was seated near me on a sofa with Mrs Churchill, who was giving a brilliant description of Ceylon merry makings. Lady Colville highly disapproved of such levities and was beginning to express herself very energetically on the subject, fidgetting on her seat too, and twisting herself, and so on, when the head servant, an Englishman, whom I remember remarking afterwards never left the room, came steadily up to her with a tray in his hand, and fixing his eye on her, he said in an odd commanding tone—'Your Ladyship will take coffee?' She was quiet in a moment, took the cup in silence, and we both of us felt that the less we spoke to her the better. In the mornings she was calmer always. I went to her dressing room after my breakfast, which I took in my own room, and she seemed to have great pleasure in making the discovery that patterns of her baby clothes would be useful to me. She collected a little bundle with extreme good nature, adding some fine calicoes etc. to cut up and she sent for a merchant, from whom I bought what else was wanting to give my neat fingers needle work enough to last thro' the rest of the voyage.

We felt it a relief to remove to Mr Telfer's, where we had a kind welcome and no company but the brother, our Captain, and Dr Eckford. We slept in a pavilion in the garden, which left me at liberty for charming wanderings about the wooded hill their cottage was built on. Little Willy had been with these good people from the first, as their only child, a boy of his own age, had been delighted to have a companion.

Here an affair was arranged of which I hardly like to speak, knowing but one side of the story. Judge of it we cannot, tho' the facts acknowledged look ill. This was to be Captain West's last voyage, he now told us ; he was to give up his ship on going home, make as much as he could of his part of her and her cargo, and then return with his wife and son and daughter to settle in the Mauritius as part owner of a sugar plantation now in the market. The two Telfers were to have shares ; Charles Telfer was to be the manager, and if they could but pick up a few thousand pounds to start with, repair the buildings, purchase more slaves, etc., etc., in a year or two it would be a most remunerating concern.

We all went to see it, an excellent plantation, canes in high order, business going on which much interested us; from the cutting of the canes in the fields, their transport on long waggons, recutting, steeping, boiling in great cauldrons, stirring, skimming, straining, drying, to the packing in the barrels, we saw the whole process, with its rum and molasses, spirit and dregs, hot and sticky, but very amusing.

Dr Eckford was enchanted, his speculating turn quite roused, his vanity flattered by the deference paid him and the idea of proprietorship, and so, cautious and canny as he was, after grave inspection of the books, consultations, calculations and so forth, he offered to buy a share or two himself, and advance the required sum, to start with at 8 per cent—the common rate of interest in the island. I wonder that did not startle him; people must be very much in want of cash when they pay such interest for the loan of it. However he saw no risk, but to make sure of all going right he resolved to remain on the spot for the next few months instead of going on to the Cape; so we sailed without him. To end the tale now, the sugar plantation was a drain on the Doctor's purse for some years. Captain West and the Telfers were equally unsatisfactory as partners, matters grew more than perplexing. The Doctor threatened a visit and legal advice, Charles Telfer cut his throat, the Secretary brother died, Captain West was ruined and the plantation bankrupt. On the Doctor leaving India for good, he called at Port Louis, found Captain West rich, sole owner of the plantation, which he had bought cheap on borrowed money and with £2,000 to indemnify the Doctor for the £5,000 the adventure had cost him.

We soon resumed our sea routine, but not altogether so pleasantly. The steward had been neglectful, and made a poor provision of fresh supplies; the table had therefore fallen off. We had privately supplied ourselves, as we did every where without making a fuss, that would have been useless, and so, faring well in the cabin, were independant of the Cuddy. We could afford a help to Mrs Churchill too; but the friendless and the dogged who fought for the value of their passage money were ill off and cross enough. Major

Floyd consoled himself by complaining to Mrs Churchill for that flirtation recommenced vigorously; I tried to frustrate much of this, and by giving up my pleasant privacy contrived to amuse the Lady sufficiently enough to keep her a good deal from the Cuddy door. She and the Colonel played Piquet and Backgammon while I worked at my tiny wardrobe. She got confidential and told me a deal of her history, poor soul. She might have been a better woman had she been better guided. Idleness was her bane. To get thro' the time she really compromised her character.

On we went, into colder weather; warm wraps were wanted as we neared the Cape—the ugly Cape I must always think it, with that flat topped Table Mountain, woodless shore, and low, objectless town. Yet we were glad to reach it, for our company was ill humoured, fare bad, Captain scowling, except to me. My Colonel, since the colder weather, had been suffering from asthma; he therefore, not being able to dress mostly kept his cabin. The voyage was beginning to be dreary. I suffered a good deal myself, only, having so much to do, I had luckily very little time to think of self.

We did not land the first day, but I bought fresh butter, bread and fruit from the boatmen. Next day the Colonel was so well he went ashore and brought many little delicacies back. He had also heard of an old brother officer being at Wyneberg, about 8 miles beyond Cape Town—Captain Wogan Browne—and had sent off a messenger to offer a day's visit; the answer was an insistence that we should come to him and Mrs Browne for the whole time we were to stay. We gladly consented and passed five very pleasant days in the small house they occupied. Poor Captain Browne was there for health, which utterly failed on his return to his regiment at Poonah, for there he died. She was nursing her only son, a fine boy, tho' with a red head. In the evenings they had a fire, such a charming sight—the fire side is surely more than equal to the moonlight stroll, and certainly superiour to a sofa under a punkah.

The deep sand prevented pleasant walking; it is loose and red, very penetrating. The scenery was disappointing, flat in general, no heath or other flowers in bloom; the cool air was the pleasure and even that was only during the night, and the dawn, and the sunset; the middle of the day was very scorching, as we found when we drove to the grape garden, and walked all thro' among the little bushes on which the over ripe fruit was hanging; a very rich and sweet grape, no mistaking it for the Constantia. When nearly baked we were conducted to a cave as cool as a well, where biscuits and several sorts of Constantia, deliciously cooled wine were presented to us. The Colonel ordered three *awms*[1] some of which we still have, altho' he has always been the reverse of niggardly in his use of it. The oddest thing I saw at the Cape was the sheep going about with little carts behind them to carry their tails in. The appendages are so large, such lumps of fat, that the animals would destroy them and impede its own progress without this assistance. The enormous waggons goods were carried in were drawn by a regular regiment of bullocks, and great noise made with the whip and the tongue of the Conductor.

My colonel bought me a dozen large ostrich feathers here and several bunches of small ones dressed as foxtails etc. for a couple of £; he also replenished our Cabin stores, as did some others unluckily. There had been little doubt from the beginning of the voyage that Archdeacon Hawtayne was not altogether in his senses. Very strange tales of the wildest outbreaks of temper had been current about him in Bombay. His timid young wife was evidently in painful awe of him, for she hardly spoke in his presence. Among the servants it was openly said that at times he used her barbarously, even to shaking and beating her, and nobody doubted that the death in childbed of our friend Kitty was owing to some shock she had received from his violence. Two facts were known, that he had been bound over by the magistrate to keep the peace towards his own head servant and that once, on the company he had invited all assembling at his house to dinner, Mrs Hawtayne was discovered, the image of a ghost, trembling on a sofa, no lights nor attendants, nor any preparations, and the Archdeacon met them with the intelligence that all his household having run away, no dinner could be forthcoming.

1. Dutch measure of 41 English wine gallons.

It was on account of health that he was returning to Europe. At first he merely appeared excited, restless, wandering in his conversation, gazing up at the stars at night, in one of which he stated that his wife was dwelling and looking down on him with pity. He was also strangely particular about the little boy, whose times of eating he regulated oddly and also had his food prepared in various singular ways—difficult enough to manage on board ship. He was sometimes foolishly indulgent of the child, sometimes harsh and unjust to him. The boy feared him more than he loved him and yet he was the unceasing object of the father's care. He had brought a native servant from Bombay whom he dismissed for some fault at Ceylon, hiring then one of the invalid soldiers.

He had gone ashore at the Cape, and among other things had laid in a great store of water in bottles—the supply from the Mauritius not having kept. A hamper at a time he got up from the hold, any Thursday he required. The Mate once or twice remarked that the Archdeacon had got on to drink a great deal of water. We all remarked that his manner was becoming much more extraordinary, there were frequent quarrels with his servant, loud disputes with the man, and scolding and punishment of the poor child. One day the little creature, who was fond of slinking up to our Cabin and playing quietly with Willy Anderson, rushed up in an agony of terrour, sobbing and screaming out 'hide me, hide me'—and after him the Archdeacon in his shirt and drawers with a whip, rushing about to strike at him. The gentlemen were all on deck. I took the boy in and closed the Cabin door, then opening the looking glass panel, which, as in Mrs Churchill's Cabin, communicated with the small one next to us, which was Willy's, I bid Mary call the Captain. The result of all this was the discovery that the bottles contained rather strong waters, under the influence of which this poor half madman became wholly mad. The Captain from hence forward prohibited any such wares entering that cabin, he possessed of all remaining bottles and after a conference with the Ship Surgeon, a Soldier, Serjeant of superiour character, was appointed to attend upon the poor man with a regular charge upon him, which indeed had become necessary if only to protect the little boy. That night he slept on cushions in Willy's cabin, there was no persuading the poor little thing to go below. I had certainly good nerves then.

The next scene was enacted by the younger Stalker, who now began to have epileptick fits, during which he foamed at the mouth and very much distorted himself. One of them he took while I was seated in the Cuddy near him. I remember gratefully the extreme consideration of all the rest of the party closing round him till they had got me to move away. The unfortunate young man's intemperate habits heightened his disease; how much his good brother suffered under this affliction.

These events carried us on to St Helena, where we were promised fresh provisions and a cow; the one brought from India was said to milk ill, it had therefore been parted with at the Cape. Another had been procured there, the Captain said, but by the most extreme mischance we had sailed without her—the fault of the Steward as before—so were the salt, bad butter, the old biscuit, and the many other deficiencies; a little hard to believe, thought most of us, and very hard to bear. Coarse tea, without milk, brown sugar full of insects, rancid butter, and maggoty biscuits were not Indiaman's fare. At dinner the meat was fresh certainly, but there were no vegetables, with the exception of pumpkin pie. Neither the Colonel nor I could attempt the breakfast. We made Malek prepare us rice and curry or *kabobs* and we flavoured water with apples or lemon, or claret afterwards. I felt this much, being generally ill enough in the mornings at this time.

There were two goats on board expected to kid shortly, which was the hope held out to the discontented—a poor one, as we proved. No wonder so much ill humour prevailed and that the officers and others declined, from the day that we left the Cape, to drink wine with the Captain.

Mrs Churchill got her soldier's wife to make her soup and apple dumplings, and such dishes as her own locker supplied materials for; but really it was very uncomfortable, not unlike starvation. She, and we, had bought tea, coffee, sugar, butter, apples, potatoes, portable soups etc. all in small quantities at the Cape from a sort of forewarning, and well it was that we did so. No body should ever go to sea with a Captain on his last voyage.

We came very suddenly on St Helena. A huge lump, rising out of the sea. A flat top and steep sides, inaccessible they seemed as we coasted round, no way of landing, apparently, till all at once a gully appeared. A zigzag slit thro' the mass of land, running down from high up inland to the sea. A small plain at the bottom just held a little close packed town, and up the steep rock on one side was a set of steps like a ladder leading to a fort upon the top, very pretty, very strange, a want of breadth about it. Several ships were in the roads, boats of all sizes and a few people wandering along the shore. The whole scene struck me as familiar; then I recollected the show box at Moy, at old Colonel Grant's, where I got the porridge breakfast, which the old Lady let me amuse myself with; prints were slid in behind, and, viewed thro' the magnifying peephole, had quite the effect of real scenes. One of these represented St Helena, and very true to nature it must have been to have fixed itself so tenaciously in a childish memory.

We landed in boats on a very loose shingle, thro' which I really could not get; unused to walking for so long, and with more to carry than was convenient, lifting the feet up out of those yielding pebbles was really too much, and at last, nearly fainting, down I lay. The poor Colonel! half a mile more of the same dreadful shingle before us under a hot sun, and no help anywhere; the rest of our party had got on far ahead. There was nothing for it but patience, the very quality in which we were, some of us, deficient. I was so distressed and tried to rouse up, but failed, so began crying. Fortunately— there generally is a fortunately if one waits for it—a second boat landed Mary the maid, to whom I was consigned and by whose stout help after many stoppages in about two hours I reached the boarding house, where the Colonel had engaged a room; there I fainted right off and passed the remainder of the day on a mattress on the floor till sufficiently revived by dinner.

It was a good house in the only street, which consisted of large and small dwellings and some shops on either side of the road that led up thro' the gully; the rock rose up pretty

straight behind the row opposite. Our row had a rushing
river between it and the side of the mountain, with a steep
bank down to the water, which made the look out from the
back windows rather pretty. Our host was also a merchant,
and a gentleman, it being the custom in this little place for all
the inhabitants to keep a sort of inn. Colonel Francis Grant
did not, therefore, marry a mere lodging house keeper's
daughter. Mr Dunn was a trader and made money by
receiving boarders, like others.

Our hostess was a little woman, rather crooked, and not
young. She had been a beauty and possessed a voice extraordinary for power and compass; her songs were therefore of
a manly cast. All Braham's 'Angel of Life' and such like; the
sweetness of tone was gone, but the spirit was there still. I did
not like so much noise myself, and thought her style would
have been better suited to the top of a mosque, from whence
she could have been heard far and near to call the folk to
prayers. Each evening we were there, she had an Assembly
of the inhabitants in addition to the home party, which
consisted of half a dozen from the *Childe Harold* and a whole
dozen from another Indiaman, after whose comforts we
indeed sighed, for they had cows, new laid eggs, fresh bread,
a good cook, and plenty of every thing.

To buy a cow at St Helena was impossible or a goat even;
milk was very scarce, and all the butter used in the island
came in crocks from the Cape. Every thing was monstrously
dear here; 2s. 6d. a pound for sago, 9s. for tea; a bit of ribbon
for my bonnet the price of the bonnet itself elsewhere. Our
bill at the boarding house was something astonishing, £3 a
day, I think, for the maid, the child, the Colonel and me and
no separate sitting room, wine extra and beer, and £5 for a
carriage we clubbed to take for the morning to visit the Lions
of the place—the Briars, the cabin where Napoleon died (the
beautiful house near it he never occupied), and his tomb.

The road wound up by the side of the stream, rising at
times very suddenly, turning sharp corners as suddenly,
frequently high above the water, so that the occasional
steepness and the precipice together made timid nerves
quake. It was pretty, tho' there was not much wooding and
the trees were low, like bushes. The Briars was a cluster of

small buildings on a knoll below the road near the river that should have passed as some small farmer's cottage had it not been pointed out to us. Upon the table land we saw the plantations round Government House, where we had been civilly invited to dine by I forget who was the Governour—for we did not go—and then, having ascended the last rise, we looked round on an immense plain bounded by the Ocean. The plain is varied by little heights, little hollows, and some wooding; drives thro' it are agreeable from more variety than one would suppose; the air is delightful. There is no access but by the one precipitous zig zag we had come, along the banks of the only river in the island, and that is a mere brook, or rather torrent; there may be rivulets but we did not see them, there are a few springs. It might be monotonous as a residence; it was certainly grand as a view. The hut Napoleon would not leave was in part fallen from decay; his own room remained, a closet 10 foot square or so, with one small window, dingy green walls. Very wretched.

A very little way off was the prettiest villa ever designed, plenty of space round it, a fine view from all sides, and such a quantity of accommodation inside. A suite of publick rooms, particularly cheerful, good apartments for the attendants, and the Emperour's own wing delightfully arranged, 7 or 8 rooms including a bath and a private staircase. His ill humoured preference of the miserable Cottage punished him severely. Certainly this most charming house, all made in England and merely put together after reaching its destination, was a residence fit for any Prince. I never heard what they did with it. It was too large for any private family, and the Governour was provided for, pulled it to pieces probably and sold the materials.

The tomb was very saddening; 'after life's fitful fever' to see this stranger grave. In a hollow, a square iron railing on a low wall enclosed the stone trap entrance to a vault, forget me nots were scattered on the sod around, and *the* weeping willow drooped over the flag. The ocean filled the distance. It would have been better to have left him there, with the whole island for his monument.

On we went again from St Helena to Ascension, miserably enough, the fare more wretched than ever, the ill humour encreasing on that account and added to on another, for we had taken on board at St Helena some new passengers, an old Mr and Mrs Blanch and a young sailor, Mr Agassiz, who had lost his health slave hunting on the Coast of Africa and was going home invalided. Mrs Churchill had varied her attentions to Mr Floyd by latterly paying a deal more to the 3rd mate than was at all fitting, a mere boy, very good looking, better employed about the ship than in gaining expertise in coquetry. The Captain put a stop to his walking arm in arm with her along the deck, but he could not check glances, asides, occasional tender encounters. Indeed she behaved shockingly, for which these two distracted about her, no sooner did fresh prey appear than she cast them off remorselessly—Captain Floyd entirely, the poor mate very nearly. Mr Agassiz she seized on and he paid her off for he became necessary to her. He bewitched her and so imprudent were they both that the Captain had to speak to him. Captain Floyd got savagely sulky, made himself odious. The mate went almost beside himself—the poor boy! heart had given itself away so confidingly and to be cast off as a worn out toy was so cruel a shock; he really pined away, acted quite foolishly. Never was such an unpleasant state of affairs.

For two days these disagreeable scenes went on; the 3rd produced graver matters to think of. About this time last year a vessel homeward bound had in this latitude been attacked by pirates, attacked and overpowered—the surviving men were made to walk the plank, the women after the worst usage left alive in the vessel which was stript and scuttled. It so happened that a cruiser came up with this doomed ship and rescued these unfortunates, several soldiers' wives and one lady, her maid and some children. The lady was the wife of an Officer who remained with his regiment at St Helena, while she returned home on business, taking her little boy and girl with her. She was nearly out of her mind, extremely ill, and on landing sent the maid, with the children, the papers and other effects belonging to them and her husband to his parents, with an injunction to the maid to tell the dreadful tale. She was herself never more heard of. Whether she died or what became of her nobody could ever find out. She said she loathed herself and would never obtrude herself on her beloved husband's sight. The maid described the Pirate as young and handsome, magnificently dressed in a fantastick style and with perfect command over a most horrible looking crew. Whether he it were who reconnoitred us, we could not say, but a most suspicious looking 'craft' bore down upon us, strangely rigged and piratically painted, coming from no regular direction. Several small merchant-men had sailed with us for company's sake, these latitudes being at this time dangerous, and they all began to cluster in our wake at this unpleasant apparition.[1] Mr Agassiz, whose employment it had been to look out for all sorts of contraband keels, said this was not a slaver. As she neared us, he ascended to the mast head and reported that she was all trim and smart and filled with a crowd of active men.

Upon this Captain West began his preparations; all the soldiers were called out in their red coats and dispersed about the deck. The two officers, suitably rigged out, marched here and there. Arms glancing in the sun's rays. The whole crew was called up in full view. Every body on board had a proper place assigned. We ladies with the children were to go down to Mrs Blanch's cabin on the lower deck when directed and our door guarded by Colonel Smith and Mrs Blanch. The soldiers' wives and children to keep below. The Surgeons went to prepare for extremities, and the Archdeacon retired to pray. Perhaps all this was unnecessary, yet it was certainly prudent, and as certainly made us very grave. Mrs Blanch, quite an old woman, was in agonies at the possibility of the treatment she might be subjected to, cried and wrung her aged hands, making her not only ridiculous but troublesome. Mrs Churchill quite shone; roused by the excitement she seemed all alive. 'Pray be quiet, Mrs Blanch,' said she. 'If the worst came to the worst *I* may be in danger enough, but I think both you and Mrs Smith will be respected!' and then she laughed one of those ringing laughs that must have reminded her of her girlhood. She had actually brought down with her some old linen she had for the voyage, scissors, and

1. There was another case of piracy in these waters at this time involving the schooner *St Helena*, which was boarded on 9 April 1830, shortly after this incident.

a housewife, etc., that she might help the surgeons, should it be requisite. Mr Agassiz and Captain West put on their uniforms, and as the English part of the Crew were always as neat as men of war's men, we must have looked rather imposing to our new acquaintance, who soon came boldly within hail. It was before the new system of conversation signals; what we had to say to each other had to be bawled thro' the speaking trumpet. We were informed by 'John Thompson of New York' that he was 'bound for the Cape and else where,' with what, we could not make out, neither did he explain how he had got so much out of his track as to be coming up from the south west on a nor' easterly course. In return we acquainted him that we were 'Captain West, R.N., in the *Childe Harold*, with troops,' which he seemed to think sufficient, for he rolled off and tho' hovering on the outskirts of our horizon for many hours, we saw no more of him nearer and next morning, he had disappeared. Our companions also left us, by degrees, and we in the poop cabin soon resumed that 'evenness and tranquillity of spirit' which not even the jars in the Cuddy could disturb, altho' the poor Colonel had a weary time of it.

From the day we left St Helena asthma had prevented his ever lying down; the hammock was never unrolled. A wrapper, a coverlet, and the easy chair were his doom. At first he could dress and take a walk on deck, latterly he was unable to catch breath enough for the slightest exertion. We had no proper food for him, sago and lemon juice only, and no medicine relieved him, his sufferings were unceasing, his weakness encreased alarmingly for want of proper nourishment; he could not manage meat in any shape. I was really in despair. The soldier's wife made him gruel but he could not bear it; there were no eggs, no milk, chicken broth only. But there came comfort. We had reached Ascension, such a dreadful place, a bare rock, and we were to lay to for a few hours to catch turtle, very abundant there. Two King's ships happened to be doing the same, on board of one of which Mr Agassiz betook himself, and mentioning to the commanding officer how shamefully our Captain was using us in the providing way, that gentleman sent to us, to Mrs Churchill and Mrs Smith, a goat in full milk—was there ever any thing kinder, a perfect stranger he was to all of us. We gave our goat in charge to Malek, who milked her himself and brought his jug of treasure to our cabins, where we divided it honestly. After supplying my Colonel, myself, and the two Willies, there was not much of my share left, but what there was I sent to Mrs Blanch. Mrs Churchill took care of Mr Agassiz, to whom we really owed this unspeakable comfort, and he used to offer his remains to the two disagreeable officers—they, far from being grateful, were indignant at getting so little, demanded their full share of what they insisted was meant for every body, in short were so turbulant that we two owners were afraid of bad consequences. After a consultation it was determined that I should explain, Mrs Churchill not quite liking to encounter Captain Floyd under existing circumstances. A good opportunity presenting itself, I set the matter at rest and amicably. I was sitting inside the Cuddy door with Mrs Blanch one evening, the two malcontents grumbling away outside. Malek was coming from the forecastle with his jug of milk. 'I say, old fellow,' said Captain Floyd, 'hand us over that fine jug of yours. Share alike and fair play, we are not going to let the old gentleman in the sulks there keep all the good things to himself etc.,' nice gentlemanly style! So I just addressed the pair very quietly, told them they were under a mistake about the goat, which was private property, presented especially to Mrs Churchill and me by a private friend, that my sick husband lived almost entirely upon her milk and that until he was supplied, I regretted being unable to offer him and Mr Bell any share of my share, which hitherto I had always given to Mrs Blanch and the little boys. Apologies, bows, smiles and a few epithets, well deserved, applied to the Captain, closed this business, of which we never heard another word, but indeed I got very anxious to reach England. The Colonel's encreasing debility under the obstinacy of his asthma, the uncomfortable atmosphere of our little cabin, always filled with the smoke of stramonium,[1] the cold, the illhumour, the bad fare, the improprieties of Mrs Churchill,

1. Narcotic drug prepared from the Thorn Apple
   (Datura Stramonium).

the devotion of Mr Agassiz, the despair of the 3rd mate, the sarcasms of Captain Floyd, all combined to render the run from St Helena most disagreeable, tho' we had a good wind. At last, off the Azores we got into what was as good as a trade wind, which sped us on I know not how many knots an hour. We were soon in the chops of the Channel, within a *foot* of never being heard of again too, for the greatest danger almost that can be run at sea we so narrowly missed here. A huge Merchantman tacking her way out, with no lights visible, nor any watch we supposed, bore down full upon us in the darkness of night. Our Captain, who was on deck, *felt* her approach or heard it, seized his trumpet first, and then the helm, and just turned us sufficiently out of the course to avoid the collision. I was lying on the sofa in the gloom of the just vanished twilight; I heard the rush of parting waters, distinguished the encreased blackness as the mass heaved past the windows, and shuddered, at I knew not what, the Captain had given us up. So very near had we been to danger. Hundreds of vessels, they say, are lost in this very way from utter carelessness on both parts. Captain West was prepared on deck, the little swivel loader to be fired if needed—only for this we had been gone. One more escape we had, from fire. The first mate next evening perceived some burning on the lower deck and entered every cabin instantly. The Archdeacon, surrounded by papers in flames on the floor, was vainly endeavouring to check the conflagration he had so unthinkingly raised—he had intended only to burn a few letters.

The coast appeared, first rocky, wild, rough, then came fields and trees, and villages and church spires; then we passed the Needles, and then, sailing on in smooth water with beauty on every side, we anchored in the roads off Portsmouth very early in the morning of some day towards the end of April 1830, St George's day, I think it was, the 23rd. Most of the gentlemen called boats and went ashore. Captain West returned with such delicious things for breakfast, fresh butter, fresh eggs, cream, fine bread. Oh how we enjoyed the feast. It gave us strength for our preparations.

Our two servants bestirred themselves busily. Malek was to remain in the ship in charge of all our heavy luggage; Mary, and the trunks selected, was to land with us. The Colonel was the difficulty; for a week past he had not been able to move hand or foot without bringing on a spasm. They said at Bombay he would never live to reach home. They said at sea he would die on the Voyage, and I believe had we not got that goat, he could not have struggled on under such sufferings. It seemed this last day as if we should never get him safe ashore.

The chair was prepared, he was carried out to it, laid in, lowered to the boat, lifted up and settled among cushions, and the rest of our party seated as could best be managed. We were half an hour or so rowing in, and we landed by the same steps on the same quay, and we had secured rooms at the same hotel looking on the harbour, from which we had started two years and a half before for India. The Captain took the rooms in the morning as the nearest to the water and so the most convenient for the poor Colonel. What was our amazement to see him when the boat struck, rise unassisted, walk up the steps, and along the small portion of the quay in his large cloke which covered his wrapper and seat himself in the little parlour without a gasp. We ordered what was to us the most luxurious repast in the world, tea, bread and butter, eggs and muffins, and did we not enjoy it, our Captain, Mrs Churchill, Mr Agassiz, the Colonel, the 2 children and I. We even played whist, and when we went to bed, the Colonel lay down and slept till morning, the first time he had ventured on such an indulgence for six weeks. We really did feel too happy, I was too happy to sleep, I was tired, too.

We had had the Custom House officers on board early, but they had not been the least impolite—quite the contrary. In the first place, they found nothing contraband, my shawls being on myself and Mrs Churchill, and my trinkets in the Captain's pockets. In the next place they looked for nothing, an old servant of Mr Gardiner's family being Chief of the party. Mr Gardiner had written to him to expedite us on our way, and the civil creature not only let all our packages pass that we wished to take to the hotel, but the trunks (which went to the Custom House) of which I gave him the keys, I am persuaded were hardly looked at—for all their contents were untumbled when they came back to me. A long paper box in which were the Cape feathers and an embroidered muslin gown my Mother had thought of just at the last for Aunt Fanny were all that paid duty—£1 on the feathers, half their cost, on the gown 25/- although we had run it up into a petticoat. The probably thought it decorous to tax something. The good old man had also ordered a set of rooms at the George, higher up the town in case they should be wanted. In short he quite welcomed us home.

Next day I actually walked *with my Colonel* about the town and found it piercing cold up on the Ramparts. I bought a straw bonnet, the Colonel a pair of gloves and a warm scarf for Willie. Before going out I had written two notes, one to Jane to say we should be with her the next day and to ask her to put up Mrs Churchill for two nights, as we really would not lose sight of her, and one to Lady, then Mrs, Burgoyne, whose husband had some command at Portsmouth. She called on us in the afternoon, and tho' very affected and a little airified was cousinly enough. We agreed to stop at her house next morning on our way to Malshanger to see her children. She lived in a pretty villa out of the town, and had all her plain children kept from school and nicely dressed to shew to us; there was good taste about her furniture and her garden, about all but herself. She herself was the same cockney looking, cockney mannered, self important little body that tormented us all as Charlotte Rose.

We were travelling most uncomfortably in two post chaises, Mrs Churchill, Louisa, and I in one, the Colonel, Willy and black Mary the maid in the other. There were three stages; we all met at the first, all met at the second, but we lost sight of the Colonel in the third. Where he had wandered his stupid postboy could not tell; very much out of the road, that was certain, for he did not reach Malshanger for an hour after we had been comfortably seated in Jane's pretty drawing room. Poor Jane, she was watching at the gate. I forget all else almost that day.

The party assembled at Malshanger consisted of Mary, her husband, and *two* children, Tom having been born the previous January, William, Aunt Bourne, and her stepdaughter, Henrietta. We were too large an addition, but it was not for long, as Colonel Smith had determined to go up to town at once to see if any Doctor could get him a bit to rights.

This resolution was hastened by an attack of asthma, the air up on those dry heights of Hampshire not at all suiting him. Asthma attacked him immediately. As his Indian servant would meet him in London, the general voice forbade my accompanying him, indeed I was in no trim for travelling. Besides I stood in need of rest after the discomforts of the voyage and the nights of broken sleep so long continued. He therefore departed on the 3rd morning, with his suite, in Jane's *basket* to Basingstoke, from thence by coach. Poor little Willy, who cried bitterly on leaving his *Aunty* was to be delivered to Miss Elphick at Kensington; she had given up the governess line, having her mother to provide for, and was trying to establish a sort of infant boarding School, which, poor soul, in spite of large help from all of us, she never succeeded in rendering a profitable speculation. Black Mary with whom I was glad to be done, for she was at times when excited rather unmanagable, was to go to the Agent's to resume her sea service, and Mrs Churchill and Louisa were to be deposited at old Mrs Churchill's. We were really glad to part with her. She was an incorrigible coquette, if not worse. After the distracting scene we had unhappily witnessed on her parting from the 3rd mate, and the very tender proceedings with Mr Agassiz, who was to see her again in London, she commenced a flirtation with my brother William, an engaged man at this time, and ought to have been thinking of good Sally, but man like, could not help philandering after a pretty woman. Mrs Churchill was really very inconsiderate, there was no actual harm in her; she was merely amusing herself, was what is called 'fast' in these days, in plain English, indecorous. She went soon after to visit her own Mother at Boulogne, Mr Agassiz her escort. More of her I never heard till some years after, when her husband got some good appointment in Bengal. She and Louisa went to India with them, and there they married their daughter to Colonel, afterwards General and then Sir John Michel,[1] well known in Canada and Dublin.

1. Sir John Michel (1804–86) married Louise Anne, only daughter of Major General H. Churchill C.B., Quarter Master General of the troops in India (D.N.B.).

William went to town but not with Mrs Churchill, he went to play host to Colonel Smith, whom he had invited to his lodgings and who carried a note from me to Mr Robert Pennington, the medical man he meant to consult. We seemed quieter at Malshanger after all these good friends were gone; but not for long. Mrs Guthrie and Mrs Basil Hall came to welcome me home, Mrs Guthrie the same kindly and pleasant person as ever; Mrs Hall kindly too, I believe, but airified by the *passing* fame[1] of her husband. They had come purposely to see me. It is nonsense to expect that early friendship will last under the shade of a total separation. We all declared we were all so happy to meet again, but I really fancied that they, like me, were very nearly indifferent upon the subject. I had never much taken to Margaret. After her marriage she became insufferable to every body but her sister—there was only Jane Guthrie, therefore, to try to care for her. She is to this day a most excellent person, but she is not in my line so that our intercourse is a very ghostlike semblance of the intimacy of our girlish days. Our Christian names in each other's mouths always sounded very hollow to my ears, altho' she and I have retained a warm interest in each other's doings. She was living among people I had never heard of and my Indian past and Irish future were then equally removed from her sympathies. Both sisters were extremely concerned about their dress, a strange affair to my unpractised eyes. Miss Elphick, too, worn a little, not exactly prospering, just able to rub on; and Mrs Gillio, with her warm highland heart. Aunt Bourne, too, had been at Malshanger all along; her rich and happy marriage had ended in a second widowhood, and she was left the charge of a step daughter, who was to her all that her own daughter could have been. Henrietta without being a beauty was very attractive in looks and manners. She was particularly suited to my Aunt, perfectly capable of appreciating her superiour-ity, and modest and tractable herself. She took to us all, particularly to John Frere, who was also with us for a while, and delighted on moonlight walks in the shrubberies with an

1. For an explanation of Basil Hall's *passing fame*,
   see II, pp. 49–50.

agreeable companion. I have always thought it a great pity these walks were not encouraged. My cousin Freres had not grown up handsome, besides there was a great want of grace in their manner. They were quaint, too, Frerish—that nameless oddity that runs thro' the race. But they were thoroughly amiable, unaffected, well brought up and altogether very pleasing, my dear little Aunt queerer and dearer than ever.

The Gardiners had taken a cottage at a pretty village three miles off down the hill, surrounded the parish church we attended; they took it for six months, and Jane and I hoped it might suit them for a longer time. It was so very comfortable, an old, good sized farm cottage, with a porch, and a draw well, and latticed windows, and a new front, with large rooms, and large windows looking on a flower garden, a well cropped kitchen garden behind. The house was furnished and the rent was low, though not a cheap country, no expensive establishment could have been kept there. They should have been tired of their wandering adventures. Their voyage in that little boat had been very boisterous. They escaped shipwreck by a mere chance; instead of landing at Liverpool they were stranded on the coast of Galloway, landed in boats, started with half their luggage for London, in post chaises, and after a London lodging and other discomforts, took a house at Ham, too near Mr Gardiner's aunt Miss Porter at Twickenham, whose interference with their domestick arrangements made their moving again almost a necessity. They tried Cheltenham, Leamington, Matlock and then eagerly responding to Jane's proposal of this cottage, which accidentally offered itself, they arrived at Malshanger, bag and baggage, to look at it. A few days sufficed to settle them most comfortably, having a talent for this sort of business. They looked very happy there, always cheerful, every thing nice about them, the children, neat and merry, dear little things. Jane and I often drove there in the basket cart with 'Goody,' and while she wandered through the village visiting all the poor people who shared her bounties, I sat quietly by Mary's work table in the window opening on the garden, where Mr Gardiner delighted in being busy, little Janey in her short white frock and broad blue sash trotting up and down the room, and baby Tommy on my knee.

All parties were anxious that my Colonel and I should settle in that neighbourhood; there was a very desirable place, Tangier, close to Malshanger, to be let, but we could not take it. The sharp air of these Hampshire heights quite disagreed with him. Besides that, duty and early attachments recalled him to his own green isle. In London, where he remained three weeks, he was comparatively well. Asthma attacked him directly he returned to us. Mr Pennington told him the disease was a consequence not a cause, but it was now chronick and would not cure, though it would be relieved, and his health, which was much deranged, should strengthen. He advised him to seek for an air that suited him, and *stay* in it and trust to time. An Indian *stay* anywhere; foolish Mr Pennington. It was plain he could not stay at Malshanger, so he left us for Dublin.

My sisters and I had a subject of anxiety in William's engagement to Sally Siddons; about this time she came on a visit to Mary, her sister Elizabeth followed to Malshanger; William, of course, was with his affianced. The news of their engagement had not reached Bombay when we sailed. I met it in England, I must say, with dismay. I feared it would really overset my father and that my Mother would give way to a violence of disapproval that would make all concerned very uncomfortable. For myself, I had yet to find out that worth would, and should, outweigh quarterings, that good sense and high principles in a woman are worth to her family more than all the more brilliant qualities, which are more attractive, and that no rank in life honourably supported ought to place a bar between a gentleman and a gentlewoman. So, liking her father and admiring her mother, our near connexion was a bitter pill. Very anxiously we all awaited our Indian letters, Jane, Mary, and I were grave, William in a fever, Sally calm. Mrs Siddons had written to my father detailing the whole progress of the attachment, which, when mentioned to her, she would not sanction without this consent. She touched on William's faults of character, but believed them to have been redeemed by the way in which he had supported adversity, which belief alone could have induced her conditionally to consent to give him such a daughter, knowing too, that she must lose her for their destination was to be Calcutta. William was keeping his terms at the Temple, Lord Glenelg having obtained permission for him to proceed as a barrister to Bengal. The last paragraph of Mrs Siddons' letter probably did no harm; it stated that Sally's fortune would at the least be £10,000.

My father received this letter alone and alone he determined to consider it before venturing to inform my Mother. This naive admission sufficiently explained his own feelings. He passed a sleepless night, and when at dawn he made up his mind to rouse his sleeping partner with the news, he found he might have saved himself all his perturbation. My Mother had heard nothing for a long while that had given her so much pleasure. A most cordial invitation to William and his Wife accompanied the consent to the marriage; Jane gave a grand dinner, the daily ones were small enough, Colonel Pennington produced champaign, and an evening of happy family cheerfulness followed. My Mother was very wise. She made the best of it, not her usual way.

It was a fine summer. I thought I should have enjoyed the power of wandering out in the open air at every hour after the imprisonment of India—and so perhaps I might, but I had not the power, for I was ill, very uneasy and not able to exert myself. I had had to hire a little maid to wait upon myself in order to secure some attendance in my room, Jane in that immense large house having but two women servants and an old Molly, who came in after weeding the shrubbery to wash up dishes. There was always company in the house, additions frequently at dinner, besides one or two regular parties of the neighbours, and two of the little Penningtons, Charles and Annie, were living there. Georgina came afterwards, and the father and mother, neither of whom I liked. I therefore fared but badly as to attendance. So I proposed to Jane to hire a maid, to wait entirely on me, do out my room etc., and to pay her board so that she would cost her nothing. Jane was charmed. She knew a young woman that would exactly suit. She would arrange it all, the plan was excellent. I hoped so, for as it was I was rather miserable. Poor little Sarah, on the 29th. May, Royal oak day, we went all to lunch with Mary and to see the villagers dance upon the green, the queen, footing it merrily in her white dress with her garland of oak leaves round her straw hat, was pointed out to me as my future maid, which not a little startled me, and Mary advised me to cry off. But as the engagement was made, and only conditional, I did not like to disappoint either Jane or her protégée, as she could easily be left when we moved if she did not suit me. But she was the nicest creature possible, a good housemaid, quick and neat at her needle, clearstarched well, was always busy and always merry and I felt sure that when I had her to myself, we should get on admirably.

As it was, I had her not, or very little. Jane expected her to be obliging, the housemaid begged for help, the Cook Nelly! insisted upon help, the little Penningtons were given over to her. So what with dressing them, and waiting on them, cleaning other rooms than mine, going messages, shelling pease, basting meat etc., I was nearly as forelorn as before. I might ring but was I answered? Sarah had just stept out to the farm for eggs, to the garden for parsley or had gone with Master Charles to lead his donkey. I daresay it was very good for me to try to wait upon myself, however, as Mr Workman of Basingstoke, who was to attend me, was not easy about me, as he told Jane, a proper monthly nurse was sent for to town, and down came Mrs Stephens, the usual assistant of Mrs Guthrie. Under her government, Sarah had to mind her own mistress, as the mistress herself, much to her own benefit, had to mind the nurse. She was a skilful person, and I do believe by her care of me she prepared me so properly for what I had to go thro', that she was the principal means of saving my life and Janey's. It was a case similar to the Princess Charlotte's, whatever that was, for I am sure I don't know.[1] I took ill on the last day of June, Saturday, the day King George the 4th. died. On Tuesday the 3rd. of July that little blessing to her parents saw the light about 9 o'clock in the morning. Poor Jane, who never left me, had given me over. The clever little strange Doctor, however, brought us both thro'—there never was a better recovery either, altho' the nurse had to leave us in 10 days being engaged elsewhere.

1. She had given birth to a still-born boy and died shortly afterwards.

Before I left my room, I had a peep of my husband on his way from Dublin to London, and he returned only to take me away, being ordered by his doctor to Cheltenham for a long course of the waters. He came back in a very pretty *britchska*[1] he and William had chosen for me; *Annie Need* and these two travelling together in it. After a few days we packed up and packed off, and then indeed I felt I was gone out from among my own kindred, and had set up independently—a husband—a baby—an end indeed of Eliza Grant.

And here I think I'll leave my Memoirs for the present. You know, dear children, what my Irish life had been, the friends we found, the friends we made, the good your dear father did. Ten months in Dublin sufficed to shew us a town life was not then suited to us. We resolved to settle among our own people, your father finding in his own old neighbourhood all those companions of his youth whom he had left there more than thirty years before. A very happy life we led there. First in the pretty cottage at Burgage which we improved without, and within, and made so comfortable, and then in our own fine house built by ourselves, such a source of happy occupation to the Colonel for years and the means of raising his tenantry from debt and apathy and wretchedness to the thriving condition in which we now have them. It would take a volume to describe our slow but regular march of improvement, never wearying in well doing, bearing patiently with ignorance and all its errours, and carefully bringing up our own dear children to follow us in doing likewise. One only trouble assailed our happy home, the want of health—that miserable asthma breaking him and breaking me and stepping in between us and many enjoyments. The purse, though never heavy, was never empty, our habits being simple. On looking back I find little essential to regret and much, Oh so much, to be truly thankful for.

Dublin, February 1854   E.S.

---

1. An open carriage with removable folding top and space for reclining when used for a journey.

Index